A UFO
Hunter's
Guide

A UFO
Hunter's
Guide

Sightings, Abductions, Hot Spots,
Conspiracies, Cover-ups, the Identified
and Unidentified, and More

Bret Lueder

WATKINS PUBLISHING
LONDON

This edition published in the UK 2013 by
Watkins Publishing Limited, Sixth Floor,
75 Wells Street, London W1T 3QH

A member of Osprey Group

Table 1: UFO Shapes and Patterns by Bret Lueder and William Henderson
Table 2: Categories of Sightings reprinted with permission of Jacques Vallée. First printed
in *Confrontations* (New York: Ballantine Books, 1990).

1 2 3 4 5 6 7 8 9 10

Interior by Kathryn Sky-Peck

Typeset in Adobe Caslon Pro

Printed and bound in Great Britain

A CIP record for this book is available from the British Library

ISBN: 978-1-78028-543-6

www.watkinspublishing.co.uk

Contents

Acknowledgments

ASIDE FROM THE MANY EFFORTS of the world-renowned researchers who have graciously contributed to this book, it could not have been done in the way it has been if it were not for the kind assistance of several key individuals: Ruben Uriarte, Marcia Schafer, Suzy Stevens, Kim Freeman, and especially Victoria Jack.

Introduction

Many of us have been born into a society where unidentified flying objects, or UFOs, are already part of popular culture. From the friendly, multicolored lights of the craft in Steven Spielberg's classic movie *E.T.* to the ominous and city-sized disks in the movie *Independence Day*, Hollywood has firmly implanted images of UFOs in the minds of people worldwide.

Energized by the influence of Hollywood, UFOs have been seen and heard across a wide spectrum of media, including musical genres, children's television cartoons, and poster art. The stereotypical image of a space alien, popularized on the cover of the famous Whitley Strieber book *Communion* (1987), can be seen on coffee cups, baseball hats, and bumper stickers—the image of an alleged UFO occupant known as a "Gray." Not coincidentally, Strieber's book was later made into a movie (1989) starring Christopher Walken as Strieber (see *www. ufopop.org*).

It wasn't until the first publicly reported sighting on June 24, 1947, in Washington State, however, that the term "flying saucer" was born. Hollywood now had a new and rich source of material to fuel its money—and some say "mind control"—machine. In his now famous book *Report on Unidentified Flying Objects* (1956), Captain Edward J. Ruppelt coined the term "unidentified flying object," or "UFOs," to better describe these various phenomena, and henceforth that has been the preferred term used to identify what appear—at least for the time being—to be indefinable. Hollywood has adopted the term as well.

For researchers, however, many questions have arisen since that fateful day: Where do UFOs originate? What do the world's governments and military establishments know about the phenomena? How long before 1947 did they know about them? Is there really a cover-up of information? Are these objects really spaceships from other planets? And the biggie: What is a UFO? These and other questions have all, so far, remained unanswered. Well, at least in public—say some.

Among the few brave researchers who offer explanations, many heated arguments arise. One claims that UFOs are from outer space, while another says that anyone who believes in UFOs is a wacko. Some more grounded researchers admit the UFOs could be from outer space or other planets, but some continue to insist that they are nothing more than misidentified planets, stars, meteor fireballs, comets, and other aerial and weather phenomena covering a wide range of situations. The arguing goes back and forth, each side claiming to have "expert" analysis and opinion. The result is mental fatigue of the highest order.

Many ufologists, or people who research UFO sightings and cases, have suffered from burnout, nervous breakdown, and other types of psychosis. Often, the information available conflicts, making the mental strain on investigations more difficult. Worse still, many have died in their pursuit of the truth. The television series *The X-Files* (1993–2002) is a good example of the portrayal of situations that arise from seemingly harmless UFO investigations. The movies *Hangar 18*

(1980) and *The Arrival* (1996) and the television series *Stargate SG-1* (1997–2007) are good examples of the kinds of situations an individual may encounter when in pursuit of UFO and/or UFO-related information.

It is true that Hollywood hypes this kind of intrigue, because it does help to sell movie tickets and advertising. But these dangers are real, with numerous accounts of life-threatening situations concerning UFOs reported by both military/government and civilian research efforts. As will become clear in the pages that follow, the study of UFOs can go from fun to deadly serious in a short time.

You only have to witness for yourself the signs posted outside of Area 51 in the Nevada desert, which state that trespassers could be shot. A common Area 51 sign reads:

WARNING: U.S. Air Force Installation. It is unlawful to enter this area without permission of the Installation Commander Sec. 21, Internal Security Act of 1950; 50 U.S.C 797. While on this Installation, all personnel and the property under their control are subject to search. USE OF DEADLY FORCE AUTHORIZED.

Perhaps most shocking, however, are the reports of the mysterious "men in black" (MiB) and the many techniques they use to harass UFO researchers, witnesses, and their families—disinformation; physical, economic, and/or psychological threat; and the forcible acquisition and intentional destruction of evidence. These MiBs have allegedly blocked or destroyed many investigations and reports and have kept competent researchers from pursuing evidence and information. All these things have been reported.

So how are we supposed to make sense of this miasma of "facts," conflicting information, incomprehensible details, and potential life-threatening danger? Many will remain in a state of denial and go about their daily lives. More power to them. Others will go running away screaming in fear that any of it could be true. They will find their way.

In the end, a brave few will handle the emotional strain this knowledge can bring; they will venture forth and seek answers to phenomena that could potentially affect every person on Earth—phenomena that have been taking place since long before 1947. Reports in California alone go back to 1896. And it has been alleged that both Nazi Germany and U.S. President Franklin Delano Roosevelt had meetings with alien races as early as 1933 (see BRANTON, aka Bruce Alan Walton, *The Omega Files: Secret Nazi UFO Bases Revealed* [2000]).

Nor is the idea that UFOs are from worlds other than Earth new. It has been with humanity since the dawn of recorded time. Cave paintings of what appear to be classic saucer-shaped disks can be found in modern-day Lascaux, France, that are thought to be 17,000 years old. Other rock art in Mali, West Africa (the Dogon tribe), Australia (the Aborigines), North America (several Native American tribes), and many spots in Europe (Celtic, Etruscan, and other early peoples) all show indications that they were visited by, learned from, and were guided by beings from other worlds, some of which are described as traveling in what today are perceived as UFOs.

In 1968, author Erich von Daniken described many "sacred sites" around the world in his classic book *Chariots of the Gods*, which later became a movie (1970). According to von Daniken, there is a global pattern of native traditions that mirrors the alleged locations of contact with the occupants of UFOs. He was the first popular writer to interpret many rock-art figures and shapes as UFOs from outer space. His compelling research and insight into the Nazca lines in Peru, the tomb lid of Lord Pacal in Mexico, and the many rock-art sites in Europe—the pictographs in the caves of Capo di Ponte in northern Italy, for instance—spawned an early wave of research from heavyweights like Zecharia Sitchin (*The 12th Planet*, 1976), William Bramley (*The Gods of Eden*, 1989), and Jordan Maxwell (*The Matrix of Power*, 2000). These early researchers were followed by a whole new generation of young scholars who associate UFOs and their occupants with the origins of humanity and society—writers like William Henry, Michael Tsarion, and Cyd Rice.

Von Daniken's work also confirms Native American thought that sacred sites are locations of UFO activity. The entire American Southwest could be described as a "hot spot," and places like England's Stonehenge, China's Shensi pyramid, and Peru's famous Machu Picchu are rife with activity as well. So too are various "vortex" areas, or dimensional doorways, like the Bermuda Triangle, the Skinwalker Ranch in Utah, and many other places around the world (see chapter 4).

Sitchin, for example, points to references of flying machines in a variety of ancient texts, including, but not limited to, the Bible, the East Indian *Rig-Vedas*, and the ancient Sumerian cuneiform texts, which are thought to be from what most mainstream authorities think is the oldest known civilization on Earth (Sumeria/Mesopotamia circa 8000–6000 B.C.E.). Sitchin also points to various passages in the Old and New Testaments—Genesis 6:1–4, where the "Nephilim . . . the sons of god came in to the daughters of men . . ."; Zecharia 5:1–2, where we find ". . . I see a flying scroll . . ."; and 2 Kings 2:9–12, where Elijah is whisked away in a "whirlwind into heaven," which some say refers to extraterrestrials riding in UFOs and contacting humans at or near many of these same sacred sites.

There are many more Biblical references, especially when researchers delve into texts that were once part of the Bible but have since been removed—*The Book of Enoch*, for example, and *The Book of the Wars of Yahweh*.

It was during and just after that fateful year of 1947, however, that the Roswell, Magdalena, Corona, and many other disk crashes and retrievals allegedly took place. This is when most researchers say that the U.S. military/government began its long—and, some say, now tired—stance that there are, in fact, no UFOs from outer space. This is when the alleged disinformation group known as MJ-12, which is still thought to be in operation today, was initiated. It is because of the disinformation and scare tactics of MJ-12, argue several ufologists, that the situation is where we find it today: with no definitive answers.

Really, we are left with more questions: If many of the world's indigenous traditions claim affiliation and interaction with ETs that ride in

UFOs, what is the role of these beings in terms of human evolution? What is the "real" picture of the cosmos? How many species are visiting Earth at any given time? And another biggie: How much is already known but concealed by secret government agencies around the world?

While governments like that in the United States have taken the position that they must keep certain secrets concerning UFOs, other countries are not so secretive. Mexico is an example of a government and a people that, together, openly embrace the UFO phenomena. Government officials appear on mainstream news broadcasts telling what they may have witnessed without the fear of public derision, a common tactic used in the United States to keep its officials and other witnesses quiet. The Japanese, Turkish, and Italian governments, as well as a growing number of others, are publicly addressing these issues in a way that fosters a safe environment for witnesses to come forth with testimony.

Some issues are still too much of a societal taboo, however. Take the highly controversial subject of abductions—a specific type of contact in which the "experiencers" are taken against their will by unknown beings allegedly not of this world. They are supposedly taken aboard various craft—solid, metallic flying machines—from the most mundane of places. The alleged beings in these variously shaped craft apparently seek out humble, spiritual, and honest people to take aboard their ships (see Appendix B).

There are tales of levitation beams that paralyze alleged abductees, sometimes levitating entire automobiles, and of different types of experiments, including the ingestion of various liquid substances. We hear of various sexually oriented experiments, frequently misinterpreted and misunderstood as the infamous "anal probe" that so often draws the typical sneers and jokes heard in modern popular culture. Some of these experiences are reported in both wonderfully positive and dreadfully negative ways. The classic works *The Secrets of the Saucers* (1955) and *Son of the Sun* (1959) by Orfeo M. Angelucci and *Aboard a Flying Saucer* (1954) by Truman Bethurum are among the many examples of these reports (see others throughout this book).

Abductions may be the most strange and controversial aspect of the UFO field. A leading theory among researchers, Native Americans, and many abductees themselves is that these alleged abductions are really hoaxed by the world's governments and their corollary military establishments for a variety of purposes. (Caution: Obtaining answers to these questions may be frightening and possibly dangerous. Many abductees have claimed that there was an alien/military context to their experiences. These events are described as "military abductions," or "Milabs.")

No matter what your preconceived notions are on the subject, when you see the vast array of cases, sightings, alleged contacts, and abductions, it becomes hard to imagine why the subject is not taken more seriously in the mainstream. But because many of the world's governments and militaries wish to keep secrets—and because militaries usually have more guns—the answers are not readily forthcoming.

There are several theories as to why any government would want to keep these phenomena secret. And there are just as many scenarios in which it is thought that UFOs are used by governments. One popular theory is that the knowledge of UFOs is covertly disseminated from a "secret" government to the public through various "agents" as a distraction from the "real" genetic experimentation, advanced technology, and/or population control going on behind the scenes. In this view, the UFO "mythology" is fabricated by the United States corporate government as a cover for other activity. Another popular theory suggests that the world's many governments—predominantly that of the United States—have actually known about the extraterrestrial nature of UFOs since long before 1947 and are afraid not only of invasion but of the ensuing public panic that the mere knowledge of the ET presence might cause as well. In this view, governments withhold secrets for the protection of their people. There are many such theories.

Despite the secrecy, however, the information is there if we choose to investigate. Famed French researcher Paris Flammonde goes so far as to say, in his dedication to *UFOs Exist!* (1976): "to Sylvia Meagher and Bernard J. Fensterwald, Jr., the courage and independence of their need to know may be numbered among the last weapons defending American freedom."

This is important work. Few have taken it upon themselves to do the research. Various factions have gone to great lengths to conceal evidence of UFOs. And authorities aren't talking. So it will most likely fall to private, independent, and certainly dogged individual researchers (like you!) to uncover and/or experience the truth about UFOs for themselves and inform the rest of the world with competent, factual, and clearly written reports. Thus, although this book can easily be used by anyone, it is especially written for and offered to those hearty souls—the real seekers of truth who are willing not only to do their homework but also to go out into the field (aka "the real world") in search of answers. It is an attempt to buttress the searchers' search, to aid on the journey to knowledge on whatever level. Keep this book close to you when you're out in the field and use its quick history, overviews of a wide variety of subjects, and research/investigator tips from the pros to help you in your search.

Because of the tangled web of information associated with the field of ufology, standard definitions often don't apply. You will see that, in many cases, it will be up to you to decide what is real and what is not. This is as much a personal journey to your own truths as it is a human journey to human truths. (Warning: Personal truths will conflict as well!)

There will be plenty of opportunities along your journey to have fun and chart new scientific ground. Whatever your motives are for delving into the field of UFOs, you will find this book a valuable resource. So bring it with you, enjoy yourself, and stay safe.

What Is a UFO?

There are many competing theories about the origins and nature of UFOs. For example, researchers Brad Steiger and Sherry Hansen Steiger list seventeen theories at their website, *www.bradandsherry.com*. In *UFO: The Complete Sightings* (1995) by Peter Brookesmith, there is a list of nine theories. Further, these theories are often categorized. In *The Mammoth Encyclopedia of Extraterrestrial Encounters* (2001) edited by Ronald D. Story, the subject is divided into "conventional (unintelligent)" and "unconventional (intelligent)" encounters.

Others use terms like "natural" versus "unnatural," "material" versus "immaterial," or "physical" versus "nonphysical" to categorize, or break down, the UFO situation. Choose whatever terms feel best to you. Below is a simplified breakdown that gives three categories of UFO manifestation:

- **External UFO theories** suggest that UFOs are phenomena that originate outside of the human mind, whether physical, ethereal, or inter-dimensional.

- **Internal UFO theories** suggest that UFO phenomena originate within the human mind—that they are psychological, spiritual, and/or inter-dimensional.

- **Internal/External UFO theories** incorporate the first two categories into one, several of which offer inter-dimensional explanations.

Many of these theories can be interpreted as originating in one or more categories, depending on your viewpoint. For example, inter-dimensional phenomena can be described as external, internal, or internal/external, depending on your definition of the word—the objects can be physical and then morph into the ethereal, or vice versa. They may also be physical in one dimension, go through a wormhole or stargate (see chapter 6), and also be physical in this dimension. Or they may be ethereal in this dimension and in others. There's really no limit to the possibilities.

I see this particular breakdown as helpful because it helps you visualize the various alleged dimensions and how a UFO may travel between them. It helps you imagine the many inter-dimensional theories quickly and easily and see the subtle differences between other dimensions that are perceivable internally, as well as ones allegedly proved by mathematicians to have originated externally. I like to imagine UFOs phasing from the ethereal to the physical worlds, or internal images from within manifesting—not just as external projections, holograms, and/or hallucinations, but as physical, 3D objects. For me, it's part of the fun with this kind of research.

External Theories

The categorical breakdown, along with what I see as the most dominant theories, is listed below.

Extraterrestrial Space Craft

This theory suggests that UFOs are physical spacecraft built and operated by an intelligent species that is not indigenous to Earth. This is by far the most common, popular, and prevalent theory. A variation on this theme suggests that UFOs are inter-dimensional in the sense that they are physical craft in our dimension and can phase into and out of other dimensions, where they are still physical in the context of that dimension (see *www.startinglinks.net/cydoniaufo/11.htm*).

Terrestrial Craft: Alien-Built vs. Man-Made

Several researchers have theories describing UFOs as being from Earth. William R. Lyne finds that there is no evidence whatsoever to indicate that visitors from other planets have come to Earth for any reason. His book *Space Aliens from the Pentagon* (1994) emphatically declares that all UFOs are physical craft made by humans using technology stolen from Nikola Tesla and smuggled to Germany before World War I. Other researchers hedge more toward the middle. For example, William S. Steinman in *UFO Crash at Aztec* (written with Wendelle C. Stevens, 1986, UFO Photo Archives) and Stanton Friedman, author of several books (see chapter 3) make the seemingly more rational case that some UFOs may be from other planets while many others are no doubt man-made.

There is also a theory that claims that there is at least one advanced species indigenous to Earth—a species that has chosen to remain invisible to the "normal" world. In this scenario, these hypothetical beings manufacture physical, metallic UFOs. Some say they reside inside the

Earth. Some say they are humans from the future of Earth. It may be that a combination of all four theories is true (see chapter 6).

Earthlights Hypothesis

First propounded in the 1970s by Paul Devereux, editor of the academic journal *Time & Mind*, this theory makes the case that tectonic stresses of various kinds in the Earth's crust can, under the right conditions, manifest in strange and elusive light forms. Particular mineral deposits are thought to influence earthlights as well. Many promising UFO sightings, upon investigation, have turned out to be some kind of light form.

Devereux told me in a personal interview:

> Earthlights seem to belong to the same family of phenomena as ball lightning and earthquake lights but can sometimes show distinguishing properties and behavior, such as unusual longevity. They are exotic energy forms, which, like plasmas, can seem metallic when seen in daylight. There is a polarity effect too, in that earthlights can occasionally appear pitch black, as can ball lightning.

These lights are often reported in conjunction with the seismic activity of earthquakes and volcanoes and can apparently interact with the atmosphere. Researcher Michael Persinger has concluded that earthlights can generate electromagnetic fields that can trigger hallucinations in some witnesses. Devereux advises: "It is important not to be misinformed, which is something ufology has suffered from for decades." For more information on earthlights, see *Earth Lights Revelation* (1989) by Paul Devereux, *Examining the Earthlight Theory: The Yakima UFO Microcosm* (1990) by Greg Long, and *UFOs and Ufology* (1997) by Paul Devereux and Peter Brookesmith.

Indigenous Atmospheric Beings

Trevor James Constable developed this compelling theory after studying the work on orgone by energy pioneer Wilhelm Reich. He found that UFOs were "space creatures" and claimed to take infrared photographs of the "plasma" beings regularly. For more information, see Constable's classic works *The Cosmic Pulse of Life* (1977) and *Sky Creatures* (1978), as well as his work at *www.trevorjamesconstable.com*. (See also chapter 6.)

Aberrant Weather Phenomena

Water spouts, tornados, rogue waves, wind shears, rare cloud formations, and electromagnetic occurrences and interactions (including earthlights) are just some of the natural weather phenomena that may explain many UFO sightings.

Many Bermuda Triangle books have good anomalous weather information. See, for instance, *The Fog: A Never Before Published Theory of the Bermuda Triangle Phenomena* (2005) by Rob MacGregor and Bruce Gernon and *The Hurricane Hunters and Lost in the Bermuda Triangle* (2007) by Tom Barnes. (See also chapter 4.)

Always check the local weather conditions at the time of any sighting or contact encounter, as well as before field excursions. You can find the information at *www.accuweather.com* and *www.nws.noaa.gov*.

Internal Theories

Internal theories require the investigator to look inward for confirmation, or denial, of any of these ideas. Although the urge will be there, the best investigators will not lie to themselves about their personal experiences and will be able to use them as a trusted reference during an investigation. Below you will find the main internal theories.

Psychological Phenomena

Whether or not a UFO originates from an external or an internal source, there is always some degree of internal, psychological impact—not just on the witness or contactee, but on society as well. Pioneering psychologist Carl G. Jung, during his communications with Major Donald Keyhoe (see chapter 2), proposed that UFO sightings may be the product of some type of mass hallucination and that they were worthy of further study (see *Flying Saucers: A Modern Myth of Things Seen in the Skies* [1978]).

Consciousness researcher and explorer Terence McKenna also sees UFOs as "an idea complex emerging in the collective psyche," but claims that UFOs were phenomenologically "real," or real to the perceiver. He argues:

> [P]silocybin reveals an event at the end of history of such magnitude that it casts miniature reflections of itself back into time. These are the apocalyptic concrescences that haunt the historical continuum, igniting religions and various hysterias, and seeping ideas into highly tuned nervous systems.
>
> *The Archaic Revival*

For more information on this theory, see *The Mind Parasites* (1967) by Colin Wilson.

Until the present era of UFOs that began in 1947, sightings and contacts were often viewed through a religious lens, attracting Catholic priests to perform exorcisms and other rituals designed to rid a person of demons or other such nefarious entities. Carl Sagan speaks of this in his *The Demon-Haunted World: Science as a Candle in the Dark* (1997), as does Jacques Vallée in his *Messengers of Deception: UFO Contacts and Cults* (2008).

In fact, it was Jacques Vallée who first introduced the idea that UFOs were either a type of evolutionary "control system" or part of one. In his classic work, *The Invisible College* (1975), Vallée suggests that

UFOs act as a way to shake up stale mass psychological patterns by triggering projections that foster new kinds of thinking—UFOs among them. He suggests a possible inter-dimensional aspect as well. Richard Haines explores this as well in his *UFO Phenomena and the Behavioral Scientist* (1979).

Inter-dimensional Craft

It is hard to trace the origins of this idea because of the crossover with dream interpretation and traditional shamanic experiences. All three phenomena have been with humanity from the beginning of recorded history, and probably before. But dreamlike states are reported in association with UFO sightings and abductions to such a degree that many subscribe to the theory that UFOs are ethereal, inter-dimensional phenomena that elude definitive description.

John Keel proposed that UFOs were "elemental intelligences" that he called "ultraterrestrials." These are described as being akin to the types of entities communicated with during some traditional shamanic experiences. Another variation is Thomas E. Bearden's supposition that the psychic stresses aroused in the dream state can manifest what are described as UFOs to a human consciousness. Jung might describe the end result of these proposed "stresses" as a hallucination. This discussion is continued by John Keel in *Mothman Prophecies* (1975), by Allen Greenfield in *Secret Cipher of the UFOnauts* (1994), and by Philip Imbrogno in *Interdimensional Universe: The New Science of UFOs, Paranormal Phenomena & Otherdimensional Beings* (2008).

Spiritual Beings

The idea that the occupants of UFOs, and possibly the UFOs themselves, are spiritually advanced beings has grown steadily in the West as more and more contactees come forward with similar messages (see chapter 2). In fact, many indigenous cultures adhere to this belief, as demonstrated by Nancy Red Star in *Star Ancestors* (2000). Now deceased *Flying Saucer Review* editor Gordon Creighton held to the notion that UFOs were used as a disguise by certain spirit beings known as "djinns," beings also described by Farah Yurdozu in her work (see chapter 3).

Orbs are also thought to be what are known as "Ascended Masters" (see chapter 5) who can take on spherical form and a variety of colors (see below). These ascended beings allegedly can also choose to activate their merkabas, or reflexive mental envelopes, which allows them to travel anywhere in the universe "outside of time." *The Book of Knowledge: The Keys of Enoch* (1973) by J. J. and Desiree Hurtak is the prime source of this esoteric knowledge.

Internal/External Theories

Internal/external theories blur the lines between what we perceive inside and what we perceive outside of ourselves. How do we tell the difference? Key internal/external theories are listed below.

Evolutionary Control Systems

The physical aspect of Jacques Vallée's "control system" is possibly some type of holographic projection technology that is used with the goal of either governmental psychosociological studies (like how to handle crowds, etc.) but may possibly be research into unknown natural phenomena as well, which implies other dimensions that are perceivable both internally and/or externally. While acknowledging both the physical and ethereal nature of many reported UFOs, Vallée takes the position that the subject warrants serious scientific scrutiny and should be studied from both perspectives.

Fred Beckman and Douglas Price-Williams of UCLA propose that Vallée's computer-detected UFO activity patterns resemble the kind of planned reinforcement schedule commonly used in the process of training, ironically reinforcing Vallée's control-system theory (see chapter 3). He believes that UFOs are one of the means by which the concepts of man are organized. It is not fully known, however, who or what is doing the controlling.

Inter-dimensional Craft

These are physical craft with the capability of traversing dimensions. Several individuals, like James Gilliland, maintain that some of these craft can phase in and out of our reality and are both physical and ethereal at the same time. The technology here is apparently so advanced that these beings/crafts can move about successfully in the dream state, as well as in the "waking" world.

Because ETs can allegedly move through the dream state with such ease, it is thought that they normally operate at or around the Delta (1.5–4 Hz) or Theta (5–8 Hz) brain wave frequencies (the frequencies of deep sleep and drowsiness, respectively) and rarely enter into the Alpha (9–14 Hz) or Beta (15–40 Hz) ranges (the frequencies of being alert and highly alert). ("Hz" stands for hertz and refers to cycles per second.) See *Cosmic Deception: Let the Citizen Beware* by Steven Greer (2002) and *Becoming Gods: A Reunion with Source* and *Becoming Gods II* (1996 and 1997 respectively) by James Gilliland for an analysis of this assumption.

Merkabas

Merkabas allegedly represent the highest achievement in consciousness expansion and expression. When individuals activate their merkabas, they unlock a latent part of human consciousness. It's like having your own universe. The shape of this "light body" looks similar to what many believe is the classic saucer shape of a UFO. J. J. Hurtak says that, once activated, an Ascended Master can physically travel "anywhere in God's Creation," literally "outside of time" and to no physical detriment.

The merkaba originates from thoughts within, yet manifests in the physical, 3D world. The *Crystal Links* website describes them thus:

> [It] is the divine light vehicle allegedly used by ascended masters to connect with and reach those in tune with the higher realms. "Mer" means light. "Ka" means spirit. "Ba" means body. Mer-ka-ba means the spirit/body surrounded by counter-rotating fields of light, (wheels within wheels), spirals of energy as in DNA, which transports spirit/body from one dimension to another.

www.crystallinks.com

Orbs

Orbs became a subject of interest in the mid-1990s. These mysterious entities are considered by many to be a spherical form of spiritual consciousness, possibly Ascended Masters. They appear to be attracted to loving, often feminine, energy and have been photographed extensively. They can appear on their own, but others claim to be able to manifest these "beings" through intention, prayer, and/or ritual (see chapter 5).

Skeptics claim that they are merely light-refraction effects from a camera's lens. But there are many photographs in existence that easily make the case that not all "spots" on a piece of film stem from light refraction. Orbs are also photographed in association with near-death experiences (NDEs). But are they external ethereal phenomena or internal, possibly hallucinogenic, phenomena? Or both? For more information on orbs, see Rickard and Kelly, *Photographs of the Unknown* (1980).

UFO Shapes

If merkabas have a distinctly saucer-on-saucer shape, and orbs are typically spherical, is it possible to glean any information from the shape of a UFO?

From a purely quantitative information-gathering approach, documenting and categorizing what may appear to be simple, mundane shapes can have dramatic results when cross-referenced with other sightings. By cross-referencing abduction cases, for example, researcher Wendelle C. Stevens has found that there may be a globally orchestrated effort to contact humanity by a specific race of beings thought to come from the Reticulan star system. Comparing the shapes of the craft reported enabled Stevens to find other similarities, leading to his startling conclusion (see chapter 2).

NASA physicist Alan Holt believes, as does William R. Lyne, that the shape of an alleged craft is important for other reasons.

> I think the shape of the spacecraft can be quite important. Elliptical or saucer-shaped would be the shapes I'd start out with. I hate to use those words because of the connotations. But what you're trying to do with the artificial energy pattern is overwhelm the natural mass energy pattern and exist in the material of the spacecraft itself. So saucer is probably best. I don't think it is an accident that the UFO phenomena we see are, by and large, saucer-shaped.
>
> Connie Stewart, *Los Angeles Herald Examiner,* June 5, 1980

Others, like Ruben Uriarte, director of the Mutual UFO Network (MUFON) in northern California, think that basic shapes help a witness to describe something for which they may have no prior frame of reference. Uriarte says:

> The myth is that very few people have seen a UFO. Yet, according to a Roper Poll conducted in 2002 for the SciFi Channel

[now Syfy], one in seven Americans say they or someone they know has had an experience involving a UFO. So in reality, almost 15 percent of the US population claims to have seen one. And of those, 14 percent say they have had, or know someone who has had, at least one Close Encounter of either the First through Third Kind [see Appendix C]. When this happens, people try to explain their sighting experience through their own perception and reality. And without anything else in their past with which to help them describe what they saw, basic shapes become the basis by which a witness can reconstruct their memory to the best of their ability. MUFON has twenty-three categories describing the objects ranging from saucers, triangles, cigar shapes, boomerang and egg shapes to categories designated as unknown or other. The goal is to capture the image through the witness's eyes as possible evidence of a visitation from another world.

Ruben Uriarte, director of MUFON in northern California,
personal interview

Other shapes used by witnesses to describe what they have seen include bells, hats, giant mother ships of various shapes and sizes, globes, arrowheads, teardrops, dumbbells, rhomboids, cylinders, bowls, footballs, cones, pyramids, and darts. In fact, almost every conceivable shape has been reported (see table 1 on page 13).

Table 1. UFO Shapes and Patterns

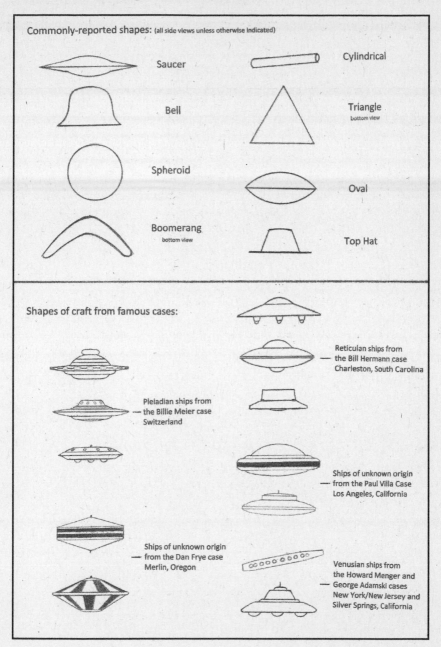

Commonly-reported shapes: (all side views unless otherwise indicated)

Saucer

Cylindrical

Bell

Triangle
bottom view

Spheroid

Oval

Boomerang
bottom view

Top Hat

Shapes of craft from famous cases:

Reticulan ships from the Bill Hermann case Charleston, South Carolina

Pleiadian ships from the Billie Meier case Switzerland

Ships of unknown origin from the Paul Villa Case Los Angeles, California

Ships of unknown origin from the Dan Frye case Merlin, Oregon

Venusian ships from the Howard Menger and George Adamski cases New York/New Jersey and Silver Springs, California

Early Sightings, Researchers, and Contactees

Part of any investigation is familiarizing yourself with the subject's history. A review of UFO investigation history reveals a convoluted quagmire of honest sleuth work and government misinformation, misdirection, and dishonesty in reporting research findings. According to many investigators, masterful mass public-relations campaigns have succeeded in diverting interest and smearing sincere investigators' work. Added to this is the constant threat of being fooled by a hoax.

Still, several diligent individuals, now deceased, persevered to form the foundation of what today is considered modern ufology. Each case, situation, or event offers UFO detectives many different lessons. In this chapter, I give one investigative tip after each section for the benefit of both quick field reference and extended philosophical consideration. These tips are gleaned from the work of the researchers indicated. For more information, see Appendix E.

Kenneth Arnold

The intrigue began with the very first "official" sighting and has continued until today.

Kenneth Arnold (1915–1984), pilot and businessman, reported the first UFO sighting on June 24, 1947, marking the beginning of the modern UFO era. By the time Arnold landed his plane in Pendleton, Oregon, his radio communications had created a media frenzy and he was greeted by several reporters and others at the airstrip. He became an overnight sensation, which alerted the Army Air Force. They immediately approached Arnold for an interview to assess any possible threat.

Officially, this is when the military became involved. However, after interviewing several other pilots about what he had seen, Arnold came to believe that the Air Force had to have known about this long before then. Not only did this event mark the beginning of the modern UFO era, but it also marked, among other things, the beginning of the now familiar battles between the various theories about the phenomena and between "believers" and "skeptics."

For example, UFO skeptic Gregory M. Kanon, in his book *The Great UFO Hoax: The Final Solution to the UFO Mystery* (1997), points out that some obvious similarities exist between Arnold's drawings and today's advanced stealth aircraft. Further, he points to an April 7, 1950, *US News & World Report* article that claimed that, after "extensive interviews," they had concluded: "They [the purported UFOs] are actual planes, soundly engineered on principles developed by the US in wartime."

On the same day in 1950, Arnold told Edward R. Murrow in a telephone interview how he felt:

> Well, I'll tell you this much—all the airline pilots, none of us have appreciated being laughed at. We made our reports essentially to begin with, because we thought that if our government didn't know what it was, it was only our duty to report it to our

nation, and to our Air Force out of it [sic]. I think it's something that is of concern to every person in the country, and I don't think it's anything for people to get hysterical about. That's just my frank opinion of it.

Ed Murrow–Kenneth Arnold telephone conversation,
www.project1947.com/fig/kamurrow.htm

In 1952, with Ray Palmer of *Fate* magazine, Arnold wrote one of the first UFO books, *The Coming of the Saucers*. He was arguably the first open critic of the military's handling of all aspects of the incident. In the end, after all the public and governmental scrutiny, Arnold was quoted as saying "If I saw a 10-story building flying through the air, I would never say a word about it" (*www.project1947.com*).

INVESTIGATIVE TIP: Every person, every corporation, and every government has an agenda. Try not to be overly naïve. Try to interview as many witnesses to an incident as possible for maximum comparison potential. There are consequences for telling the truth.

KENNETH ARNOLD

Frank Scully

Frank Scully (1892–1964), writer for *Variety* magazine, was the author of one of the first UFO books, *Behind the Flying Saucers* (1950). His set of articles for *Variety* in 1949 was the second set of published articles on the subject, the first being that of Arnold and Palmer in *Fate* in 1948. In *Behind the Flying Saucers*, Scully explored several pertinent issues of the day, setting the early standard of research for the many books to follow—the kinds of people to interview, the kinds of science to apply in an investigation, and how to tell when you are being lied to by the authorities.

Scully talked with astronomers, astrophysicists, and engineers, as well as with a variety of specialists including pilots, both civilian and military, in an early effort to make sense of the Aztec crashed-disk case in which, on March 25, 1948, a disk-shaped craft allegedly crashed on a mesa twelve miles east of Aztec, New Mexico. There were two other alleged crashes associated with Aztec as well. Scully was also one of the early proponents of saucers flying by some kind of electromagnetic propulsion, a common theory today.

Because he was first on the scene with a book, he was also the first writer/reporter to undergo severe public scrutiny and engineered discrediting from the newly formed MJ-12 secret governmental, military, and civilian organization set up to assess and "handle" the UFO "problem." However, despite extended efforts to smear Scully's reputation and discredit his story, many believed he was telling the truth and that his sources, although controversial, were legitimate. For example, British author Timothy Good devoted a chapter to championing Scully's integrity in *Above Top Secret* (1987).

This was also the beginning of the battle between the "Saucerians," who believed there was a government cover-up of UFOs, and the "Pentagonians," who did their best to convince the Saucerians and the rest of the world that UFOs do not exist, let alone come from other planets. Scully and his book have inspired thousands of individuals to seek explanations for their own experiences. This—inevitably, in many cases—led to confrontation with some type of government and/or military authorities. This brings us to one of many investigator/research tips that can be gleaned from Scully's work.

INVESTIGATIVE TIP: I advise readers to treat any official comment as no more to be considered than old newspapers blowing in the wind.

FRANK SCULLY, *BEHIND THE FLYING SAUCERS*

Donald E. Keyhoe

Donald E. Keyhoe (1897–1988) was a retired Marine major and an aviation writer. By the time the phrase "flying saucers" was coined in 1947, Keyhoe was an experienced aviator with a career in the military and experience as a freelance writer. In 1950, when aviation publication *True Magazine* asked him to investigate the 1949 phenomena, launching the third set of published articles on the subject, he was a skeptic. But his very first investigation convinced him that the Army Air Force must have known what was going on with UFOs.

After over 800 eye-witness reports, testimonies, and interviews, Keyhoe became one of the first writers to become convinced that the U.S. government and military were withholding pertinent data regarding UFOs. The fact that he was a retired Marine added credibility to his information and claims. He became the director of the civilian National Investigations Committee on Aerial Phenomena (NICAP) in 1957 and, in that capacity, was the first to encourage congressional hearings on the matter.

Although Keyhoe had written extensively in the fiction genre well before his interest in UFOs, it is his five UFO books that have garnered him the most notoriety. They are *The Flying Saucers Are Real* (1950), *Flying Saucers from Outer Space* (1953), *The Flying Saucer Conspiracy* (1955), *Flying Saucers: Top Secret* (1960), and *Aliens from Space* (1973).

As the first writer to consider the psychological and spiritual ramifications of contact with an alien species through UFOs, Keyhoe initiated what has since become the famous exchange with psychologist Carl Jung, the progenitor of the theory of the "collective unconscious." Most interesting is that Jung admitted that he could not tell whether or not UFOs were real physical objects or some type of mass hallucination, and that there was not enough information to make a valid assessment of the phenomena. Yet later, he said that he thought that there was something physical at work, although wouldn't say what he thought that was (see Jung's *Flying Saucers: A Modern Myth of Things Seen in the Skies* [1959]).

Jung recognized Keyhoe's dilemma and offered some basic investigative advice: "There are two aspects to any experience, (1) pure fact and (2) the way one conceives of it." Several good books have been authored on this subject, including *UFOs and the Bible* (1956) by Morris K. Jessup, *UFO's: A Scientific Debate* (1972) edited by Carl Sagan and Thornton Page, *The Invisible College* (1975) by Jacques Vallée, and *Divine Encounters* (1995) by Zecharia Sitchin.

INTERVIEW TIP: A witness's perceptions are, to varying degrees, colored by their cultural beliefs: spiritual, religious, political, moral, etc.

DONALD E. KEYHOE

James E. McDonald

Dr. James E. McDonald (1920–1971) was an atmospheric physicist at the Institute for Atmospheric Physics. According to Ann Druffel, author of *Firestorm!: Dr. James E. McDonald's Fight for UFO Science* (2003), McDonald is seen as the first credible and established U.S. scientist to consider seriously the possibility that UFOs originate somewhere other than Earth. He was also the first eminent scientist to work with civilian researchers and organizations "toward a common goal." Railing against the Air Force's handling of many sighting cases in Project Blue Book (1947–1969), McDonald consequently became antagonistic toward a prominent member of the project, Dr. J. Allen Hynek. He continued his rejection of the Air Force's final conclusions in their Condon Report, which was issued in 1969. McDonald (along with other prominent ufologists) made fierce criticisms of the committee's leadership and bias, but to no avail. The Condon Report couldn't find explanations for nearly one-third of the cases it examined, but Edward Condon, in his introduction to the report, flatly stated that UFOs didn't exist and that serious science had nothing to gain from studying the subject (from *Projectcamelot.org/mcdonald.html*).

INTERVIEW TIP: Respect is part of correct interviewing and investigation. In *Firestorm!* I describe how Rex Heflin was interviewed by several non-respectful scientists at a Los Angeles/NICAP Subcommittee meeting in the later 1960s. If these scientists had the ability to interview with respect (even though they might be non-accepting of the validity of Heflin's photos), the meeting might have had better results than it did.

ANN DRUFFEL, PERSONAL INTERVIEW

McDonald had a reputation at the university as a highly energetic and thorough researcher and was well respected even by his critics. By the time of his untimely death by alleged suicide in 1971, McDonald had published fifty technical papers on atmospheric physics in magazines like *Nature* and *Science* and was an early pioneer of weather modification. He also wrote sixty other papers. For example, he wrote a paper on his own research findings that a lighter baseball bat would produce more home runs, a finding still appreciated by today's home-run kings.

McDonald wrote another forty papers on UFOs. His impassioned pleas before Congress for the need to study UFO phenomena invoke images of Fox Mulder on television's *The X-Files*. In the end, whether McDonald's death was a suicide (as his family believes it was) or the result of a deliberately engineered attempt to grind away at his psyche and control his mind (as some have alleged), Druffel paints a painful picture of unfortunate emotional disappointments—associated not just with his work, but also with his personal life—stemming largely from the UFO aspect of his research.

Maintaining an emotional balance in your life, especially in the face of the kinds of information that researchers face when dealing with the subject of UFOs, is paramount to being a fair and impartial investigator and is imperative to being a healthy human being as well. McDonald's life and work offer modern investigators many lessons. What seems to have stood out to witnesses he interviewed, however, was his ability to stay calm and to maintain both emotional and intellectual neutrality.

Joseph Allen Hynek

Dr. Joseph Allen Hynek (1910–1986) was an astronomy professor at Ohio State University. Because of his reputation as a leader in his field, he was picked to be the astronomical consultant to the Air Force's Project Blue Book from 1948 to 1969. From there, he went on to found one of the leading civilian research organizations, the Center for UFO Studies (CUFOS) in 1973. He wrote two landmark books: *The UFO Experience: A Scientific Inquiry* (1972), in which he invented the close-encounter classification system, or "CE I–III," and his highly praised *The Hynek UFO Report* (1977).

A much maligned figure among early proponents of open scientific scrutiny of UFO phenomena, Hynek was treated—and there is some justification for this—as the figurehead for government/military misinformation, disinformation, and feigned indifference.

McDonald, repeatedly frustrated with Hynek's seeming unwillingness to come forward with information, wrote him a letter that stated, in part:

> I think when the facts are all set forth, Don Keyhoe will appear, in the deeper sense of the term, a far better scientist than you, when your respective contributions to progress in the UFO arena are finally toted up. Keyhoe will get praise and you'll get some of the criticisms you've felt free to aim in his general direction over the years of your Air Force consultancy.
>
> Ann Druffel, *Firestorm!*

Hynek appears to have opened up more as time went on, and he was respected by his colleagues, despite having to weather years of verbal shots by serious civilian researchers. In the end, Hynek was able to see the things that fellow researchers like McDonald and others were trying to tell him about the military's dubious, publicly released "findings" in both Project Blue Book and the Condon Report. In the recently discovered Introduction to his third and last book, *Night Siege* (available at *www.cufos.org*), he concluded:

> Intellectual adventure is not sterile when there is the continual ability to seek answers to challenges. . . .The Boomerang and the Holocaust are but striking samples of what happens when the collective mind willfully disregards evidence when "it can't take it." The entire modern UFO syndrome is another: here we have utterly ample evidence of the global nature of the UFO phenomenon. Thousands of instances and over many countries the evidence for the UFO phenomenon is clear, but those in position of policy and authority (FAA, educators, scientists etc) are deaf or purposely obtuse.

INVESTIGATIVE TIP: Don t be afraid to go slow and work in a methodical way. The old adage "slow and steady wins the race." often applies in UFO field investigation.

J. ALLEN HYNEK

George van Tassel

George van Tassel (1910–1978) was an aviation engineer, pilot, and contactee. In 1951, after he had moved his family to Giant Rock, California in the Mojave Desert in 1947, van Tassel began having alleged UFO contacts after meditation sessions in underground rooms hewn beneath the mammoth boulder. During these visits, van Tassel received information that was to change the world.

Here, he was given the knowledge of "cell rejuvenation" in the form of the Integretron—"a machine, a high-voltage, electrostatic generator that would supply a broad range of frequencies to recharge the cell structure" (see *www.integretron.com*). He went on to found and host the first UFO expositions known as the Giant Rock Space Conventions from 1953 to 1970 and founded the Ministry of Universal Wisdom, which became the blueprint for most of the contactee and channeled cosmic philosophies that followed.

Van Tassel's basic premise was that human beings were hybrids—both from Earth and not from Earth—who were seeded on the planet by extraterrestrials thousands of years ago. Humanity has erred, he claimed, in creating the moral, environmental, health, and economic situations it faces today. So it needs to raise its vibration in order to embrace a future of harmony rather than war and destruction.

Van Tassel was also the first contactee to profess that he had futuristic health technology (the Integretron) to use for the benefit of humankind. This has since been identified by psychological profilers as part of the contactee modus operandi—the pattern of behavior typical of this kind of person—and an aspect always to consider in any investigation (see Appendix B).

Van Tassel wrote five books, starting with the classic *I Rode a Flying Saucer* (1952), and followed by *Into This World and Out Again* (1956), *The Council of Seven Lights* (1958), *Religion and Science Merged* (1968), and *When Stars Look Down* (1999), a posthumous release.

INTERVIEW TIP: Always consider the state of consciousness of any interview subject. Know why they are happy, sad, angry or nervous, etc.

GEORGE VAN TASSEL, *WWW.INTEGRETRON.COM*

George Adamski

George Adamski (1891–1965), contactee and author, was the first popular speaker about UFOs and his alleged contact experience. He is often associated with Howard Menger, Frank Stranges, and Omnec Onec because of their similar "Venusian" contact contexts. He coauthored *Flying Saucers Have Landed* (1953) with Desmond Leslie and wrote *Inside the Spaceships* (1955).

Like van Tassel, Adamski founded another cosmic philosophy organization called the George Adamski Foundation in Vista, California. He taught a Utopian worldview, claiming that humankind was not living within universal laws and that it had to correct its behavior if it were to survive. The theory falls in line with popular Ascended Master doctrine, as well as with much channeled material. Many of his early disciples waned in their support toward the end, feeling that his lectures were more show than truth.

Adamski may have had more accusations slung at him, both during and after his life, than any other individual figure in UFO history. There are a large number of websites with banners like "Profiles in Pseudoscience: George Adamski" and, in 1955, the U.S. government sought to sue him for fraud.

Author Richard M. Dolan, in his now classic *UFOs and the National Security State: Chronology of a Cover-up, 1941–1973* (2002), writes: "In 1955, Thomas Eickhoff tried to force the US government into suing UFO contactee George Adamski for an act of fraud in the US mail system. The pretext: Adamski claimed to be in contact with beings from Venus and was using the US Postal Service to help sell his books." They were unsuccessful. The apparent lack of witnesses who could testify due to reasons of "maximum security" was enough to end the case.

INVESTIGATIVE TIP: Consistency—in witnesses, in your professional actions, and throughout your life—is paramount to foster public and professional credibility.

GEORGE ADAMSKI

Gray Barker

Gray Barker (1925–1984), theatrical film booker, author, and publisher, wrote the famous book *They Knew Too Much About Flying Saucers* (1956). This was the first book to describe the phenomena of Men in Black—mysterious men who approached UFO witnesses, scientists, researchers, and possessors of alleged UFO fragments and harassed them in several ways. In fact, the book coined the phrase "Men in Black" and introduced the world to the dark side of the UFO field.

In the book, Barker also popularized the term "the three men," which became a common nickname for MiBs, referencing the three mysterious men who visited Albert K. Bender, founder of the International Flying Saucer Bureau in Bridgeport, Connecticut, in a now famous 1953 event. These men were apparently polite but strongly insinuated that Bender should drop the whole search for UFOs—or else. Bender later chronicled his story in *Flying Saucers and the Three Men* (1963).

In 1956, however, Barker was the first to bring the story to light, which paved the way for many later books and movies, among them Jenny Randles's *The Truth behind Men in Black: Government Agents—or Visitors from Beyond* (1997), Timothy Green Beckley's *Mystery of the Men in Black: The UFO Silencers* (1990), and Jim Keith's *Casebook on the Men in Black* (1997). These and other credible researchers managed, in a field with very few verifiable facts, to make a convincing case for the MiBs. On the other hand, documentaries like Ralph Coon's *Whispers from Space* (1995) gave an unflattering portrayal of Barker as a closet gay who liked to drink a bit too much. Movies like Hollywood's *Men in Black* (1997, 2002) starring Tommy Lee Jones and Will Smith are also worth review.

Writer John Sherwood, among others, called Barker a hoaxer and cited much proof to support his claim in a now famous article for *Skeptical Inquirer* called "Gray Barker: My Friend, the Myth-Maker." In it, Sherwood claims to have helped Barker create hoaxes and myths in print. This, according to detractors of Barker's work, is justification enough to throw out all the writer's work in the field.

Based on a survey of more recent work on the MiBs, however, their patterns of behavior—their harassment of those associated with a variety of mysterious events, their usually black attire, and their choice of vehicle (usually late-model Cadillacs)—seems to point to the fact that Barker's first book was dead-on, despite his later, and admittedly more questionable, work.

Consequently, Barker's 1956 book, *They Knew Too Much About Flying Saucers*, offers several lessons for the aspiring investigator, among them:

- Don't forget to smell the ground at ground level when investigating alleged landing sites for indicative odors.

- Try to gain the trust of any witnesses by talking sincerely with them.

- Be emotionally prepared for strange and often threatening phone calls at all hours of the day.

Perhaps most important of all, however, is the tip offered below.

MOTIVATIONAL TIP: After they {new UFO investigators} discover the volume of work involved in checking on an endless progression of tiring, undramatic, or even deliberately faked data, their enthusiasm is often short-lived.

GRAY BARKER, *THEY KNEW TOO MUCH ABOUT FLYING SAUCERS*

Philip Klass

Aviation writer Philip Klass (1919–2005) is known as the world's leading UFO skeptic. His is one of the most recognized names in ufology. He was an award-winning writer who also received the Lifetime Achievement Award from the Royal Aeronautical Society in London for his integrity.

In a 1993 debate on *Larry King Live* with David Jacobs, a Temple University professor who wrote a book suggesting that more than one million Americans have been abducted and taken aboard UFOs for study, Klass observed:

> If aliens are invading our bedrooms, impregnating our teenage girls; if they're abducting little children, cutting flesh samples out without even putting Band-Aids on; if you're not safe anywhere on the face of the Earth—then it is something that this nation needs to mobilize.

Claudia Levy, Washington Post, August 11, 2005

In this comment, it is easy to see that Klass came to the same conclusion about UFOs as many other researchers. The differences arose when he could find no credible evidence to support the idea that UFOs were from outer space. He argued that the only thing science had learned in fifty years of UFO research is that intelligent, credible witnesses can easily mistake Venus, meteor fireballs, and other weather phenomena for UFOs. It was this type of comment that earned Klass the disdain of UFO abductees and contactees.

Klass and Hynek even disagreed on occasion. In a 1953 incident involving a military helicopter over Mansfield, Ohio, a "red light" kept pace with the Huey and then turned on a collision course. After going into a dive drop, the UFO hovered over the dropping helicopter and flashed a green beam into the interior of the aircraft. Klass argued that what the soldiers in the helicopter had really seen was a shooting Orionid meteor. Hynek countered by saying that Klass's theory was "untenable" and argued that the "red light" could not possibly have been a meteor.

RESEARCH/RESOURCE TIP: One of the characteristic fingerprints of pseudoscience is that the passage of time provides no additional basic knowledge of an alleged phenomena.

THE MAMMOTH ENCYCLOPEDIA OF EXTRATERRESTRIAL ENCOUNTERS

John Mack

Dr. John Mack (1929–2004), professor of psychiatry at Harvard University, was considered the preeminent researcher of alleged UFO abductions. Mack was controversial at Harvard, not only because he sought to integrate spirituality with psychology, but also because of his early study of 200 alleged UFO abductees in the 1990s. For the first time in its history, Harvard launched a fifteen-month investigation of the man's professional protocols. Although they were not well-received, the faculty found no unethical or inappropriate behavior in his abduction studies.

In his book *Abduction: Human Encounters with Aliens* (2004), a summation of his findings from his abduction study, Mack propounded his now famous and controversial theory that UFOs are "more spiritual than physical. But still real."

MOTIVATIONAL TIP: If you believe what you have found is real and true, stick with it.

JOHN E. MACK

His conclusions that abductee experiences led to a change in their worldview and that those changes were for the better of the individual are both foundational and controversial. Many abductees are opposed to his idea that their experiences should be considered within the larger global traditions of visionary quests, or "walkabouts," in which a young person takes some type of journey to become an individualized and socially accepted member of society. Mack even claims: "The alien encounter experience seems almost like an outreach program from the cosmos to the consciously impaired."

Mack died shortly after being run over by an allegedly drunken man in London in 2004—a controversial life and a controversial death. Some think he was murdered, but no concrete evidence of that has ever come to light. His conclusions stand in contrast to fellow abduction-phenomena researcher Budd Hopkins, who accepted the physical reality of aliens in alleged victims' experiences.

In Mack's classic book *Passport to the Cosmos: Human Transformations and Alien Encounters* (1999), he laid out his societal philosophy that the Western world should turn away from materialism, as well as what he thought was his final word on the subject.

Leonard H. Stringfield

Leonard H. Stringfield (1920–1994) was another ex-military man who pioneered mainstream crash/recovery research and opened the door for many others. He self-published seven Status Reports over the course of his life, which are now considered classics in the field. The reports outline many characteristics of the alleged occupants of crashed disks and are where many of today's popular conceptions about these phenomena first originated.

This is also where Hollywood got its images of small gray aliens with elastic, scaly, mesh-like skin similar to that of a chameleon, iguana, or other lizard-like reptile. The popular idea of reptilian aliens grew from this and was reinforced by the media and movies, including *Communion* (1988) starring Christopher Walken, *Enemy Mine* (1985), *They Live* (1988), *Star Trek's* Gorn, and many others.

As far as resumes go, not many can stack up to Stringfield's. He held several public relations, editing, publishing, and/or writing positions in organizations like Civilian Research, Interplanetary Flying Objects (CRIFO), National Investigations Committee on Aerial Phenomena (NICAP), and the Mutual UFO Network (MUFON). He also acted as a civilian investigator for the military and had a special code number with which he could contact his military liaisons at Air Defense Command in Dayton, Ohio.

Stringfield's major works in the field include his famous newsletter *Inside Saucer Post . . . 3-0 Blue*, which he wrote and published for

CRIFO in the 1950s, the book *Situation Red: The UFO Siege* (1977), as well as seven Status Reports: *Retrievals of a Third Kind* (1978), *The UFO Crash/Retrieval Syndrome* (1982), *UFO Crash/Retrievals: Amassing the Evidence* (1982), *The Fatal Encounter at Fort Dix–McGuire* (1985), *UFO Crash/Retrievals: Is the Cover-up Lid Lifting?* (1989), *UFO Crash/Retrievals: The Inner Sanctum* (1991), and *UFO Crash/Retrievals: Search for Proof in a Hall of Mirrors* (1994). Stringfield's work demonstrates how having good connections can increase research capabilities and offer a wider variety of opportunities to obtain pertinent data.

INVESTIGATIVE TIP: Networking is key for information gathering in UFO investigations.

LEONARD H. STRINGFIELD

Carl Sagan

Dr. Carl Sagan (1934–1996), astronomer, physicist, author, and television host, was known for his PBS science specials, most notably the science series *Cosmos*. But Sagan has a lesser-known history in the world of UFOs as well. While he is well-known for his pioneering work in the mainstream fields of exobiology and artificial intelligence, he was also pivotal in the not-so-mainstream formation of SETI (search for extraterrestrial intelligence). For pro-UFO researchers, this is where the controversy begins.

For example, renowned researcher Stanton T. Friedman (see chapter 3) sees Sagan as a government-cover-up sympathizer because of his public support of SETI, something Friedman refers to as the "silly effort to investigate." Another controversy arose from the part Sagan played in Project Blue Book, the much-maligned Air Force program to "investigate" UFO phenomena. Sagan also disagreed with renowned abduction researcher and medical psychologist John Mack, saying that he did not "use the scientific method." Mack countered by arguing that Sagan discounted valuable emotional content from abductee testimony. One thing you cannot argue, however: Sagan has always been consistent.

Sagan never denied that he was open to the possibility that some UFOs could originate from other worlds; he just denied that there was hard evidence for it. He never denied the possibility of alien abduction; he just denied that there was any hard evidence of such events. He was, however, a proponent of the idea that UFOs and abduction experiences represented a question, not for hard science, but for religion, theology, and superstition. In other words, he believed that these events—sightings, contacts, abductions, etc.—all happened in the mind of the experiencer.

Sagan wrote several books, including the Pulitzer Prize–winning *The Dragons of Eden: Speculations on the Evolution of Human Intelligence* (1977), *UFO's: A Scientific Debate* (1972) edited with Thornton Page, *The Demon-Haunted World: Science as a Candle in the Dark* (1997), *Contact* (1997), and *Cosmic Connection: An Extraterrestrial Perspective* (2000).

RESEARCH/RESOURCE TIP: Extraordinary claims require extraordinary evidence.

Carl Sagan, *Cosmos* TV series, 1980

Wendelle C. Stevens

Lieutenant Colonel Wendelle C. Stevens (retired Air Force, 1923–2010) was an author, lecturer, and publisher who did a lot of work collaborating with other international and American investigators to chronicle UFO and abduction phenomena. He was a part of the reporting and investigation of some of the most famous modern contact stories ever recorded, including the Billy Meier case in Switzerland (see chapter 4), the abduction at Maringa, Brazil, and various alleged Venusian contacts. A first edition of his book *UFO: From Venus I Came* (1990), coauthored with Omnec Onec, has fetched over $1,500 on Amazon.

Stevens did major investigative work on the Billy Meier case, along with Lee and Brit Elders, who wrote and produced the two now famous coffee-table books called *UFO . . . Contact with the Pleiades,* volumes I and II (1979, 1983). Some of the best UFO photographs ever taken come from this case, and they led to Stevens becoming world renowned for his UFO photo collection. Stevens went on to pen six other books, continuing the series: *UFO Contact from the Pleiades: A Preliminary Investigation Report* (1982), *Contact from the Pleiades: A Supplementary Report* (1983), and *Message from the Pleiades: The Contact Notes of Eduard Billy Meier,* volumes I–IV (1988–1995). All are now out of print and worth hundreds of dollars each if you can find them.

Stevens's work has proven invaluable to later researchers for many reasons. Perhaps most important of all is the way he cross-references seemingly unrelated abduction cases. He's found similarities of contact testimonies suggesting a concerted global effort to reach humanity by an other-world species—reports of the same kind of being wearing similar uniforms with similar insignia, for instance. Contactee/abductees have even reported that their captors have referenced other contact events, indicating such a concerted global effort.

**INVESTIGATIVE TIP: Cross-reference as much informa-
tion as possible not only to test the authenticity of
testimony and other data, but also to bring forth more
deeply ingrained patterns of behavior, both of the con-
tactee/abductee and their alleged abductors.**

WENDELLE C. STEVENS

Milton William ("Bill") Cooper

Milton William Cooper (1943–2001), former Air Force and Navy officer, radio personality, political activist, author, and lecturer, was reared in an Air Force family and served with the Strategic Air Command. He held a secret clearance working on B-52 bombers, KC-135 refueling aircraft, and Minuteman missiles. He was a member of the Office of Naval Intelligence and was awarded several medals for his leadership and heroism during combat, including two for valor.

Cooper produced several documentaries covering subjects like the Kennedy assassination and secret black projects that have built flying disk-shaped craft. He was an internationally acclaimed radio personality, broadcasting *Hour of the Time* on WBCQ worldwide shortwave. He is also the author of the now classic tome *Behold a Pale Horse* (1991), which is considered one of the most controversial and bestselling underground books in the UFO field of all time.

Shortly after Cooper's publishing house, Harvest Trust, published Michele Marie Moore's *Oklahoma City: Day One* (1996), Rush Limbaugh read a White House memo on the air that named Cooper "the most dangerous radio host in America."

In the Clinton administration, Cooper's FBI file was part of what came to be known as "Filegate." Shortly after this discovery, President Clinton ordered all federal agencies to begin investigating and harassing him through prosecution. Cooper considered Clinton's pronouncement the greatest compliment he had ever received.

After years of filing FOIA (Freedom of Information Act) requests and researching the IRS, Cooper brought suit against the agency in federal district court in Phoenix, Arizona, to force them to produce proof of jurisdiction and delegation of authority, which the IRS was unable to do. To short-circuit Cooper's attempt to reveal the true nature of the criminal IRS, and to carry out the orders of the White House, it is believed that the agency lied to a grand jury, thereby keeping him from testifying, and secured indictments against both him and his wife.

In March 1999, Cooper sent his family out of the United States for their security. Cooper was later killed under mysterious circumstances by the Apache County Sheriff's Department during a raid on his home in November 2001.

CAUTIONARY TIP: What happens when you broadcast the truth is you piss everyone off.

WILLIAM COOPER,
HOUR OF THE TIME RADIO BROADCAST, 1991

Karla Turner

Dr. Karla Turner (1947–1996) was a professional educator, scholar, and author. She was also an abductee. Turner was widely respected in the UFO community for her research on alien abduction. She earned a Ph.D. in Old English studies and taught at the university level in Texas for over ten years. In 1988, however, after she and her family endured a series of experiences and recollections that forced them to acknowledge that they were abductees, she began her abduction research.

In the eyes of many ufologists, abductees are "flakes"—people with mental problems who have nothing to do with UFOs. Or worse, they are seen as so far "out there" that many refer to them as "tinfoil-hat people" or "channelers" from another planet. Some feel that they are absolutely not to be taken seriously.

Turner understood this and sought to change the perception. She was instrumental in bringing malevolent alien abduction—reptilian and mantis, among others—into the forefront of anomalous research and making it an accepted and legitimate part of the field. Further, she and her work are credited with bringing credibility to abductees, which has helped to remove societal stigmas and paved the way for more alleged victims, formerly too ashamed to come forward, to speak out.

She has also done pioneering work in the area of "Milabs," or military abductions—black operations in which a secret group abducts individuals and performs some type of mind-control operation on them or waits until abductees are dropped off by their alien abductors and then re-abducts them for mind-controlled debriefing (see chapter 5).

Turner wrote three books: *Into the Fringe* (1992), *Taken: Inside the Alien-Human Abduction Agenda* (1994), and *Masquerade of Angels* (1994), which was cowritten with psychic Ted Rice. Turner was working on another book when she became ill in early 1995. Although many suspected it, it was never shown whether or not her abduction experiences had anything to do with her illness—a fast-acting, unknown form of cancer.

INTERVIEW TIP: Investigators who have not had personal experiences with the phenomenon may not be able to tell the difference between what is a real memory or what is an illusion. But the abductee understands that it may very well be both at once: both mental and illusory.

KARLA TURNER

Modern Research, Researchers, and Contactees

Today's UFO investigations are as muddled, convoluted, and perplexing as the research field's history. With pitfalls like threats and interference from government agents, possible contact with exotic and often toxic substances, potentially harmful advanced technology, and self-financed field excursions, it is really a wonder that there are so many competent researchers and investigators currently active.

Nonetheless, many a brave soul has persevered and gone on to add to the colossal body of research data on UFOs readily accessible to any aspiring investigator. Many of the people listed below—and this list is far from comprehensive—have joined civilian research organizations like MUFON, CUFOS, or NICAP in order to benefit from the easy access to archival information found on their respective websites. Some have gone on to represent these groups. Still others have chosen to remain independent, working with these organizations on a case-by-case basis.

As an independent investigator, you can find a wealth of information on the Internet (see Appendix E), and there are scores of books and DVDs on a wide range of related topics as well. Research has branched out in many directions, and there are many areas where new, fresh thinking is sorely needed if certain cases are ever to be cracked. In fact, some cases will never be resolved, but this has not stopped the incredibly curious, competent, and capable investigators who continue to try. The truth is out there.

Ruben Uriarte

Ruben Uriarte—author, speaker, and MC—is state director and deputy director for International Investigations/Activities for the MUFON in northern California. He has been interviewed on many Bay Area and national radio shows and television documentaries on the subject of UFOs. Uriarte has coauthored a series of books with researcher Noe Torres about major UFO crash incidents that have occurred along the southwestern United States border with Mexico.

The Other Roswell: UFO Crash on the Texas-Mexico Border (2008) discloses for the first time the eyewitness testimony of Colonel Robert B. Willingham (Ret.), who says that he chased a UFO across Texas, saw it crash to the Earth near Del Rio, Texas, and later visited the crash site. Uriarte and Torres appeared in a first-season episode of the History Channel's *UFO Hunters* television series to further explore the case. They also appeared in the *UFO Hunters* episode entitled "Crash and Retrieval," which was based on the research the authors did for their book *Mexico's Roswell: The Chihuahua UFO Crash* (2007, 2008). The authors served as technical advisors for the program, which first aired on February 20, 2008. On July 11, 2008, clips from the program were shown on CNN's *Larry King Live*.

As one of MUFON's leading investigators, Uriarte has also researched crop circles, animal mutilations, and even the mysterious *chupacabra*. He appeared and was an official consultant on the Learning Channel show *Monster Hunters*, which aired in 2000. A group of "remote viewers" (see chapter 6) was brought in to assist. Although the Beyond Boundaries Expedition to Puerto Rico did not locate any of these elusive creatures, Uriarte felt that they found "so much testimony that one is left with the impression that this elusive creature does exist."

As a bilingual lecturer and member of OMIFO, Mexico's version of MUFON, Uriarte has not only been instrumental in bringing top Latin American researchers to America, but, in doing so, he has also been able to bridge the gap between research in the United States and many Central and South American countries. His international diplomacy has also helped him become one of two masters of ceremonies (author Robert Perala is the other) at the annual Bay Area UFO Expo.

INTERVIEW TIP: Learn the art of questioning: asking questions in unique ways, reading body language, and keeping quiet and letting the person talk are just a few of things necessary to master this skill set.

RUBEN URIARTE, PERSONAL INTERVIEW

Nancy Red Star

Nancy Red Star is an author, filmmaker, and Native American "Runner." The Native American viewpoint is a truly valuable one when it comes to explaining the UFO phenomenon, about which different cultures hold different views. In Red Star's classic work *Star Ancestors: Indian Wisdomkeepers Share the Teachings of the Extraterrestrials* (2000), she chronicles several tribal traditions from the Western hemisphere about how Natives have had ongoing, peaceful, and positive interactions with many different kinds of beings.

Some of these beings are physical, material beings, including what many in the modern world refer to as aliens, or extraterrestrials. Some are encountered aboard their vehicles, or flying saucers. Some are ethereal, energetic beings—what Red Star refers to as "ultraterrestrials"—confirming what Keel described to the Western world in the 1960s. She chronicles how these beings impart wisdom in many forms, heal a variety of maladies, and bestow prophecy on shamans to help their respective societies.

Red Star's *Legends of the Star Ancestors: Stories of Extraterrestrial Contact from Wisdomkeepers Around the World* (2002) reveals that the pattern of peaceful interaction with UFOs—whatever they are, or wherever they are encountered—is a global phenomenon. The Native perspective, in general, focuses more on the spirituality of these interactions, calling into question the age-old themes of the nature of reality and consciousness, the purpose of our lives, and our place in the bigger picture. Often, UFOs and their occupants are viewed as a mirror of the Native peoples and their cultures—a true mirror of the Self.

Fear is commonplace in the study of UFOs in the West—and justifiably so, considering the various levels of danger that have been reported. According to the Native view, however, there need never be any fear associated with UFOs because they are just a reflection of the society that perceives them. The common belief is that the world's governments and subordinate militaries view UFOs with fear because that is what is inside of them.

MOTIVATIONAL TIP: By showing myself that I can find out about this information, I am demonstrating that anyone can find out for themselves, if they look hard enough. And that is what people need to do: find out for themselves.

NANCY RED STAR, PERSONAL INTERVIEW

You can find out more about Red Star's work on her website at *www.nancyredstar.com*.

Linda Moulton Howe

Researcher, documentarian, and lecturer Linda Moulton Howe has received local, national, and international awards, including three regional Emmys and a national Emmy nomination. Her film *A Strange Harvest* explored the worldwide animal-mutilation mystery that has haunted the United States and other countries from the mid-20th century to today, gaining her recognition in the paranormal research fields. While her work delves into many areas of the paranormal, it was her study of animal mutilations that led to her study of crop circles and UFOs, which are sometimes seen in close proximity to animal mutilations (see chapter 5).

Howe's website (*www.earthfiles.com*) is a clearinghouse for information on a variety of subjects. You can do your own research or enter blogs and chat in real time with like-minded people. From this site alone, you can bring yourself up to speed in many areas of paranormal/metaphysical research.

Howe has received the Aviation and Space Writers Association Award for Writing Excellence in Television. That kind of talent is what prompted HBO to engage her in 1983 to do a UFO documentary. She tells the story in her now classic *Animal Mutilations: The UFO Factor* (1988). Researcher/attorney Peter Gersten of Citizens Against UFO Secrecy set up a meeting with Special Agent Doty from Kirtland Air Force Base in Albuquerque, New Mexico, in April of 1983. Howe says Doty told her that he had been asked by his superiors to show her the briefing papers; she could ask questions but could not take notes.

The agent told Howe that she was being shown the briefing papers because the government intended to release to her several hundred feet of color and black-and-white film, including footage of crashed disks, alien bodies, and an alleged landing at Holloman Air Force Base. The film was intended to be used in her HBO UFO documentary.

When it came time to receive the film, however, Agent Doty claimed that there were "political delays" and that he was off the project.

The film was never released, prompting Howe to speculate: "Perhaps that was the government's goal all along. . . . I'm not sure how much of what I saw and heard was misinformation or fact." As a result, she reported the astounding information in *Animal Mutilations* as "speculation." The experience holds many lessons for UFO investigators, but chief among them is the tip below.

RESEARCH/RESOURCE TIP: A good rule of thumb is to accept all information reported and evaluate it later. Be clear as to whether the information you are reporting is fact or speculation. The risk of being perceived as a "dupe" is too great to make a mistake.

LINDA MOULTON HOWE, *ANIMAL MUTILATIONS*

Farah Yurdozu

Farah Yurdozu, a Turkish investigator and third-generation abductee/contactee, is the first female investigator of UFOs in Turkey. She has written seven English/Turkish books, among them *UFOs are Coming/UFOlar Geliyor* (1993), *Life is a Horror Movie/Yaşam Bir Korku Filmidir* (1999), *UFO Truths and Lies/UFO Gerçekleri ve Yalanları* (1999), *Confessions of a Turkish Ufologist* (2007), *You Are Your Soulmate* (2007), *UFO Forbidden Zone/UFO Yasak Bölge* (2008), and *Love in an Alien Purgatory* (2009). She has also been an outspoken advocate of Turkey's "real" history—the theory that its society originated with an alien hybrid being named Oguz Kagan over 2,200 years ago (see her website at *www.farahyurdozu.com*).

Yurdozu maintains that the founder of the modern Turkish Republic, Mustafa Kemal Atatürk, was the first exopolitical leader of the world and that he traced the origins of the Turkish peoples through Mu, or Lemuria, and back to the nation's cosmic ties to the Sirius star system.

In the United States and Latin America, Yurdozu utilizes her fluent English and Spanish to bridge cultural gaps between East and West in well-presented and informative lectures. In them, she maintains that her family's contact has been ongoing for at least three generations. She also argues that the people in her country view these alleged beings as "jinns," or a specific type of spirit for which they show great respect and reverence. And most surprising, from a Western standpoint, is that the Turkish government and its people are not secretive about the subject.

Yurdozu's gifts as a psychic medium were recently featured in the Learning Channel's paranormal investigation TV series *Dead Tenants*. She is a columnist for the leading semi-monthly UFO publication *UFO Magazine* and a journalist/producer at Jerry Pippin Internet Radio. Though her work reflects a passion for all aspects of the paranormal, her main area of study is abductions and close encounters. As a result, she says, "the meaning of being a UFO/paranormal researcher is a constant self-education."

SPECIAL KNOWLEDGE/SKILLS TIP: A good researcher must have a very open mind about world cultures, religions, old traditions and new scientific developments. Also, a basic knowledge of how to identify fake videos and photographs is always a must for a real UFO investigator.

FARAH YURDOZU, PERSONAL INTERVIEW

Ann Druffel

Ann Druffel is a paranormal researcher, author, and lecturer who dates her interest in the UFO question back to 1945 when, as a schoolgirl, she and her mother viewed a bright yellowish UFO very high in clear blue skies over Long Beach, California.

The incident sparked a lifelong interest in Earth mysteries of all kinds. She was one of the first investigators for NICAP, remaining with that organization from April 1957 to 1973. During those years, she became acquainted with the renowned atmospheric physicist James E. McDonald (see chapter 2) and participated with him in several UFO cases during his six years of public UFO research.

After NICAP's controversial demise, Druffel joined MUFON, with which she is still actively associated as an investigator. She is a frequent contributor to their journals and serves in other official capacities today. She also joined the Center for UFO Studies (CUFOS) and contributes articles on California sightings and other UFO subjects to *International UFO Reporter* (IUR). She was a U.S. consultant and regular contributor to the British research journal *Flying Saucer Review* (FSR) through 2004. She has authored six books and contributed more than 200 articles and columns to top UFO journals. The breadth of her career shows the value of having a scientific, or scientifically oriented, background if you seek to investigate UFOs (see *www.anndruffel.com*).

Druffel has also done extensive work in the field of alien abductions. In *How to Defend Yourself Against Alien Abduction* (1998), she presents many true accounts drawn from her present database of 120 "resisters" that demonstrate how nine simple mental and physical techniques can drive away these harassing creatures.

In general, Druffel hypothesizes that the so-called UFO phenomenon is actually two separate phenomena: sightings and abductions. The sightings of solid metallic craft of varying descriptions should be investigated by science, she maintains, arguing that the government cover-up "is illogical."

Druffel considers so-called abduction scenarios to be separate phenomena related to, but not the same as, the "possibly" extraterrestrial UFOs. Since most abduction scenarios take place in altered states of consciousness, she doubts the validity of much testimony due to the lack of solid scientific proof.

Stanton T. Friedman

In 1978, nuclear physicist, author, and lecturer Stanton T. Friedman
became the original civilian investigator into the Roswell Incident—the
now famous (or infamous) disk crash that occurred in early July 1947.
Crash at Corona (1992), which he coauthored with Don Berliner, is considered to be the definitive study of the event. Another Friedman book,
Top Secret/Majic (1996), outlines the document trail of the event, allegedly proving that the ultra-secretive MJ-12 group had been controlling
UFO information ever since the sightings went public in 1947. This
group has allegedly had a strong influence on the public perception of
both the Roswell and Aztec cases. He and many others allege that the
group is still in operation today.

Since he began speaking on the topic in 1967, Friedman has covered a wide variety of UFO cases that he summarizes in *Flying Saucers
Are Real*. He has a long list of accomplishments in the field aside from
the ongoing Roswell case: crucial analysis in the deciphering of the legendary "star map" from the Betty and Barney Hill abductee case from
the early 1960s and inquiry into the Delphos "physical trace" case. He
openly challenges any and all Air Force personnel to refute what he

calls "irrefutable evidence" of the existence of flying saucers and the fact that some of them are from outer space. That challenge has gone unanswered. These are just some of the things that have made Friedman an international icon for UFO researchers.

Friedman also wrote *Captured! The Betty and Barney Hill UFO Experience* (2007) with Kathleen Marden, niece of Betty Hill. She was his coauthor on *Flying Saucers and Science* (2008) and *Science Was Wrong* (2010) as well. He has provided written testimony to congressional hearings and appeared twice at the UN. The city of Fredericton, New Brunswick, declared August 27, 2007, to be Stanton Friedman Day. His website (*www.stantonfriedman.com*) is loaded with official documents and other information.

RESEARCH/RESOURCE TIP: Because many people today lack integrity and will say whatever they think will forward their ends and that nobody will check, it is a very good idea to pin people down on their degrees (which degrees from what school, when) and military background. Get a birth date so you can check records; colleges and the military. Many people have lied about their degrees to me. Also, obituaries give names and locations of married daughters and names of funeral homes, which keep extensive records.

STANTON T. FRIEDMAN, PERSONAL INTERVIEW

Robert O. Dean

Command Sergeant Major Robert O. Dean (retired 1976) first became interested in UFOs while in the military, from 1949 to 1976. Dean is a highly decorated combat veteran of both Korea and Vietnam. In 1967, while part of NATO's Supreme Headquarters Allied Powers Europe, or

SHAPE, he began extensive work within the Army intelligence community and became privy to a document now known as "The Assessment," subtitled "An Evaluation of Possible Military Threat to Allied Forces in Europe." After this, he received a Cosmic Top Secret security clearance and became one of "those in the know."

Most of Dean's work can be found on video, which seems contradictory for a man who has refused to use the Internet for security reasons. His work centers around enabling military veterans to speak openly about their experiences and UFO knowledge within a military context without fear of ridicule, defamation of character, prosecution, or loss of pension.

Currently, after over forty years of UFO research, Dean focuses on its spiritual ramifications for all of humanity. Reflecting on these issues, he asks his standing-room-only audiences worldwide to look within in order to prepare for what he feels is the inevitable first open contact with an extraterrestrial species. In his calm, warm, and heartfelt presentations, he makes the case that, with the coming Earth and paradigm changes, humanity will be forced to learn who it really is, both as a species and as individuals.

INTERVIEW TIP: Listen to everything the witness has to say. Even the most far-out observations have often been found to be true and valid. This subject stretches the limits of our complacent traditional world view. Apparently nothing is impossible. Don't disregard anything as absurd or impossible because, if you think about it, the very existence of human beings on this planet is absurd and impossible.

ROBERT O. DEAN, PERSONAL INTERVIEW

Nick Pope

Nick Pope is former director of the British government's UFO project at the Ministry of Defense (MoD). He was initially skeptical about UFOs, but his research and investigations, as well as his access to classified government files on the subject, soon convinced him that the phenomena raised important defense and national security issues. During his tenure, he was trained in media by the MoD so that he could appear on TV as an official spokesperson; he also learned to draft news briefs and press releases.

Pope left the MoD in 2006 after twenty-one years. Although best known for his work on the MoD's UFO project, he undertook a wide range of different jobs in the course of his career, the last of which was in a security-related area. He was formerly the military affairs consultant for *Eye Spy Magazine* and provides commentary on a range of defense, security, and intelligence-related areas—although the Official Secrets Act places obvious limits on what he is able to discuss. He contributed to the History Channel series *That's Impossible* in his capacity as a defense analyst, commenting on the military applications of fields like robotics, nanotechnology, and weather modification.

While investigating UFO sightings for the MoD, Pope was often accused of being part of a government cover-up to hide the truth about UFOs. He became interested in conspiracy theories more generally and the related issue of the psychology of belief. He has looked into various conspiracy theories, including those surrounding the assassination of JFK, the moon landings, the death of Princess Diana, and 9/11. He found that, when examined in detail, these conspiracy theories are based on factual inaccuracies or misinterpretations, together with fundamental misunderstandings about the way in which governments operate.

RESEARCH/RESOURCE TIP: Do not be conclusion led in your investigations. Set aside your personal beliefs and go where the data takes you. Learn as much as you can about the Freedom of Information Act and, where appropriate, make timely, narrowly focused requests to try to secure sighting reports, radar data, and other relevant information from official sources. Try to build a network of experts who can help with specialist advice on imagery analysis, astronomy, meteorology, military affairs, and other relevant fields of knowledge.

NICK POPE, PERSONAL INTERVIEW

Jacques F. Vallée

Today a successful industrialist, astronomer, computer programmer, and author, Jacques Vallée saw his first UFO as a teenager in Pontoise, France (see *www.jacquesvallee.net*). He corroborated the event with another neighborhood boy: It was "a traditional saucer, silver plated, reflecting the sun, with a kind of transparent dome top." Years later, after college and during his astronomical work, Vallée observed more UFOs. But his superiors decided to deny the observations and destroy the evidence.

Outraged, he headed for the United States in 1962 to practice astronomy at the University of Texas at Austin. He worked at the McDonald Observatory on the first project of the detailed computerized cartography of Mars for NASA. He then decided to contact J. Allen Hynek (see chapter 2) and to study at Northwestern University. From then on, he worked side by side with Hynek, who introduced him to Quintanilla and Woody, the persons in charge of Project Blue Book. Vallée began to study UFO phenomena seriously and later established that UFO landings tend to occur in what he called "sorry zones."

He went on to propose a system of classification of the observations of UFOs (see Appendix C).

Vallée is credited with the idea that UFOs are psychological phenomena that work as a type of barrier or mental control system that steers the spiritual evolution of humans (see chapter 1). His ideas and personality are so distinct within the field that renowned movie director Steven Spielberg chose him as a model for the character of Lacombe, the French scientist portrayed by actor François Truffaut in the famous movie *Close Encounters of the Third Kind* (1977).

Vallée has written several classic works: *Passport to Magonia: On UFOs, Folklore, and Parallel Worlds* (1968); *The Invisible College: What a Group of Scientists Has Discovered About UFO Influences on the Human Race* (1975); and *Messengers of Deception: UFO Contacts and Cults* (1979). He has also written several newer well-respected works, like the three-part series *Dimensions: A Casebook of Alien Contact* (2008), *Revelations: Alien Contact and Human Deception* (2008), and *Confrontations: A Scientist's Search for Alien Contact* (2008).

CAUTIONARY TIP: When interpreting information of any kind, whether it is from a scientific analysis or the oral testimony of a witness, always be careful of two kinds of bias: anthropomorphism, or the tendency of investigators to interpret data in terms of human traits, and cultural bias. For example, if a witness reports that an entity has four appendages and an investigator interprets this as being a humanoid alien without having more specific data about the appendages, this is what is known as anthropomorphizing the information. The same thing can happen with cultural bias, or the tendency of investigators to interpret data with a slant toward the investigator's cultural heritage. For example, if a witness reports that an entity had a long, round, cylindrical object that it put in its

> mouth and a Mexican or American investigator interprets
> the long round cylinder-like object as a burrito without
> having more specific data, this would be known as being
> "culturally biased."

JACQUES VALLÉE

Raymond E. Fowler

Raymond E. Fowler is a science educator and author whose career included a tour with the U.S. Air Force Security Service and twenty-five years with GTE Government Systems.

Fowler's contributions to ufology are respected by UFO researchers throughout the world. His investigative reports have been published in congressional hearings, military publications, newspapers, magazines, and professional journals in the United States and abroad. He served as chairman of the Massachusetts Subcommittee for the National Investigations Committee on Aerial Phenomena (NICAP), as an early-warning coordinator for the U.S. Air Force–contracted UFO Study at the University of Colorado, and as a scientific associate for the Center for UFO Study (CUFOS). In later years, he has served as director of investigations on the Board of Directors of MUFON and was the editor of their *Field Investigator's Manual*.

Fowler has also been featured on hundreds of radio and TV shows in the United States since 1963, including *The Dave Garroway Show*, *The Dick Cavett Show*, *The Mike Douglas Show*, *Good Morning America*, *Unsolved Mysteries*, and *Sightings*, as well as a number of network television and syndicated documentaries on UFOs.

Author of eleven books on the subject of UFOs and paranormal phenomena, Fowler is a classic example of a by-the-book investigator. Among his books are *UFOs: Interplanetary Visitors* (1974), *The Andreasson Affair* (1979), *Casebook of a UFO Investigator* (1981), *The Watchers* (1990), and *The Allagash Abductions* (1993).

Fowler built the Woodside Planetarium and Observatory in Wenham, Massachusetts, which was written up in *Sky & Telescope* magazine. He moved to Kennebunk, Maine, in 2002, where he has built another observatory and continues teaching courses in various science subjects in his home classroom for the Kennebunk Adult Education Program.

SPECIAL KNOWLEDGE/SKILLS TIP: An essential period of learning and practical training can be accomplished by first becoming thoroughly familiar with the contents of a comprehensive field investigator's manual. I would recommend the *MUFON Field Investigator's Manual* and *The UFO Handbook*. {Also} a period of on-the-job-training with an experienced investigator is a must.

RAYMOND FOWLER, *CASEBOOK OF A UFO INVESTIGATOR*

Barry Chamish

Barry Chamish, formerly a member of the Israeli military, is now a journalist, author, and lecturer. Although he has written only one book on UFOs—*Return of the Giants* (1999), an investigation of the 1987–1999 wave of Israeli sightings of six-foot- to nine-foot-tall, bald, humanoid aliens—his excellent reporting and insight have garnered several television appearances and worldwide recognition (see *www.barrychamish.com*).

The NBC series on paranormal phenomena, *Sightings,* based four episodes on Chamish's work, and, in 1999, Fox TV devoted a half hour of prime time to exploring his detailed examination of the events described in his book. The sightings became an international sensation, garnering the attention of actor Shirley MacLaine, who personally visited an alleged landing site on an Israeli beach, along with several hundred other "pilgrims." When the events subsided, he decided to stop reporting on the subject. Further, he quoted Israeli Air Force pilots when he was a soldier in the same Air Force. He got them to talk off the books. But once he was out of the service, he says, his sincere Air Force quotes dried up.

Chamish made an important contribution to the UFO dialog, claiming that UFOs may play a role in international intrigue and possibly in the shaping of Jewish and world history. Currently, his celebrated and award-winning writing focuses on the secret history and corruption of the Israeli government. Because of this subject matter, he is considered Israel's most controversial writer.

In ufological circles, his work is seen as a bridge between UFO scholars of ancient history like Erich von Daniken, Zecharia Sitchin, and William Bramley and modern fringe political analysts.

INVESTIGATIVE TIP: Treat each incident as a journalist; corroborate testimony, gather evidence, especially videotapes. If you have only one person's testimony, without a tape, you don't have a case . . . . Initially, treat every case as a hoax until you are convinced by the facts that it can't be. You are allowed to speculate only if you say that's what you are doing. If dealing with the authorities, try to have a private meeting. What they say in the office comes from policy, not the heart. The real internal enemy of UFO research is writers who will believe anything. Be critical, tough, and thus believable. If not, time will catch up with you and you'll be dismissed.

BARRY CHAMISH, PERSONAL INTERVIEW

Timothy Good

Author, lecturer, and documentarian Timothy Good became interested in UFOs in 1955, when his passion for aviation and space led him to read a Donald Keyhoe book. He was inspired to begin his own research in 1961, after reading Ruppelt's now famous book. Since then, he has amassed a wealth of evidence, including several thousand declassified intelligence documents.

In January 1989, following the dissolution of the Soviet empire, Good became the first UFO researcher from the West to be interviewed on Russian television. He was invited for discussions at the Pentagon in 1998 and at the headquarters of the French Air Force in 2002. He has also acted as consultant for several U.S. congressional investigations. He is known to millions through his numerous television appearances and has coproduced several documentaries on the subject of UFOs.

Good's first book, *Above Top Secret: The Worldwide UFO Cover-up* (1987)—fully revised and updated as *Beyond Top Secret: The Worldwide UFO Security Threat* (1996)—became an instant best seller and is regarded widely as the definitive work on the subject. His other books in the field include *Alien Liaison: The Ultimate Secret* (1991), *Alien Base: Earth's Encounters with Extraterrestrials* (1998), and *Unearthly Disclosure: Conflicting Interests in the Control of Extraterrestrial Intelligence* (2000). He has also edited a number of books on the subject, including the bestselling *Alien Update* (1993). His latest book is *Need to Know: UFOs, the Military, and Intelligence* (2007).

Born in London, Good completed his formal education at the King's School, Canterbury. He is a celebrated violinist who has played internationally and for composers like Leonard Bernstein, Benjamin Britten, Igor Stravinsky, and William Walton. He has also freelanced as a session player for television dramas, commercials, feature films, and recordings with pop musicians. Among those with whom he has recorded are Phil Collins, Depeche Mode, George Harrison, Elton John, Paul McCartney, Rod Stewart, and U2.

SPECIAL KNOWLEDGE/SKILLS TIP: In America, there is no lawful provision allowing the detainment of one of its people. There either has to be a warrant, complete with a verified complaint (meaning that a damaged party has to sign it before a judge issues the warrant); you are either under arrest or you are free to go. Statutes, Codes and Rules are given the color of law, but are not law. Authorities use these legal rules if one does not actively claim their rights. So if you know your rights, it will be much more difficult for law enforcement, military police and/or covert government agents to successfully harass you in the field.

TIMOTHY GOOD, *ALIEN CONTACT*

Melinda Leslie

Melinda Leslie is an abductee, UFO/paranormal researcher, and event organizer/consultant. As an admitted abductee since the late 1970s, Leslie has been able to bring her personal experiences to her own abduction research. She formed the Orange County Paranormal Researchers (OCPR) group, which specializes in the consciousness aspects of UFOs, abductions, and other paranormal investigations.

Leslie's particular work centers around the collection of evidence of the alleged military and covert intelligence involvement in various abduction scenarios. She is also particularly interested in evidence pertaining to the vast array of psychological and spiritual ramifications of these events. She has earned a reputation for patient and kind assistance of abductees on these levels.

As a speaker, Leslie has lectured for numerous organizations and conferences, appeared on several prominent radio programs, and appeared on and served as a segment or project consultant to numerous television shows, including *The Other Side, Encounters, Strange Universe,* and *Sightings.* She was the associate producer of both the San Francisco and Los Angeles 1994 and 1995 UFO Expo West conferences and assisted in producing and/or served as a consultant to many additional well-known UFO conferences, including the Bay Area UFO Expo, the International UFO Congress, and the Mount Shasta Convergence Conference.

Leslie's research and experiences have been written about in nine books: *Camouflage Through Limited Disclosure* (2006) by Randy Koppang, *UFOs and the National Security State,* vol. II (2009) by Richard Dolan, *MILABS: Military Mind Control and Alien Abduction* (1999) by Helmut Lammer, *Flying Saucers 101* (2000) by Harold Burt, *On the Trail of the Saucer Spies* (2006) by Nick Redfern, *One in Forty: The UFO Epidemic* (1997) and *Extraterrestrial Visitations* (2006) by Preston Dennett, and *Abducted by Aliens* (2008) by Chuck Weiss. She is also a contributing author to the book *Paranoia: The Conspiracy Reader* (2010) and an expert in EVP (electronic voice phenomena).

INVESTIGATIVE TIP: Evidence, evidence, evidence. In real estate they say the three most important things are location, location, and location. Well, in ufology it's evidence, evidence, evidence. Or at least it should be. Before you take on any aspect of the UFO subject or start an investigation, be sure you are focused on gathering and documenting the evidence first and foremost. If not, you need to ask yourself why you're in this; it does nothing to move the ufology field forward. Sure, gathering and documenting evidence is difficult, tedious, and boring work, but getting to the truth is all that matters, and the truth about UFOs and the extraterrestrial presence is anything but boring.

MELINDA LESLIE, PERSONAL INTERVIEW

A. J. Gevaerd

A. J. Gevaerd is a journalist and editor who, by the age of fourteen, was already pursuing the mysteries involved in UFO phenomena and was a devoted investigator of flying saucer sightings and alien contact with humans. He started lecturing about UFOs in 1978. In 1985, at the age of twenty-three, he decided to quit his career as a chemistry teacher to devote himself to his UFO research full-time.

Gevaerd is the founder and editor of the Brazilian *UFO Magazine*, the only one published in his country and, after a twenty-six-year history, the longest-lasting magazine about ufology in the entire world. The publication now has two companions, *UFO Special* and *UFO Documental*. All three magazines are monthly, with a circulation of over 30,000 all over Brazil and Portugal. Gevaerd is also the founder and national director of the Brazilian Center for Flying Saucer Research (CBPDV), the largest UFO organization in South America, with over 3,300 members.

Gevaerd has investigated over 3,000 UFO cases personally and leads a team of over 400 experts who are members of *UFO Magazine*'s editorial board. As a national and international speaker, he has lectured countless times in dozens of cities in Brazil and conducted investigations and lectures in fifty countries.

In 1983, Gevaerd was appointed by J. Allen Hynek as the representative of the Center for UFO Studies (CUFOS) in Brazil. He is presently one of the international directors of the Annual International UFO Congress, Laughlin, and Brazilian director for both MUFON and Skywatch International.

Gevaerd has been interviewed regularly by national and foreign radio talk shows, including Whitley Strieber's *Dreamland*, Errol-Bruce Knapp's *Strange Days . . . Indeed*, George Noory and Art Bell's *Coast to Coast AM*, and *The Jeff Rense Program*. He has also served as consultant to many TV documentaries produced in Brazil, especially by the largest network, Globo.

Bruce Maccabee

Dr. Bruce Maccabee is a retired Navy physicist, UFO researcher, author, and lecturer who has been active in UFO research since the late 1960s when he joined NICAP. He remained active in NICAP's research and investigation until its demise in 1980. He became a member of MUFON in 1975 and was subsequently appointed as state director for Maryland, a position he still holds. In 1979, he was instrumental in establishing the Fund for UFO Research and was its chairman for thirteen years. He presently serves on the National Board of the fund.

In 1972, Maccabee began his career at the Naval Surface Warfare Center, where he worked on optical data processing, aspects of the Strategic Defense Initiative (SDI), and Ballistic Missile Defense (BMD) using high-powered lasers. His UFO research and investigations, however, are unrelated to this work. These have included the Kenneth Arnold sighting (June 24, 1947); the McMinnville, Oregon, "Trent" photos of 1950; the *Gemini* 11 astronaut photos of September 1966; the New Zealand sightings of December 1978; the Japan Airlines (JAL1628) sighting of November 1986; the Gulf Breeze flap in Florida, 1987–1988; the "red bubba" sightings, 1990–1992 (including his own sighting in September 1991); the Mexico City video of August 1997; the Phoenix lights sightings of March 13, 1997; and many others. He has also done historical research and was the first to obtain the "flying disc file" of the FBI—a real "X-File."

Maccabee is the author or coauthor of nearly three dozen technical articles and more than a hundred UFO articles and is a part-time columnist for the U.S. edition of *UFO Magazine*. He wrote the last chapter of *The Gulf Breeze Sightings* (1990) by Edward Walters and Frances Walters (see chapter 4) and the UFO history chapter of the German book *UFOs: Zeugen und Zeichen* (1995). He also co-authored *UFOs Are Real, Here's the Proof* (1997) with Edward Walters and wrote *The UFO/FBI Connection* (2000) and the novel *Abduction in My Life* (2000). He is listed in *Who's Who in Technology Today* and *American Men and Women of Science*.

SPECIAL KNOWLEDGE/SKILLS TIP: Maccabee managed several aspects of the Gulf Breeze sightings investigation for the book. While directly handling the photo analysis of each photo using "standard acceptable field-measurement practices" and both optical and digital enhancement equipment utilizing his background as an optical engineer, he also knew when to call in other specialists. For example, when it came time to evaluate the key witnesses, Maccabee called in clinical psychologist Dr. Dan Overlade who then performed the standard set of psychological tests like the Wechsler Adult Intelligence Scale Revised, the Minnesota Multiphasic Personality Inventory, the Thematic Apperception Test, the Draw-a-Person Test and the Rorschach Test.

EDWARD WALTERS AND FRANCES WALTERS,
THE GULF BREEZE SIGHTINGS

Bill Birnes

Bill Birnes is an author, lecturer, and UFO hunter, and owner and publisher of the U.S. edition of *UFO Magazine*. His contributions to ufology are extensive and sometimes controversial. Known for its well-rounded set of perspectives, Birnes's magazine has been an institution in the field since the 1980s and is home to such noted columnists as Stanton Friedman, radio talk show host George Noory, and Larry W. Bryant of CAUS notoriety. It also boasts an all-star roster of military, ex-military, and civilian UFO researchers and/or experiencers.

Birnes was pivotal as a consultant for the History Channel in three episodes of the television series *UFO Files:* "UFOs in Russia," "USOs, Underwater Submersible Objects," and "Black Box UFOs." His working relationship with the History Channel extended to include the *UFO Hunters* weekly television series. Each week, he and his team of researchers travel to the sites of world-famous UFO events, where they use high-tech equipment and cutting-edge investigative techniques to explore the alleged events and attempt to arrive at answers about what really happened.

Birnes is well qualified to lead such a team, having written and edited over twenty-five books and encyclopedias in the fields of human behavior, true crime, current affairs, history, psychology, business, computing, and the paranormal. He is a frequent radio and television talk show guest, having appeared on *Good Morning America, Dateline NBC, Entertainment Tonight,* and *Coast to Coast AM.* Among his books are *The Day After Roswell: A Former Pentagon Official Reveals the U.S. Government's Shocking UFO Cover-up* (1988), *Unsolved UFO Mysteries: The World's Most Compelling Cases of Alien Encounter* (2000) with Harold Burt, *The UFO Magazine Encyclopedia: The Most Comprehensive Single-Volume UFO Reference in Print* (2004), *Worker in the Light: Unlock Your Five Senses and Liberate Your Limitless Potential* (2008) with George Noory, and *Journey to the Light: Find Your Spiritual Self and Enter into a World of Infinite Opportunity* (2009).

Birnes holds a law degree and received a Ph.D. from New York University in 1974.

INVESTIGATIVE TIP: Go after every conventional explanation first and exhaust each one. Make sure you have covered every conventional base thoroughly before suggesting any anomalous explanation. Eliminate the conventional and then deal with what remains.

BILL BIRNES, PERSONAL INTERVIEW

Jenny Randles

Jenny Randles, paranormal/UFO investigator, author, and lecturer, was born in the Rossendale Valley of Lancashire, not far from Pendle Hill, home of British witchcraft. This area, rich in UFO sightings, is now known locally as UFO Alley. Randles was apparently born to investigate.

Randles joined Britain's oldest and largest national UFO group, the British UFO Research Association (BUFORA), and subscribed to *Flying Saucer Review* magazine around 1968. After high school, she became a full-time writer and researcher into strange phenomena, funding her own work. Then, in 1973, she became an investigator for BUFORA and is an honorary life member.

Randles sees the actions of some ufologists as extremely irresponsible and has helped to forge a code of practice to govern how they should interact with the public, the media, and authorities. She has also developed a protocol for how to protect witnesses.

Randles's books include *UFO Reality* (1983), *The UFO Conspiracy* (1987), *From Out of the Blue* (1993), *Alien Contacts and Abductions* (1994), *Alien Contact: The First Fifty Years* (1997), *The Truth Behind the*

Men in Black (1997), *The Complete Book of Aliens and Abductions* (2000), and *The Little Giant Encyclopedia of UFOs* (2000). In 1996, the Discovery Channel hired her as an official consultant to their four-hour series on UFOs. She has edited *Northern UFO News* since 1974 and is the British consultant to the Hynek Center for UFO Studies (CUFOS) journal, the *International UFO Reporter*.

MOTIVATIONAL TIP: I love puzzles and enjoy the cross between being a detective, social worker, and scientist that the quest for truth behind the paranormal involves. I do not believe or disbelieve. I listen to the evidence, wonder what it means and go and try to figure that out. If that answer is a mundane one, then I consider this result to be a success, not a disappointment. But, whilst much of the supernatural is open to prosaic explanation, I do believe that there are some surprises waiting to be uncovered, possibly even ones that will revolutionize the planet.

JENNY RANDLES, PERSONAL INTERVIEW

Jerome Clark

Jerome Clark, former editor of *UFO* (U.S. edition) and *Fate* magazines, board member of CUFOS, and editor of their quarterly publication, *The International UFO Reporter*, has published several books and a three-volume UFO encyclopedia encompassing every conceivable aspect of UFOs.

Clark appeared on a 2005 prime-time U.S. television special to discuss the early history of the U.S. military's UFO investigations, as well as on episodes of NBC's *Unsolved Mysteries* series and on the syndicated series *Sightings*. In 1997, he was prominently featured on the A&E

Network's documentary *Where Are All the UFOs?*, which examined the history of the UFO phenomenon. In the 1970s, Clark embraced some paranormal ideas to explain UFOs and other unusual phenomena. He was influenced by the "ultraterrestrials" theory of John Keel and the so-called inter-dimensional hypothesis that had been championed by Jacques Vallée. Clark even cowrote a book on the subject with long-time friend Loren Coleman.

In recent years, Clark has championed a sort of open-ended agnosticism, choosing to focus on phenomena that are purported to have some degree of documentable support—whether physical evidence or reliably reported events. He has argued very cautiously in favor of the extraterrestrial hypothesis—not as proven fact, but as a working hypothesis—choosing to focus on the UFO cases he regards as the most promising: those with multiple witness and/or cases where there is said to be physical evidence.

INVESTIGATIVE TIP: The study of the UFO phenomenon can be broadly grouped into two categories: (1) investigation of UFO sightings themselves in the field and (2) study of the reports and/or witnesses. Within these categories are numerous separate tasks. Witnesses need to be interviewed in a manner that will provide the most reliable sighting details. Physical trace samples may be taken using careful protocols, with measurements and photographs of the site. Government agencies often will be contacted to obtain supplementary information (weather data, radar records). Reports must be carefully written to compile an accurate database for future use.

JEROME CLARK, "THE WHITE PAPER"

From 1976 to 1989, Clark was the editor of *Fate* magazine. Since 1985, he has served as the editor of the *International UFO Reporter*, the official journal of CUFOS. He is also the editor of the *Journal of UFO*

Studies and wrote *The UFO Encyclopedia: The Phenomenon from the Beginning* (1998), which appeared in two volumes. His other works include *The UFO Book: Encyclopedia of the Extraterrestrial* (1997); *Unexplained: Strange Sightings, Incredible Occurrences, and Puzzling Physical Phenomena* (2003); *Encyclopedia of Strange and Unexplained Physical Phenomena* (1993); *Unnatural Phenomena: A Guide to the Bizarre Wonders of North America* (2005); and *Strange Skies: Pilot Encounters with UFOs* (2003).

Timothy Green Beckley

Known as "Mr. UFO" and "Mr. Creepo," Timothy Green Beckley is an eclectic savant who has also worked as an author, lecturer, and film producer. He got an early start in UFOs in 1957 after being inspired by reading an issue of *Fate* magazine. He published the *Interplanetary News Service Report*, with a young Jerry (Jerome) Clark and Lou Farrish serving as assistants. He entered the publishing field in the late 1960s with *UFOs Around the World* (1966) by Edward J. Babcock and has gone on to author several books himself, as well as to publish many other works from different authors. He founded Global Communications, a news/feature service that sells well-researched articles on UFO and other paranormal phenomena to tabloids like *The National Enquirer* and today is still a leader in the publication of books in these genres.

Beckley is the editor of the online *Conspiracy Journal* and has written for several men's magazines like *Hustler*, *Genesis*, and *Saga*. He wrote an ongoing column for *Flying Saucer Magazine* called "On the Trail of Flying Saucers."

Beckley's noted works include *Subterranean Worlds Inside Earth* (1992), *Mystery of the Men in Black: The UFO Silencers* (1990), *The Conspiracy Summit Dossier: Whistle Blower's Guide to the Strangest and Most Bizarre Cosmic and Global Conspiracies!* (2009), *MJ-12 and The Riddle of*

Hangar 18: The New Evidence (2003) coauthored with Sean Casteel, *The Smoky God and Other Inner Earth Mysteries* (1996), and the classic *Book of Space Brothers* (1969).

EQUIPMENT TIP: If some flying saucers are from inside the Earth—as propounded by Dr. Raymond Bernhard in the early 1960s and others—exploring caves may become pertinent. Always hire a professional guide, or spelunker; wear the proper attire, bring the proper gear and at least enough food and water for several days.

TIMOTHY GREEN BECKLEY

Top Cases and Hot Spots Around the World

Aztec, New Mexico. Laredo, Texas. Magdalena, New Mexico. Paradise Valley, Arizona. Kecksburg, Pennsylvania. All of these places are well-known alleged crash sites of UFOs in the United States. There have been many reports in Brazil, England, and Russia as well, and most countries of the world have stories, if not official cases under investigation, of alleged crashed UFOs.

After World War II, the number of reported crashes skyrocketed, reaching at least 150 worldwide by 1980. There were sixty more incidents reported in the 1990s. Ryan S. Wood has written and compiled the most comprehensive work on the subject, called *MAJIC Eyes Only: Earth's Encounters with Extraterrestrial Technology* (2005). Reports of these kinds of events are ongoing, with the total number climbing into the hundreds. Here are some of the better known.

Roswell, New Mexico

Of all the cases worldwide, by far the most researched, documented, and controversial is the case from July 3, 1947, in Roswell, New Mexico. Many books have been written about this enigmatic event. The ultra-secretive MJ-12 group, or Majestic Twelve, was founded to "handle" the crashed-disk phenomenon and the alleged occupants, which resembled tiny humans. In December 1984, television producer Jaime Shandera allegedly received a roll of 35 mm film through the mail with secret documents on it that outlined the secret group.

The monumental event in Roswell set the precedent for the members of MJ-12 to troubleshoot the multiple problems that can arise in defining the role of government in controlling UFO information in day-to-day life. It has been alleged by several authors that the U.S. government/military actually captured advanced alien technology, and possibly live and deceased alien bodies, and wants to keep that secret from the rest of the world, including its own citizens. Roswell enabled them to determine the best ways of keeping secrets—utilizing the media, disinformation, murder, and intimidation—while at the same time secretly reverse-engineering the alien technology in order to apply it to national defense or secretly integrate it into corporate ventures for huge profits. The "invention" of fiber-optic technology is alleged to have been gleaned from reverse-engineered alien crashed disks.

Top Secret/Majic (1987) by Stanton Friedman, *Crash at Corona* (1992) by Don Berliner and Stanton Friedman, *UFO Crash at Roswell* (1991) by Kevin Randle and Don Schmitt, *The Day After Roswell* (1997) by Colonel Philip J. Corso with William J. Birnes, *The Roswell Legacy: The Untold Story of the First Military Officer at the 1947 Crash Site* (2008) by Jesse Marcel Jr., and *The Ultimate Guide to the Roswell UFO Crash: A Tour of Roswell's UFO Landmarks* (2010) by Noe Torres, et al, are just a sampling of the work available to study this all-important case.

Military Hot Spots

Since 1947, UFOs have commonly been seen above or near military bases worldwide. Military installations are the sites of nuclear weaponry and intense radar activity and are allegedly storage places for downed alien technology. In several cases, extraterrestrial biological entities, or EBEs, have allegedly been found dead or captured alive and harbored at these places. The Roswell Army Air Base is arguably the most famous of these. Wright-Patterson Air Force Base in Ohio is thought to be the final destination of the wreckage and alien bodies from the Roswell case and is also the home of the famous Hangar 18, subject of the now famous movie of the same name.

A variety of incidents have taken place around military installations. One of the most famous is the "NORAD flap." Between October 27 and November 11, 1975, several sightings, severe power malfunctions, and multiple-witness sightings happened at military bases in Loring, Maine; Wurtsmith, Michigan; and Malmstrom and Minot, North Dakota. Skeptics think the incidences were contrived—a joint U.S. and Canadian military exercise that sought to test the public reaction to UFO phenomena.

UFO/military interaction is common in other countries, like Brazil, Iran, and China. In Russia, for example, in the summer of 1961, a "mother ship" was detected over a base in Rybinski. Several smaller craft emerged, which alerted the base commander to fire missiles at the UFOs. Mysteriously, the missiles were harmlessly detonated. When the smaller craft reentered the mother ship, power was restored to the base. Richard Dolan's landmark work *UFOs and the National Security State: Chronology of a Cover-up, 1941–1973* (2002) offers a remarkable list of global military/UFO events.

Possibly the most infamous event happened in the woods of Rendlesham Forest near Bentwaters Royal Air Force Base in Suffolk, East Anglia, England. It started on December 26, 1980, and climaxed two nights later with security surrounding a "fog-like" glob hovering in the nearby forest. A UFO eventually flew over the fog, entered it, and disappeared from view. Eventually, three humanoids appeared and were part of a peaceful stand-off with unarmed military personnel.

Because Bentwaters was a U.S./British/NATO-run base, military intelligence soon became involved. This is where the "darkness" enters into the incident, say Peter Robbins and Larry Warren, coauthors of the only firsthand account of the event, *Left at East Gate* (1997). This case is great for beginners because of its overall "sweep," covering a wide variety of investigative aspects like military intelligence involvement, trace cases, organic material transformation, abductions, historical pertinence, and violent military mind-controlled debriefing. *From Out of the Blue* (1991) by Jenny Randles and *UFOs: Generals, Pilots, and Government Officials Go On the Record* (2010) by Leslie Kean also explore this event.

CAUTIONARY TIP: Because of the controlling nature endemic in any military intelligence situation, what potential there was for these men to grow spiritually {from the contact experience} was short-circuited by the nature of the controlling of the information after the fact . . . from standard military procedure {what has been described as mind control}. The aliens were not malevolent. It was the human-on-human aspect that was so dark.

PETER ROBBINS, PERSONAL INTERVIEW

Top Cases, The Billy Meier Case

Highly popular Swiss contactee Eduard "Billy" Meier claims to have had contacts all his life in preparation for his "mission" to spread the knowledge and awareness of extraterrestrials. His role, allegedly assigned him by a group of ETs from the Pleiades star system, was to keep humanity from annihilating itself with advanced technology, given their lack of spiritual development to handle it. The Swiss organization known as the Semjase Silver Star Center (FIGU) was set up to carry out the mission. There are branches in several countries.

It was not until January 1975, however, that the contacts began to intensify. "Plejarens" Semjase, Menara, Alena, and others contacted Meier over 400 times, creating a pool of evidence unmatched by any similar case. With the aid of the aliens, Meier captured what have become known as the best UFO photos ever taken. Eight video strips and numerous sound recordings add to the compelling evidence. He was allegedly able to take photos of two of his visitors, as well as take shots from space while traveling in their spacecraft.

Semjase explained on one occasion that Meier was the reincarnated Biblical prophet Ezekiel and that he was to lead the world in a consciousness transformation and help usher in a new age of enlightenment. The contacts continue today and a few persistent researchers have performed their own investigations, building upon, corroborating, and sometimes refuting the original investigation done by Wendelle Stevens, Lee and Brit Elders, and Tom Welch.

The Elders and Welch published the first two coffee-table books—*UFO . . . Contact from the Pleiades*, volumes I and II—then Stevens went on to help publish much more of Meier's lengthy notes in eight volumes. *And Yet . . . They Fly!* (2001) by Guido Moosbrugger and the "unofficial" *The Essence of the Notes* (2005) by Maurice Osborn (the only indexed version of Meier's contact notes) are two more recent examples. Michael Horn, the official FIGU representative in the United States, does some interesting work as well.

Whatever he was, Billy Meier stands at the center of one of the best-documented, well-researched, and well-tested UFO contact cases in modern history.

RESEARCH/RESOURCE TIP: For those who want to research UFOs and claims of contact with extraterrestrials, the main focus should be on . . . actual evidence. Nowadays, clear UFO photos, films, video, etc. are easy to hoax using technology not available to Meier when he was first bringing his evidence forward (from 1964 to 1980). And it should be noted that most UFOs, when they're not secret military craft, can be explained by natural phenomena. So a higher standard of proof would be specific, uniquely significant and accurate information that couldn't have been known by, or provided to, the so-called contactee by any known means or source. Of course, this is where the Meier case is also unique and extremely important. You can find an abundance (over 26,000 pages) of invaluable information (much of which I often refer to as prophetically accurate scientific and world-event-related information) and clear spiritual teaching at *www. theyfly.com* and sites linked from it.

MICHAEL HORN, PERSONAL INTERVIEW

Hot Spots, Area 51

Emmy award–winning journalist George Knapp first broke the story of Area 51 in 1989, when alleged former government employee Bob Lazar broke his oath of silence about the base on KLAS-TV in Las Vegas. His reporting on the military base, located in the Nevada desert, was selected by United Press International as Best Individual Achievement by a Reporter in 1989. The base, also known as the "Groom Lake" facility, was started in 1955 as a place to test the at-the-time secret U2 spy plane. Since then, it has become *the* testing site for military "black ops" technology and "captured" alien hardware (see *www.area51.org*).

The U.S. government has denied the existence of this facility even up to the present time, despite the fact that there are several satellite photos of buildings, airplanes, and airstrips, and video of Janet Airlines planes carrying Area 51 employees to and from the base several times a day. There are also a plethora of amateur photographs.

Until 1995, the two best places to view the base were from the vantage points of Freedom Ridge and White Sides peaks. The Air Force has since made those sites off-limits to the public, and now only the distant Tikaboo Peak, twenty-six miles from the base, is suitable for viewing with telescopes and/or binoculars. Be careful, however. If you come close to the perimeter, you will be watched by military police. And if you persist in behavior that they find threatening for any reason, they will advance on your position and perform a search. Most people are set free after an interrogation and any film, high-tech equipment, and/or weapons (licensed or not) are confiscated. So it is best to know your rights for your own protection.

Concurrent with the alleged activity at Area 51 are claims by Lazar and others that there are not only several types of actual alien craft hidden in underground bunkers, but also actual aliens interacting with humans and participating in joint high-tech projects as part of an alleged treaty from 1954—we get their technology and they are allowed to abduct humans for their own purposes. Despite claims by researchers William Cooper and Phil Schneider, this theory has so far proven to be just a rumor.

Whether the alleged sightings of craft are of Earth-made machines or alien-derived technology, the area is rife with UFO activity. There is so much ongoing activity that the entire area has been made into a tourist trap. You can visit the Little A'Le'Inn and the Area 51 Museum.

And Highway 375 has been renamed the "Extraterrestrial Highway" by the state of Nevada.

CAUTIONARY TIP: Do not assume that everything— or anything—you see in the sky out there is a UFO in the figurative sense. Groom Lake is where all manner of advanced aircraft are test-flown. If there were ever any genuine UFOs out there at the base, they have almost certainly been moved somewhere else by now due to all of the attention the facility has received over the past twenty years. Also, don't hassle the camo dudes. The men who guard the perimeter of the base are just doing their jobs and following orders. They will not mess with you unless you mess with them. If you cross over the line or march past the warning signs, you will be detained by the security teams and will likely be arrested once the sheriff arrives. What's worse, they will seize video cameras and tapes so that the footage of your momentous bust will not be available to post online, making the arrest all the more pointless. Lastly, take it all with a big grain of salt. There are a lot of crazy stories about Area 51 that have absolutely no basis in fact. You can try to contact Nellis AFB to ask about Groom Lake, but they will not answer any questions other than to confirm that there is an "operating location" out there somewhere.

GEORGE KNAPP, PERSONAL INTERVIEW

Top Cases, Gulf Breeze

The events at Gulf Breeze, a tiny stretch of Florida gulf coastline near Pensacola, are known as the "most astounding multiple sightings of UFOs in U.S. history." On November 11, 1987, Edward Walters was working in his home office when he noticed a glowing bluish-gray craft hovering in his backyard. Walters ran to his office to grab his Polaroid camera and snapped a photograph. Moments later, he says that he was hit with a blue beam that lifted him off the ground. Then he heard a voice telling him that he wouldn't be harmed. He resisted and was finally freed from the beam. Since then, he hears a "hum" inside his head every time a craft is near. It is this advance alert that has enabled him to take so many photographs.

On December 2, Edward and his wife, Frances, were visited by a four-foot-tall creature with big black eyes. A startled Edward was able to get a less-than-clear picture of it. He was able to take another picture of the craft and its paralyzing blue beam. And again, just before sunrise on December 5, he heard the hum and knew the UFO was near. Then he heard the voice telling him: "Do not resist . . . Zehaas."

Walters later used a special four-lens, light-sealed Polaroid camera given to him by MUFON investigators that allowed for easier determination of distances. An array of "experts" analyzed the photo and video evidence, and psychologists performed evaluations on the witnesses as well. But many questions have not been answered, which leaves ample room for investigators to chart new ground in the case. For example: Why would Walters tell three different versions of the first encounter on November 11, 1987? Was he able to remember further details upon each next account?

The area around Gulf Breeze has been witness to hundreds of sightings since November 1987 (see *www.ufocasebook.com/gulfbreeze.html*). The Walters' account and the now legendary photographs of the events at Gulf Breeze are chronicled in their book *The Gulf Breeze Sightings: The Most Astounding Multiple Sightings of UFOs in U.S. History* (1989). Some of the most thoroughly documented photo analyses were done in this case by veteran researcher Dr. Bruce Maccabee (see chapter 3). Other books on the events include *Gulf Breeze Double-Exposed: The "Ghost Demon" Photo Controversy* (1990) by Zan Overall; *War of the Words: The True but Strange Story About the Gulf Breeze UFO* (2006) by

Craig R. Myers; and the Walters' second book, *UFO Abductions in Gulf Breeze* (1994).

INVESTIGATIVE TIP: Since all photographic cases should be considered potential hoaxes, it is essential that investigators operate independently from those whose claims they are checking. An operation that gives claimants sufficient advance warning to cover their tracks (if there are tracks to be covered) is seriously flawed.

CUFOS, *THE GULF BREEZE SIGHTINGS*

Hot Spots, Mexico City

In July 1991, in conjunction with a solar eclipse predicted by the Mayan calendar, a variety of UFOs were reported and videotaped by multiple witnesses over and around Mexico City. This was the beginning of what was to become possibly one of the most robust waves of sightings in the modern era. And it is still going on today.

The next major encounter occurred in March 2004, when, during an antidrug task force maneuver, a Merlin C26A military surveillance airplane was approached by "an object" that was visible on the plane's FLIR infrared camera, but not with the unaided eye. Suddenly, the four-man crew reported that there were two objects; then there were eleven of them surrounding the Merlin. There was never a visual sighting by the crew, yet the FLIR captured the entire event on infrared film. The captain ordered all the airplane's lights shut off. The UFOs departed soon afterward.

The incident sparked what has become a precedent-setting press conference between Mexican military officials and a civilian UFO research group. It was Secretary of Defense Clemente Vega Garcia who contacted noted Mexican journalist Jaime Maussan and his research group and asked them to perform their own independent analysis. The historical press conference was held on May 11, 2004. It has been universally interpreted as a call for the rest of the world's governments to come forward with whatever knowledge they have about UFOs for the benefit of all.

Maussan, the host of Mexico's *60 Minutes*, has been vaulted to celebrity status as he goes about investigating sightings, encounters, and experiences of all kinds on Mexican and international television. He and other Mexican investigators like Antonio Huneeus of *Open Minds TV* think there could be a correlation between the increasingly prevalent UFO activity in Mexico, and possibly around the world, and the various prophecies and stellar predictions made by that country's ancient indigenous Mayan and Aztec civilizations.

Recently, the activity continued, even as Maussan, Huneeus, and several other speakers were gathered in Mexico City for the 2010 World UFO Summit held on March 19 and 21, 2010. During the exposition, witnesses reported several small white UFOs hovering over and around the World Trade Center building. There have been many other documented events in this ongoing flap. For more information on this and other UFO events in Mexico, see the *Journal of Hispanic Ufology*.

SPECIAL KNOWLEDGE/SKILLS TIP: If we learn to understand the many indigenous Mexican calendars—their chronologies and corollary prophecies—we may be able to predict, and be prepared to document, a UFO sighting.

Top Cases, Skinwalker Ranch

Possibly the most bizarre collection of UFO occurrences happened at a remote ranch in northeast Utah known as the Skinwalker Ranch because of its association with what the local Ute Indian tribe call "skinwalkers." Skinwalkers are evil beings capable of doing great harm to humans. They are allegedly able to shape-shift—hence the nickname, skinwalker. The Utes believe that the Navajo put the "curse" of the skinwalkers on them in ancient times and that is why the dark beings supposedly terrorize the area.

Hunt for the Skinwalker: Science Confronts the Unexplained at a Remote Ranch in Utah (2005), by veteran journalist George Knapp and scientist Colm Kelleher, chronicles the various ongoing activities at the location—from classic UFOs to dark entities that manifest from a vortex in the middle of the air, to Bigfoot- and lizard-like creatures, to mysterious and sometimes ominous orbs of varying color. Research teams have been baffled as to what may be causing any of these phenomena, and several landowners have been driven off because of them.

The best guess is that the ranch is the location of an interdimensional portal that allows for the passage of any beings that have the ability to move from one dimension to another. This is a popular theory—but just a theory, as far as science is concerned. Studies at the location are ongoing and have provided a wealth of raw data.

CAUTIONARY TIP: I am strongly opposed to anything that encourages outsiders to go there {Skinwalker Ranch}. I discourage people from going there because there have been so many trespassers on the property. They have made life miserable for the property managers.

GEORGE KNAPP, PERSONAL INTERVIEW

Hot Spots, Volcanoes

Around the world, mighty and majestic volcanoes have been known as places where UFO sightings and contacts occur. While mountains and mountainous regions in general have been places of mysterious, supernatural, and divine events throughout history—volcanoes included—it is in more recent times that they have become known as UFO hot spots.

The reasons for this are not known, but there are several theories as to why UFOs would frequent such volatile geographies. Some think they are entrances to underground bases and/or cities. Others believe that the occupants of the craft are performing some kind of tectonic plate work to thwart a devastating earthquake—possibly hyper-dimensional work in conjunction with ley lines or power points (see chapter 5). Or, they could possibly be performing a variety of other scientific tests, just as a team of human scientists would if they had the opportunity to fly to another planet and do their work.

Mount Shasta in northern California has a past rife with a variety of these activities. The alleged underground city of Telos is supposedly home to a fleet of "silver disks," and descendants of the lost continent of Lemuria are said to emerge from the mountain, shop at local stores, and pay for goods with strange gold coins. Weird lights are consistently reported from many places on the mountain, and UFO sightings are too numerous to count. But this is not just happening at Mount Shasta.

On January 27, 2010, the Turrialba volcano in Costa Rica was the setting for some video footage taken by an employee at the Volcanic and Seismic Observatory. The video shows what appears to be a silvery disk-shaped craft meandering in the vicinity of the caldera. On February 13, 2010, more footage was taken at Mexico's Popocatepetl volcano. And of course, the hottest hot spot in 2010 was the Eyjafjallajökull volcano in Iceland. Some absolutely amazing footage can be seen on YouTube, which is arguably the best source for this kind of information (see also *UFOs from the Volcanoes* [1993] by Egon W. Bach).

Perhaps the most frequent activity at any volcano, however, occurs in southern Washington State near the southern base of Mount Adams in Trout Lake. Contactee James Gilliland has built a meditation and study sanctuary there that is known as the Sattva Sanctuary. The "UFO Ranch" there is home to Gilliland's UFO research organization, Enlightened Contact with Extraterrestrial Intelligence, or ECETI. Attendees at Gilliland's first-ever UFO convention in August 2006 claimed multiple sightings on all four nights of the event.

CAUTIONARY TIP: When investigating a UFO site near a volcano, many camping and hiking rules apply: Bring several days worth of food and water, wear the proper climbing/hiking gear, never go into dangerous areas alone, bring walkie-talkies and a medical kit, and be watchful for underground gas vents that may be toxic and sometimes lethal if inhaled. In Hawaii, this gas is known as "vog," short for "volcano fog," and it can cause a variety of sicknesses and even death. And, of course, bring a camera.

Top Cases, Nazi UFOs

Many believe that Germany was in contact with aliens from the planet Aldebaran in the Taurus star system and, with alien guidance, were able to develop our world's first human-made flying saucers (see *www.nazi-ufos.com*).

Researcher Wendelle C. Stevens maintains that he was approached by one Vladimir Terziski in 1988 at Stevens's first International UFO Congress in Laughlin, Nevada. What Terziski showed Stevens concerning an alleged Nazi UFO program—including full-color photos of not only German but also American craft—blossomed into a mythology that is hard to believe.

Stevens chronicles the story in his book *Nazi Flying Disks of the German V-7 Weapons Development Program* (UFO Photo Archives, 2007). In short, the rise of Hitler and the Nazis coincided with the formation of the Thule Society, in which a female channeler apparently made contact with an entity from Aldebaran. The aliens wanted to help humanity end warfare and figured that, if Earth people had fast, cheap transportation, then the planet's populations could learn to get along.

When the channel learned that a gun turret was being installed on one of the Hannebu-series craft, however, it alerted the aliens, and they withdrew. Not having their alien support, Germany eventually lost the war and escaped by submarine to establish a military saucer and underground submarine base called New Schwabenland in Antarctica.

Several good books have been written on the subject, including *Hitler's Flying Saucers* (2003) by Henry Stevens; *Arktos: the Polar Myth in Science, Symbolism and Nazi Survival* (1996) by Jocelyn Godwin; and *The Omega Files: Secret Nazi UFO Bases Revealed* (2000) by BRANTON. There are also several good documentaries, like the rare VHS-formatted *UFO: Secrets of the Third Reich* (1996), and a number of DVDs, including *Nazi UFOs, How They Fly: Exposing German Tesla Free Energy* (2004), and *Hitler's Secret Flying Saucers* (2004).

Researcher and inventor William R. Lyne, in his controversial book, *Space Aliens from the Pentagon* (1994), makes the case that all of the UFOs seen since 1945 are of German origin and are based in Antarctica. He also maintains that there are no extraterrestrial visitors to planet Earth and that the world's elite, a large part of whom are affiliated with the U.S. government, has used the ET scam to divert attention from key technology—Tesla's free-energy machine—and so continue their stranglehold on the world's economies through oil.

RESEARCH/RESOURCE TIP: Since many eyewitnesses to the production of Nazi flying disks are now deceased, both in Germany and Argentina, many of the children of these former factory workers are holding an untold amount of documentary evidence. New documents from the children of former Nazi sympathizers in Argentina point to the notion that there is a city called New Berlin in Antarctica that is home to over 300,000 people.

WENDELLE C. STEVENS

Hot Spots, Xinjiang Province, China

Xinjiang Province, located on the border between China and Russia in northwest China, played host to a wave of sightings from the late 1960s, and these, some say, continue even now. It was in 1970, however, that an apparent peak of activity was experienced.

In April 1970, it was reported internationally that Russia and China had a minor "border skirmish" in a habitually sensitive border area. However, it was later learned that the cause of the incident was a fleet of UFOs seen over Mongolia in the area of Ulan Bator. Commanders on both sides thought the aerial display was from newly activated secret aircraft from the other side. Tensions boiled over when, on April 24, a Russian bomber disappeared without a trace, causing the Russians to send out 200 aircraft to search the last known location of the missing plane. When the pilots arrived there, however, they reported that not only was there no sign of the bomber, but also there were "over twenty" large, silver disks traveling at high speed and altitude.

Troops were actually sent to Mongolia from both sides, and a bloody battle ensued. When it was later realized that the disks were not from either side, the powers that be decided to report the event as a border skirmish.

This report appears in the rare and out-of-print book—the first of its kind in the West—*UFOs Over Modern China* (1983) by Wendelle C. Stevens and Paul "Moon Wai" Dong. The narrative was pieced together from other reports from Argentina, Italy, and Japan. Why? Because information was not available until 1976 due to a regime change after Chairman Mao's death. The Stevens and Dong book chronicles 600 sightings across China that took place between 1940 and 1982, reporting from evidence that was subsequently made available.

Xinjiang, in particular, has seen its share of UFOs. In 1958, a diesel-plant employee witnessed a luminous object so bright that it barred his vision; on three consecutive nights in early October 1976, a cream-colored fireball streaked across the sky in front of several Agriculture

Department employees; in November 1978, a man reported seeing a bluish-white object move across the sky as he and his family were watching a "cinema." The object changed shape and color, morphing from a ball shape to that of a gourd, before disappearing from sight.

China has a rich history of UFOs, as described in Hartwig Hausdorf's 1998 book *The Chinese Roswell: UFO Encounters in the Far East from Ancient Times to the Present*. Until the 1980s, there were no Chinese research organizations able to perform investigations using science, logic, and testimony. Instead, sightings were handled more like ghost sightings and were reported to priests. In May 1980, however, the Chinese government launched an investigation with the help of Wuhan University. Some have implied that it provided cover for the government. Whatever the case may be, the newly created investigations task force was called the Chinese UFO Studies Association, which had several branches throughout the country. It was later reformed into the Chinese UFO Research Organization (CURO).

Professor Sun Shi Li, former member of the Chinese diplomatic corps, is currently president of CURO, which has grown to 4,000 active members and a total affiliated membership of 40,000, making it arguably the world's largest UFO organization. Check out YouTube for over 2,000 videos of UFOs over China, including a huge UFO "pyramid" that appeared on January 28, 2010.

RESEARCH/RESOURCE TIP: Politics can often influence sighting and contact reports in a variety of ways. Governments have many agendas they wish to keep secret, whether they directly involve UFOs or not, and will go to great lengths to skew, hide, or destroy evidence. In the case above, both the Chinese and Russian governments used the sightings as a cover for their Earthly skirmish to prevent a negative global public relations backlash over the conflict.

Top Cases, The Montauk Project

Montauk Point, Long Island, New York, is home to what many consider the prime event in UFO history because of the possible ramifications of the variety of experiments undertaken at the location.

Standard research argues that the notorious Montauk Project, which secretly tested advanced weapons, was begun in the 1970s and "officially" discontinued in August 1983. Fringe research suggests, however, that the advanced technological, mind-control, and magical experiments started in the early 1940s and continue even today at the underground Camp Hero Army/Air Force Base located at Montauk Point. Today, the area is designated as a New York State Park.

The place has been the site of various kinds of activity throughout known history. For example, there are ongoing UFO sightings, periodic ghost sightings in local buildings, and strange creatures that have washed up on shore. There is a series of pyramids on the northeastern shore of the peninsula that are, today, almost totally covered by sand. At least one picture of them is known (see *Pyramids of Montauk: Explorations in Consciousness* (1995) by Preston Nichols and Peter Moon). Montauk Indian history has it that the pyramids belonged to an advanced civilization that vanished after a cataclysmic event; the Montauks claim to be descendants of that race. Some think that the pyramids could be remnants of Atlantis.

Montauk Point is sacred homeland to the Montauks, who lost possession of it under suspicious circumstances in the early 1900s to a slick "secret" U.S. government. They believe that Turtle Bay, situated at the tip of the point, is the center of the universe and that Montauk Point is situated on a key "power point," or an intersection of ley lines (see chapter 5). The advanced race favored the location for its ability to enhance their planned ritual experiments with Earth energies.

More recently, the crash of TWA Flight 800, on July 17, 1996, has raised questions. There was speculation at the time that the flight was shot down by either a missile or a particle beam that was being tested at the secret facility. Weird radio and electromagnetic (EM) transmissions have been detected emanating from the base; these are thought to be attempts to induce hypnosis in the local population. If you are looking for a UFO or other paranormal-type investigation, Montauk has it all.

An enthralling series of four books has been published by former victims/survivors of various Montauk Project experiments. Escapee Preston Nichols, in association with Peter Moon (also associated with the Montauk Project), has collaborated on the first three: *The Montauk Project* (1992), *Montauk Revisited: Adventures in Synchronicity* (1994), and *Pyramids of Montauk* (mentioned above). The fourth, *The Black Sun: Montauk's Nazi-Tibetan Connection* (1997), is by Peter Moon alone. Moon continues to write about his experiences with the Montauk Project and L. Ron Hubbard's Scientology, among others things, in his own series of books.

The Montauk Project series chronicles the stories of several of the captured psychics who were used against their will and forced to participate in time travel. They describe inter-dimensional and often abusive ritual mind-control experiments using technology from the Sirians (humanoid aliens from the star Sirius), as well as equipment based on the work of Nikola Tesla and Wilhelm Reich (see chapters 5 and 6). Nichols was a high-tech genius whose talents became useful to the Montauk Project in the fields of mind control, popular (or "pop") music, and "psychotronics"—a field pioneered by both Tesla and Reich.

Psychotronics is the practice of interfacing human consciousness with a machine for the purpose of mind control, the physical manifestation of objects, or the opening of inter-dimensional portals, wormholes, and/or small black holes, all of which were found to enable time travel (see *The Music of Time* [2000] by Preston Nichols and Peter Moon). Controversial magician Aleister Crowley is thought to have opened a portal through a rite known as the Amalantrah Working, which he performed at Montauk in 1918. It is thought that this may have allowed extraterrestrials and their craft into this dimension (see chapter 7).

Nichols and Moon wrote about Al Bielek, another scientific and technological genius and mind-control victim, and Duncan Cameron, a super-psychic used in a wide variety of experiments and nefarious tasks. They tell how the people who were overseeing these experiments did not know what they were doing and how things got out of control. The experiments were attempting to alter the past in order to change the future. The theory is that they not only conjured up a UFO that manifested inside the underground facility, but also wound up creating a time-loop lock—when two time portals that are open at the same time and synchronously connected cannot be shut down. In this case, it was the August 12, 1943, Philadelphia Experiment that was the open portal and in time-sync with another experiment that took place on August 12, 1983, at Camp Hero, Montauk Point.

It was Cameron who was first able to free himself by psychically unleashing "Junior," aka "The Beast," a Sasquatch-like biped created with the intent to crash the program and shut down the portal on the Montauk end. Then he was able to help Nichols, Bielek, and one Stan Campbell (aka Stewart Swerdlow), a kind of super-psychic known as a "mentalist," to escape as well. Swerdlow says that if a "psychic" can go into the future and read the blueprint for that reality, a "mentalist" can go into the future and alter the blueprint to create a desired outcome of events. Swerdlow went on to write his own Montauk series as well.

All the individuals associated with the Montauk Project have detractors. Different versions arise depending on the witnesses sampled; dates and participants are confused. For example, Bielek has been openly challenged on a number of occasions. In 2003, three researchers (Marshall Barnes, Fred Houpt, and Gerold Schelm) claimed that Bielek was nowhere near the USS *Eldridge* at the time of the Philadelphia Experiment, as he claimed that he was. In 2007, producer Michael Houtzager released a PC-based collection of interviews with Bielek and others entitled *Al Bielek: The Philadelphia Experiment and Montauk Survivor Accounts*, in which he reports various inconsistencies in Bielek's story.

Still, Bielek's story endures and he stands by his incredible claims. He maintains that he was Ed Cameron, brother of super-psychic Duncan Cameron, during the time of the Philadelphia Experiment in 1943. Bielek claims that after the experiment was closed in 1948, Ed Cameron was removed from the Army, brainwashed to hide evidence of the experiment, and reborn as Al Bielek. He was later reunited with his brother Duncan at Montauk to participate in the more recent Montauk Project events.

According to many researchers, the Philadelphia Experiment, also known as Project Rainbow, was a U.S. Navy project designed to experiment with making one of their ships, the destroyer-class USS *Eldridge*, invisible to radar. Some of Tesla's EM field generators were installed on the vessel as the power source for generating the cloaking field around the ship. The crew was totally unprepared for what happened to them during and after the trial.

As the legend goes, when the massive EM field enveloped the ship, physical matter began to lose its integrity. Crewmen began to "float" in and out of the bulkheads, and many lost consciousness. When the test was done, many seamen were found trapped inside solid steel, as if fused directly to it. Many went stark raving mad, and it was later learned that EM fields can cause insanity. This was the advent of EM "mind control" as a viable way to influence mass consciousness.

The U.S. Navy also learned that they didn't just cloak the *Eldridge*; they actually sent it out of this dimension to another time and place. The ship is said to have appeared briefly in a Norfolk, Virginia, shipyard and then disappeared again. The "official" position of the U.S. Navy, posted at the Office of Naval Research website in 1996, states that the Navy "never conducted studies into radar invisibility" (See *www.onr.navy.mil*).

However, the number of eyewitness accounts, weird coincidences, and conveniently missing data in "official" records are tough to deny and make a strong case that the experiments did, indeed, occur. Navy man Richard Schowengerdt actually claims to have successfully created the technology to make a man invisible (see "To See the Invisible Man" by

Robert Guffey, *UFO Magazine* 22, no. 3 [March 2007]). The "official" Navy position thus may not be true.

A number of movies have been made about these events, including *The Philadelphia Experiment* starring Kirk Douglas (1984). Books on the topic include *The Philadelphia Experiment: Project Invisibility* (1979) by Charles Berlitz and William L. Moore; *The Philadelphia Experiment Murder* (2001) by Alexandra Bruce; *Secrets of Antigravity Propulsion: Tesla, UFOs, and Classified Aerospace Technology* (2008) by Paul LaViolette; and *Secrets of the Unified Field: The Philadelphia Experiment, the Nazi Bell, and the Discarded Theory* (2008) by Joseph Farrell.

CAUTIONARY TIP: Be wary of what comes to you easily and be suspicious of those who seek you out with their "secret and unique" information that no one else has. There are many wannabes out there and many who purposely put out disinformation. Be discerning. Go by how you feel about the information and the person relaying it to you. Trust your instincts and first thoughts.

STEWART SWERDLOW, PERSONAL INTERVIEW

Hot Spots, The Bermuda Triangle

The Bermuda Triangle is arguably the most famous 440,000-square-mile section of ocean in the world because of the many mysterious happenings that occur within its unofficial boundaries. The generally accepted parameters of the legendary area are from Miami, Florida, to San Juan, Puerto Rico, and the island of Bermuda. U.S. government agencies like the Coast Guard, the Navy, and the Board on Geographical Names, for example, do not recognize the area as a distinct geographical feature, and there are no "official" maps of it.

Yet stories of sea monsters, missing vessels, and strange lights have been reported in these waters since 1492, when Christopher Columbus wrote the oldest known account of intrigue in conjunction with the area. He claimed to have seen dangerous seaweed (the Sargasso Sea) and mysterious lights in the region.

In more modern times, the triangle boasts a rich history of missing ships and planes, including the ship *Epevier*, which carried the peace proposal that delayed the end of the War of 1812; a mysterious unidentified ship and missing crews reported by the captain of the schooner *Ellen Austin* in 1881; and the USS *Cyclops*, which disappeared in 1918 along with 309 men—an event the U.S. Navy refers to as the "greatest mystery of the seas."

The rich history of the Bermuda Triangle did not become globally infamous, however, until the disappearance of the famed Flight 19, a training squadron of five Navy torpedo bombers, in December 1945. The mystery of what caused the flight's disappearance and presumed crash endures today: Was it pilot error? Or possibly an equipment malfunction? Or could it have been aberrant weather or some other yet-to-be-explained phenomena?

Many have speculated about why so many strange occurrences happen in this region. Some think there is a dimensional portal, or vortex, in the area that causes time and space distortions (see *www.gravitywarpdrive.com*). Associated with this is the "time tunnel" theory, in which electrically active clouds known as "electric fog" suddenly appear and envelope an aircraft, turning it into a type of antenna. This is said to cause electrical equipment to fail, rendering directional navigation useless and distorting time.

Others believe that the Bermuda Triangle is the site of the famous lost continent/city of Atlantis. In this theory, allegedly lost technology survives beneath the waves in the form of a giant "fire crystal" that periodically turns on and creates the often-reported time and space distortions and other magnetic disturbances (see chapter 5).

Others adopt the "stargate" theory—the same phenomenon depicted in both the movie *Stargate* (1994) and in the television series *Stargate SG-1* (1997–2007)—which claims that the same intermittent activation of a submerged piece of technology (in this case, a stargate) causes the various anomalies reported. As this theory goes, this stargate, and others around the world, are portals to other places on Earth, other planets, and/or other dimensions. Montauk Project survivors like Preston Nichols, Al Bielek, and Stewart Swerdlow have all given eyewitness testimony about the existence and practical use of such technology. As far as the general public is concerned, however, there is no such thing as a stargate.

No one disputes that there are magnetic anomalies in the Bermuda Triangle. There are disputes, however, about what causes them. As case in point, the Bermuda Triangle is supposedly one of only two places on Earth where magnetic north and geographic north are in alignment on a compass. The other is the Dragon's Triangle in the north Philippine Sea, south of Japan (see the 2006 episode of the History Channel's *UFO Files* series entitled "The Pacific's Bermuda Triangle"). However, others claim that these "agonic lines"—lines of no magnetic variation—are mobile and neither line currently passes through either of these water regions.

Scientist Ivan T. Sanderson, founder of the Society for the Investigation of the Unexplained, has proposed other theories to account for magnetic anomalies. In 1972, Sanderson propounded the theory of the "Twelve Vile Vortices," or the twelve locations around the world where there are more missing vessel and airplane reports, more mysterious lights in the sky, and more magnetic anomalies than anywhere else. This indicates, he claims, that these areas are placed on the Earth's energy grid and connected by ley lines (see chapter 5).

The twelve Vile Vortices are the North Pole, the South Pole, the Bermuda Triangle (Caribbean Sea), the Dragon's Triangle (southeast of Japan), Easter Island (South Pacific), Zimbabwe Megaliths (southeast Africa), South Atlantic Anomaly (off the east coast of Brazil), Mohenjo Daro (Pakistan), the Algerian Megaliths (north Africa), Wharton Basin (Wallaby Fracture near the east coast of Australia), the Hebrides Trench (northwest of Scotland), and Hamakulia (near the East coast of Hawaii). Other claims indicate more sites, including Alaska, the Loyalty Islands north of New Zealand, and the Giza pyramid complex in Egypt. Even the U.S. government, through the National Oceanic and Atmospheric Administration, sees "geomagnetic lines of flux" from the sea floor as the source of the described magnetic anomalies.

Still others think the many disappearances of planes and ships can be attributed to UFOs. For example, Puerto Rico, the supposed home to the *chupacabra* (see chapter 5), is a known hot spot for UFO activity and anchors the southern point of the Bermuda Triangle. Moreover, not only is Andros Island a known UFO hot spot, but also there is speculation based on testimony of former employees that the U.S. Naval Base known as AUTEC, or Atlantic Undersea Test and Evaluation Center, located there is a jointly run human military and alien space base. Witnesses report that both UFOs and USOs (unidentified submerged objects) come and go there regularly. The History Channel's *UFO Hunters* series did an excellent 2009 episode on AUTEC entitled "Underwater Alien Bases" (see chapter 6).

However, despite ongoing testimony of UFO sightings, various magnetic field tests, and questionable military endeavors (see *Into the Bermuda Triangle* [2005] by Gian Quasar), skeptics scoff at these assertions and have identified many natural phenomena that may account for the many reports of missing ships and airplanes. Among the best theories are human error and the gas bubble theory, which suggests that trapped pockets of methane gas can periodically be released from the seafloor in the areas within the triangle. The gas, they claim, can quickly rise to the surface and reduce a ship's buoyancy, sinking it. Another popular and logical theory is that extreme weather conditions like funnel spouts, flash rain storms, and rogue waves are the culprits.

A rogue wave occurs when three sets of waves moving in juxtaposed directions or simultaneously converging create one enormous wave. This is known as "superposition." Japanese fishermen call rogue waves "triangle waves" because they can appear as a large triangle, or pyramid.

The first-ever photograph of a rogue wave was captured in 1980 when a ninety-foot wave spilled over the deck of the oil tanker *ESSO Languedoc*, nearly sinking it.

Author Charles Berlitz wrote a few of the early, now classic, books on the subject. In *The Bermuda Triangle* (1974) and *The Dragon's Triangle* (1989), he put forth the notion that the paranormal played a key role in the many occurrences in both areas. On the other hand, *The Bermuda Triangle Mystery—Solved* (1995) by Larry Kusche made the opposite case—that natural phenomena like volcanic activity and the weather conditions mentioned above could account for most of the happenings in both triangles. And so today, the debate goes back and forth.

Despite some solid arguments to the contrary, "believers" still look to the Bermuda Triangle as a place of wonder. Sailors see it as an area where safety is of the utmost concern simply because of common ocean-going hardships; pilots see it as an area where tricky magnetic anomalies make their journeys unpredictable and unsafe.

Whether the area has supernatural qualities, is a UFO hot spot, or is merely a naturally dangerous geographic zone, the legend of the Bermuda Triangle is known and respected worldwide by sailors, pilots, and researchers alike.

CAUTIONARY TIPS: Prepare in advance for magnetic anomalies:

- **For pilots: If a magnetic anomaly knocks out your compass or other navigational equipment, you may need to reorient yourself visually and fly to safety. Try to get a map of the area in advance and memorize what it looks like from the air. Do this in multiple directions if possible; memorize maps from multiple directions, because you may not be able to predict the direction of orientation in an emergency.**

- **For mariners:** Include in your equipment a nonelectrical navigation device like a sextant to lead you and your vessel back to safety in case of an electrical failure due to a magnetic anomaly.

Top Cases, Varginha, Brazil

Several cases of crashed UFO sites in Brazil are chronicled in books like *UFO Abduction at Maringa* (1984), *UFO Abduction at Botucatu* (1985), and *UFO Contact from Planet Acart* (1987). The interior Mato Grosso region of Brazil is a well-known hot spot and is allegedly an area where there is at least one inner-Earth entrance.

It is the small, rural town of Varginha in the southern state of Minas Gerais, however, that is the site of arguably the world's most important, most studied, and most controversial case. On January 20, 1996, three female witnesses saw what appeared to be an injured alien being crouching by a wall. The three witnesses all reacted in different ways, but all fled in terror. Rumors spread and gained steam when military vehicles and personnel were witnessed by some hunting and capturing one, or possibly more, ET beings.

Brazilian researchers like Ubirajara Rodrigues, director of the Institute of Ufological Research, and many others have researched this case perhaps more than any other single case. Still, there is apparently much more to this case than has so far been reported. Researcher Roger Leir demonstrated this with his recent investigation, which he outlined in his book *UFO Crash in Brazil* (2005). Leir shows that, while it is never the best situation to investigate a case so long after the initial event, there are still ways to glean new and pertinent information. For example, it has been rumored that the Brazilian military killed one being and captured at least one other and then shipped it/them to the United States. It was rumored that there was an alien autopsy and even crash debris from a small (school bus–sized) cigar-shaped craft.

Leir was able to confirm, through eyewitness testimony from the doctor who performed it, that an alien autopsy did, in fact, happen. Also, by the way in which several interview subjects acted in response to certain questions, he was also able to see for himself the results of the pressure apparently put on alleged witnesses by "authorities," who are generally thought to be the Brazilian military. Although he was not able to find physical evidence, his interviews provided more corroboration for many aspects of the incident.

The picture that unfolds is dramatic. One possible interpretation of the information is that a cigar-shaped craft had technical trouble and crashed, or landed, in Varginha. Several beings may have escaped or been released to avoid death; these were spotted by a number of witnesses in different parts of the town. The military was apparently already tracking the craft and were quick to capture and, in at least one report, shoot an alien being.

One military man allegedly died from direct contact with one of the beings. Corporal Marco Chereze's family has yet to be provided with a convincing explanation by the military for what occurred in Varginha or what happened to Corporal Chereze. In what has become typical military fashion, they have maintained that "what witnesses saw were not aliens, but rather 'an expectant dwarf couple' and 'a mentally handicapped dwarf'"! For more details, see Nigel Watson's "Death by UFO," *Fortean Times* 147 (2001).

INTERVIEW TIP: I found the testimony of the deceased military police officer's wife to be most illuminating. . . . Watching her movements during the questioning was most interesting because it was obvious, even to a non-student of NLP {neuro-linguistic programming}, that she was hiding a great deal of information. Her negative comments indicated a high probability of intimidation and resultant fear . . .

ROGER LEIR, *UFO CRASH IN BRAZIL*

Hot Spots, Kwazulu-Natal Province, South Africa

South Africa, home of the 2010 World Cup soccer tournament, is also home to a plethora of UFO activity. *UFO Contact from Koldas* (1986) by Carl van Vlierden and Wendelle Stevens arguably details the most famous South African case. The event described in this book, now out of print, was rechronicled by van Vlierden in *The Twelve Planets Speak!* (1989).

In 1960, contactee "Edwin" got a new boss at the factory where he worked in Durban, KwaZulu-Natal. They got to be friends and spent time together fishing. On one occasion, Edwin reported that his boss, "George," took out a radio-like device and began directing the movements of lights in the night sky. George later revealed that he was really Valdar from the planet Koldas, which was located in an antimatter universe. The full story is enthralling.

The story of contactee Elizabeth Klarer is equally fascinating. Until her death in February 1994, Klarer maintained that she had had UFO sightings since she was a child. She had her first contact as a child in 1957, when, as she was "riding along" the Drakenburg range near the Mooi River, near Rosetta, KwaZulu-Natal, a disk hovered over her and she saw an attractive man standing in full view in a portal on the craft.

The gentle and alluring alien seemingly courted Klarer, who soon became the mother of a hybrid. She claims to have traveled to Akon's home planet Meton in Proxima Centauri but that she could not handle the thin, pure atmosphere. She returned to South Africa, where she spent the rest of her days living a meager life until her death in 1994. The story, told in *Beyond the Light Barrier: The Autobiography of Elizabeth Klarer* (2009) is rich in details and reads like a romance novel.

On May 20, 2006, Africa's leading news source reported that earlier that day, "numerous eyewitnesses" in Port Shepstone on the south coast of KwaZulu-Natal had observed "an unidentified flying object crashing into the sea." Authorities from the National Sea Rescue Institute (NSRI) had apparently been tracking the situation, as land, sea, and air rescue teams were quickly brought to the scene to investigate. After an all-out twelve-square-nautical-mile search, nothing was found.

RESEARCH/RESOURCE TIP: Weather radar data from the National Weather Service can be used when investigating UFO sightings. Getting the data from the NWS and viewing it on your computer is free, easy, and fast. NEXRAD (from Next-Generation Radar) data can be downloaded from the NWS's National Climatic Data Center online inventory (search for "nexrad inventory") ... Look under "radar resources" for free viewing programs you'll also need. Plan to spend time reading the background information and learning what you're doing.

— RALPH HOWARD, GEORGIA MUFON

5

Associated Phenomena, A–L

Abductions

This is a type of contact in which people are taken against their will to some location—often a UFO—and reportedly undergo various types of communication and experiments. Many kinds of abductors have been reported. For example, not only are human military personnel and Gray aliens reported as abductors; mantis, insect, and reptilian aliens have been reported as well.

Are these experiences real, tangible events? Or are they a product of some type of psychological effect? Could they be both? Or could they be more?

Reports first started surfacing in the early 1950s. As more and more experiencers "came out," we learned that there were much older reports as well. One of the early events widely reported was the Betty and Barney Hill case, which involved many weird sightings and encounters, as well as a legendary star map—a drawing showing the place of origin of their abductors (see John G. Fuller's *The Interrupted*

Journey [1966]). Another early international case was the 1957 Villas-Boas case in Brazil. This involved testimony that claimed the abductor seduced the abductee.

Alien Discussions: The Proceedings of the Abduction Study Conference (1994), arguably the seminal work in the field, is a must-read for history of the subject. It is a compilation of the many lectures given by an all-star panel of researchers into the phenomena at the Massachusetts Institute of Technology in Cambridge, Massachusetts. Many other noted researchers have done work in this field as well—Budd Hopkins, Leo Sprinkle, and John Mack (RIP) are legends in the field, as are Karla Turner (RIP), David Jacobs, Barbara Lamb, and Yvonne Smith. All of their works are respected (see chapter 2).

Many theories have been presented and many protocols have been devised. Dr. Jacobs, for instance—one of only two college instructors to run pro-UFO-related classes at a reputable university—has concluded that there must be an ongoing, human-alien hybrid breeding program being conducted by extraterrestrials. Jacobs has devised the first scientific typology of the phenomena. His book *The Threat: Revealing the Secret Alien Agenda* (1999) describes his work.

Another theory is that these experiences are actually military abductions faked as alien abductions. These are described as taking place in two ways: Either the military is faking alien abductions so they can carry out secret biological experiments on the general population, or they wait for genuine alien abductees to be returned and re-abduct them for mind-controlled debriefing (see chapter 3 and Appendix B). *Abducted by Aliens* (2008) by Chuck Weiss and the movie *The Fourth Kind* (2009) starring Milla Jovovich both explore these possibilities.

INTERVIEW TIP: Regardless of what you believe about the UFO or ET experience someone may share with you, know that for them the experience is probably very real and therefore deeply personal and deeply emotional. As the interviewer you are providing an ear for someone who may not have anyone else they feel they can talk to about their experience. Your first objective in interviewing someone shouldn't be to help yourself (or for your entertainment), but to help them. Be compassionate and understanding of the person's beliefs and emotions. Also, anybody's experience is filtered through their own belief system, so be compassionate of their beliefs, especially if they aren't your own! Additionally, the person sharing with you may ask you to do something for them, or you may offer to help them again or to provide them some information. If so, it's equally important to follow through with your promises and provide them the information you said you would or be willing to speak with them again if they need it. After you have compassionately allowed the person to freely share, then as an investigator or researcher, you must follow through with gathering and documenting any evidence they may have. This may require searching for it or uncovering it from a reluctant witness. Again, your being compassionate will go a long way toward the witnesses' willingness to provide you with it. While your responsibility to the interviewee is to be compassionate and helpful, your responsibility to ufology is . . . what?. . . evidence, evidence, evidence. So, always follow through after the interview!

MELINDA LESLIE, PERSONAL INTERVIEW

Advanced Technology

What drives, or powers, a UFO? This question has been at the forefront of ufology since its inception. While it is unclear just how far back the United States and other world militaries became aware of the UFO phenomenon, many of them, in particular that of the United States, quickly developed "crash retrieval" units designed and specially trained to handle such situations (see *Crash: When UFOs Fall from the Sky: A History of Famous Incidents, Conspiracies, and Cover-ups* [2010] by Kevin D. Randle).

The goal? To retrieve useable alien propulsion systems and other high-tech hardware and adapt it to military purposes and other new inventions to sell to public and private sectors. This profit, in turn, goes on to fund a number of secret government and military projects—like the Montauk Project, for example. The DVDs *UFOs and Disturbing Secrets: Project Bluebook Report #13* (2007) and *UFO Highway: The Dulce Interview, Human Origins, HAARP & Project Blue Beam* (2010) by Anthony F. Sanchez, Adad Morales, and Norio Hayakawa both discuss these possibilities.

Many new "inventions"—fiber optics in the 1980s, faster micro-processors in the 1990s, mind control, time travel, and inter-dimensional travel—are all thought either to be derived from direct meetings and/or exchanges with aliens or retrieved from downed UFOs (see *Extraterrestrials–U.S. Government Treaty and Agreements: Alien Technology, Abductions and Military Alliance* (2008) by Maximillien De Lafayette).

Contactees have described witnessing a variety of advanced technologies as well during their experiences aboard alien craft—from super-potent nutritional drinks to furniture that appears and disappears in an instant; from ray guns and force fields to indestructible yet bendable metals and teleportation devices. David Hatcher Childress describes some of them in *Technology of the Gods: The Incredible Sciences of the Ancients* (2000), as does Kenneth Behrendt in his book *Secrets of*

UFO Technology (2007). The DVD *Alien Technology* (2006) hosted by Stacy Keach presents evidence of this as well.

Many of the Montauk Project survivors claim that it was technology from the Sirians (from the star Sirius) that gave the U.S. military the ability to open gateways to other dimensions. Hitler is thought to have had technology exchanges with aliens from the planet Aldebaran, located in the constellation of Taurus, which enabled the Nazis to develop flying disks during World War II (see chapter 4). The controversial Bob Lazar also claimed to be aware of the U.S. military's scientific endeavors in antigravity propulsion systems at Area 51, derived from direct contact with both aliens and downed craft.

Of course, when it comes to antigravity, the Croatian-born Nikola Tesla (1856–1943) is the premiere inventor. The list of this man's achievements is long. He is credited with the invention of alternating current (AC), today's standard in electrical power delivery, as well as wireless power transmission and free-energy machines. Tesla was also the first to detect strange signals from outer space that he thought were most likely emanating from either Venus or Mars, predating SETI by decades (see chapter 7).

Tesla's less mainstream inventions include Tesla coils, giant electrical coils that can generate and deliver gigawatts of power (large even by today's standards), "death rays" or "particle beams" that employ electromagnetic or scalar technology, and "psychotronic" machines that are capable of interfacing with human consciousness, digitizing individual thoughts and preparing them to be amplified or focused onto a target depending on the intentions of the user.

Biographer Margaret Cheney reports in her biography *Tesla: Man Out of Time* (1981), that the FBI was called to the inventor's New York hotel room shortly after his death—reportedly from a "coronary thrombosis"—bringing a locksmith to open his safe. "Tesla's safe was opened and the contents examined," she writes. But Cheney does not say what happened to the contents of the safe.

Some researchers say that the U.S. government confiscated the man's scientific papers, thereby withholding many inventions from the public—free energy and antigravity are good examples. Inventor and author William Lyne maintains that it is Tesla's free-energy machine that the U.S. government stole and is secretly using in not only free-energy technology but also man-made flying-saucer propulsion (see chapter 1).

Of course, once it was learned that some of Tesla's machines could be used to control individuals through mind control—or alter time, for example—these devices were quickly taken out of the public view and used in further secret tests and activities. These possibilities have been explored in several books, including *Angels Don't Play This Haarp: Advances in Tesla Technology* (1995) by Nick Begich and Jeane Manning, *Incredible Technologies of the New World Order: UFOs—Tesla—Area 51* (1997) by Commander X, *My Inventions: The Autobiography of Nikola Tesla* (2010) by Nikola Tesla, and *Occult Ether Physics: Tesla's "Ideal Flying Machine" and the Conspiracy to Conceal It* (2010) by William R. Lyne.

Wilhelm Reich (1897–1957) was another advanced technology giant whose psychotronics, weather modification, and UFO work were employed during the Montauk Project. The Austrian-born Reich was the purveyor of an all-permeating universal energy that he called "organic" or "orgone" radiation (OR). This was a life-generating force—the same one, he surmised, that is responsible for orgasms. He invented an orgone accumulator (ORAC)—a box layered with specific metals that appeared to capture and store OR discharged by what he believed were microscopic life forms called "bions."

Reich's inquiry into the reasons why this was so led him to conclude that OR was generated not only by bions but by the sun as well, and then naturally absorbed through the skin. Reich developed an "orgonoscope" to detect the presence of OR in nature, an "orgone field meter" to test the level of OR in a human body, and an OR free-energy machine that was stolen in 1948. This culminated in the development of a life-size ORAC that was thought to perform various kinds of healings. There were mixed results.

Reich's theories that the levels of OR in the atmosphere determined weather patterns, cloud formations, and the northern and southern lights, that OR was the vehicle by which the manifestation of light occurred, or that it was the energetic glue that brought all the separate forces together into a Unified Field theory were popular among a small segment of the scientific community and garnered enough support to found the Reich Institute in Rangeley, Maine in 1950.

In 1951, Reich was ready to perform the first of two major experiments into the nature of OR. The results of the first experiment were published in a report entitled *ORANUR Experiment: First Report 1947–1951*. In these experiments, Reich, curious to see what would happen when OR and nuclear energy were combined, added some extra layers of lead to an ORAC and placed a minute amount of a radioactive isotope inside. Afterward, dark clouds formed over the institute for weeks, vegetation withered, and assistants became ill. By 1952, UFOs began to appear as well.

Reich discovered that there was a counteragent to OR that was created under specific circumstances—an agent called "deadly orgone radiation," or DOR. Not only did DOR cause bad weather and illnesses in both humans and plants; it was determined by Reich that it was also a kind of exhaust put out by UFOs. He put forth the notion that there was a direct relationship between the amount of DOR in the atmosphere and the presence of UFOs.

Following this thread, in 1954, he built a device known as the "cloud buster" that drew DOR out of the atmosphere, giving him the power to alter the weather. Reich was also able to attract UFOs when using the apparatus. He became aware that darker, rain-like clouds were often used as cover for UFOs. When pointed at one of these clouds, Reich's cloud buster dissipated the cloud and disrupted the flying craft. After he did this several times, the UFOs disappeared for good. He even feared that he might start an interplanetary war if he did not stop aiming the cloud buster at them.

That same year, Reich tried to warn the U.S. Air Force about the problem of UFOs and how they should be handled. But all this really did was to alert the government that Reich was someone who needed to be removed from the public view and his work studied in secret. By the time his second report, entitled *Contact with Space: ORANUR, Second Report* (1951–1956), was published, the powers that be were ready to move in on him, his holdings, and his institute.

Because of the fear of competition from Reich's ORAC machines, however, many claim that it was the Food and Drug Administration (FDA) that was behind the suit brought against Reich (others claim it was the American Medical Association, or AMA). They claimed that, by selling his ORAC machines across state lines, Reich was in violation of interstate fraud laws. Why? Attorneys argued that, because there was no such thing as OR, his packages were fraudulently labeled. He was convicted and sent to a federal penitentiary. His employees were ordered to stop production of the machines and to destroy any remaining ones. He died on November 3, 1957, two days before he was to be released on parole. The work and equipment that remained in his Long Island laboratory are reported to have been stolen.

For more information on Reich, see *Wilhelm Reich vs. the U.S.A* (1974) by Jerome Greenfield; *The Orgone Accumulator Handbook: Construction Plans, Experimental Use, and Protection Against Toxic Energy* (2007) by James DeMeo and Eva Reich; *The Science of Orgonomy: A Study on Wilhelm Reich* (2010) by Pierre F. Walter; and *The Secret History of Extraterrestrials: Advanced Technology and the Coming New Race* (2010) by Len Kasten.

Alien Implants

Dr. Roger Leir tops the extremely short list of surgeons who have extracted physical pieces of foreign bodies from human patients that are made from materials unknown to modern science. Leir's book *Casebook: Alien Implants* (2000) chronicles several cases where metallic and/or biological implants have been surgically removed from patients, some of whom claim to have been abducted by aliens. In other cases, the abductees were not aware of the abduction until one or more implants were detected inside of them.

These implants have been detected almost everywhere in the human body, but predominantly in the feet, and especially in the toes, legs, knees, and thighs. They are also commonly reported in the hands, forearms, and brains. They are usually surrounded by a tough membrane that interfaces with the implantee's nervous system through "proprioceptors," special nerve cells that specifically send messages to the brain "on bodily positioning." Several types have been extracted. Some are all metallic; some are half metallic and half biological; others are all biological. In two cases in which Dr. Leir performed surgery, the implant moved to avoid the scalpel.

In another case, Dr. Leir used a gauss meter to test for electromagnetic fields and excess radiation around an implant while it was still in the subject's body. He found that it was emitting radio waves at 19 gigahertz, 14 megahertz, and 8 hertz and that it generated a magnetic field measuring "m10 gauss." Writer Steve Colburn calls alien implants "potentially, the most important source of physical evidence to prove the reality of the abductions" (see "Alien Implant Removal and Study," *Open Minds Magazine* 1 [2010]).

Author David Jacobs, in his book *The Threat: Revealing the Secret Alien Agenda* (1999), makes the case that implants are used by the alien races performing hybridization in order to track individuals and relay mental and emotional information—in other words, mind control (see chapter 6).

There are apparently nonphysical, ethereal, or spiritual implants as well. Some claim that you have to be "gifted" with some type of psychic ability to see these devices. Several contactee/abductee types claim to be able to detect these nonphysical implants psychically and perform psychic surgery to remove them. Stewart Swerdlow, for example, maintains that every human being is equipped with what he calls the "standard array" of six implants, both physical and ethereal and of varying nature (see chapter 4). Others have additional implants for "special" tasks, he says.

Contactee Lee Patrick Hanks has developed a three-stage methodology to detect and remove spiritual implants. First, he performs a clearing of the Light Body. Then he identifies and removes negative programming and mental loops. Finally, he reconnects the subject's eighth chakra for complete spiritual realignment. Swerdlow, Hanks, and many others are available for one-on-one sessions for a fee.

EQUIPMENT TIP: Gauss meters, or magnetometers, are used to measure the strength of a magnetic field. They use an electronic chip called a Hall-effect device, which gives off a tiny electrical current when exposed to a magnetic field. The current is amplified with electronic circuitry and a meter shows the number of gauss (the units of magnetic field strength). These devices are used to detect and measure magnetic fields in scientific experiments, in industry, and even in people's homes.

A UFO Hunter's Guide

Ascended Masters

Saint Germain, Maitreya, and Quan Yin are but a few of the hundreds of human beings who have supposedly died, transcended physical reality, and ascended to a level of a "higher vibration," or "frequency." Their goal is to assist in the spiritual and consciousness evolution of humanity on Earth.

These Masters are said to be the spiritual liaisons between the coarse, dense, three-dimensional world we call "reality" and the higher spiritual realms of less-dense forms. They are thought to be able to appear physically or as apparitions in their human form, or in small, distinctly colored balls of light known as orbs. (See *The Orb Project* [2007] by Miceal Ledwith and Klaus Heinemann, *ORBS: Their Mission and Messages of Hope* [2010] by Klaus Heinemann and Gundi Heinemann; "Behind the Lens: What Are Those Orbs," *UFO Magazine* [April 2008] by Guy Pellicola; and *Chasing Orbs: An Adventure into the Mysterious World of Orbs* [2010] by Melanie France.) Starting in 1930, the Ascended Masters, who are often associated with angels, began to present the philosophy of Ascended Master St. Germain through a series of books—the *I Am Decrees* I, II, and III, which are now classic works.

Physical, three-dimensional Earth helpers like Elizabeth Clare Prophet and Mark Prophet have written a whole series of books on this subject (see *www.tsl.org*). J. Z. Knight, who channels the Ascended Master Ramtha (see *www.ramtha.com*), is just one of the many individuals who describe faster vibratory realities where many spirits dwell and where the connections between all living entities are more clearly seen.

Everything associated with these beings is part of what is called "The Violet Flame"—a spiritual fire that can supposedly transmute any negative energy into spiritual light. The idea is to propagate this violet flame on Earth in the three-dimensional "sludge," until there is no more negative energy. In this way, the Earth and its inhabitants will be ready to transition into what is believed to be the fifth dimension and another physical location in space. The DVD *Secret Signs and*

Invocations to Contact Count Saint Germain and Other Ascended Masters (2004) starring William Alexander Oribello portrays what this transition may be like.

Not all of these beings are "of the light," however. Dark reptilian Ascended Masters have also been reported to attack victims spiritually, leaving evidence of a variety of physical effects, including bruises, scratches, and open wounds presumably made by claws, as well as both mental and emotional trauma. The Ascended Master philosophy dictates that if all of the negative energy is consumed and transformed into the Violet Flame, no dark, negative beings will survive.

The Internet is a good resource for Ascended Master students, with YouTube providing a number of videos. It has also become a portal for bloggers. Check out the many "Riza" videos. Skeptics claim this whole Ascended Master world is part of a governmental mind-control program (see *The David Icke Guide to the Global Conspiracy* [2007]).

Cattle Mutilations

Since 1967 and the "Snippy the Horse" case in the San Luis Valley, which stretches across southern Colorado and northern New Mexico, cattle ranchers around the world have been finding one or more of their cattle or other livestock dead and mutilated in grotesque and odd ways. It was first thought that the mutilations were caused by some sort of predator. However, upon closer inspection, some interesting characteristics were found that negated the predator theory.

In the Snippy case, rancher and witness Nellie Lewis first made the connection between these mutilations and UFOs when she reportedly saw a UFO hovering over their ranch the day before they discovered the dead Snippy. Christopher O'Brien, author of *Secrets of the Mysterious Valley* (2007), reports that, in the San Luis Valley alone between 1992 and early 1999, hundreds of UFOs and mysterious black helicopters have been seen in conjunction with these incidents. He calls this the largest wave of "high strangeness" activity—a variety of weird activities happening simultaneously—in the history of the United States.

In July 2009 in Pampa, Argentina, a rash of mutilations were reported that had all of the now familiar characteristics: The cows were drained of their blood (known as ex-sanguination); no tracks were found near the carcass; and specific body parts were missing, apparently removed with neat and precise cuts that cannot be duplicated with today's top surgical technology and surgeons. O'Brien notes:

> Generally the mandible is exposed, the tongue is gone, and the reproductive tract has been excised and removed. Oftentimes an eye is gone, or an ear. If it's a cow, the udder is gone, generally. If it's a bull, the genitalia are gone. And always, with a few exceptions here and there, there's no evidence of predators or scavengers or tire tracks. Nobody heard anything; the dogs didn't bark. The animal is often found nowhere near its own tracks.
>
> Christopher O'Brien, *www.ourstrangeplanet.com*

Other common characteristics include increased radiation on and near the carcasses and predators not going near them. Increasingly, these events are reported in conjunction with UFO sightings and, more rarely, crop circles.

In one bizarre case from February 7, 2009, near Springfield, Missouri, investigators witnessed a freshly discovered cow mutilation. They swept their metal detector over the carcass and got a hit—meaning that metal was detected—in the beast's neck. After recalibrating and retesting multiple times, the hit was still present. The object measured 90 percent platinum. So they tested the findings again. This time, the hit was gone. The detector was randomly swept over the cow and they got another hit near the ear and sinus cavity. Then that disappeared as well, but was found again moving back toward the jaw.

Dumbfounded, the researchers decided to move the carcass back to a lab for further testing. Weather prevented them from removing it until the next day. When they went to move the dead cow the next day, they were astounded to find that it had been further mutilated—all of its internal organs had been removed "up to the uterus." No satisfactory explanation for these events has ever been provided, although researchers like K. W. Storch ("Animal Mutilation: the ever-so-mystifying case of the disappearing implant," *MUFON Journal* 115 [March 2011]) have tried.

Other wild cases include a cow whose brain was missing with no break in the cranium, spines that were excised in impossible ways, and carcasses that didn't rot, even in heated rooms.

Linda Moulton Howe has been instrumental in bringing this issue to public awareness with her two acclaimed DVDs, *A Strange Harvest* (1980) and *An Alien Harvest* (1989), as well as through her website *www.earthfiles.com*. There have also been some classic books written on the subject, like *Mute Evidence* (1984) by Daniel Kagan and Ian Summers, *The Cattle Mutilators* (1980) by John J. Dalton, and the now out-of-print classic *Mystery Stalks the Prairie* (1976) by Roberta Donovan.

Because of the many reports of mysterious black helicopters that are assumed to be from some secret military unit, most have come to the conclusion that cattle mutilations are the result of secret government weapons technology. O'Brien says:

> I think the majority of these cases are very slick teams of quasi-military-equipped scientists who are monitoring the spread of Mad Cow disease in the food chain and monitoring above-ground environmental pollutants.
>
> Christopher O'Brien, *www.ufomag.com*

The four leading theories that attempt to explain this are the following:

1. Satanic cults (a few early cases were linked to these cults)

2. Mass hysteria

3. Secret weapons testing (either biological or bacteriological)

4. Extraterrestrial testing of some kind, most probably genetic in nature

The last two theories are seen as the most likely scenarios, yet extensive fieldwork has yielded few definitive conclusions. For more information, see *The Ranchers Nightmare: Mysterious Murder of Livestock* (2006) by Jim Hickman and "Cattle Killers," a 2009 episode of the *MonsterQuest* series on the History Channel.

INVESTIGATIVE TIP: Do not overlook the value of a good sketch. Some witnesses are better able to describe their experiences if they can draw the images they are not able to vocalize. Also, some of the best information from contactees of all types comes while they are under hypnosis and are able to sketch images.

LINDA MOULTON HOWE

Crop Circles

Crop circles are mysteriously formed symbols embedded in crop fields. There is evidence of these formations in the Western world from as far back as the 17th century in England, where they were known as "faery rings." And the evidence goes back even further in the non-Western world. For example, in South Africa, the indigenous peoples claim to have viewed these symbols for thousands of years, referring to them as "God's symbols" and holding celebrations when they appear.

In the late 1970s, a variety of "unexplained ground markings" (UGMs) in the fields of southern England began to appear regularly. The first books written on the subject were *Mystery of the Circles* (1983), followed by *Controversy of the Circles* (1989) and *Crop Circles: A Mystery Solved* (1990), all by Jenny Randles (see chapter 3). Paul

Fuller, former editor of the now defunct *The Crop Watcher* journal, propounded the idea that hoaxes could account for as many as 99 percent of them. The other 1 percent were said to be explained by some kind of wind phenomena, most likely a whirlwind. After exposure of the work of the two most famous hoaxers, known as "Doug and Dave" (Brits Doug Bower and Dave Chorley), who stirred up a media blitz in the mid to late 1980s claiming to be responsible for all the formations in England up until that time, the early interest in the phenomenon faded.

However, right about the same time—between 1990 and 1991—and seemingly in response to the lack of public interest, the circles took a step up in complexity and were commonly interpreted as being more intricate "pictograms" that conveyed more complex data. Someone, or something, it seems, was trying to communicate to humans through the circles.

There are several theories as to the cause of these formations, including hoaxes, whirlwind vortices, plasma vortices, Earth energies, ETs and/or UFOs, an underground civilization, military experiments, or even a God force. Both UFOs and mysterious "orbs" have been sighted, photographed, and video-recorded in close geographical and chronological proximity to formations. Orbs are thought to be either remote-controlled devices of advanced technology or possibly living beings. The *Oliver's Castle* video shot by John Whaley on August 11, 1996, shows two orbs creating a crop circle.

Crop circle researcher and filmmaker Patty Greer, in an article for *UFO Magazine* 24, no. 2 (March 2011), says:

[The Oliver's Castle video] is believed by many to be real and has also been debunked for years. For no apparent reason, I asked my film editor to slow the footage down and play it backwards. What we found is a direct and visible line of communication that goes between the two balls of light right before the circle is laid down.

www.pattygreer.com

Some think crop circles are created with some kind of electromagnetic beam technology. American/British researcher Freddy Silva has reported that there are photographs of beams of light coming straight down from the sky where, later, crop formations appear. Australian researcher Brian Sullen calls these beams of light a "sound stylus or pen," as high-pitched sound in the range of 6 kHz has been recorded in his country.

It is more common to hear about the positive effects of entering these symbols. Silva has reported that hundreds of healings have been attributed to being inside a crop circle formation, as well as phenomena like consciousness expansion, feelings of euphoria, and psychic abilities (see chapter 6). However, what is not as widely known is that some people do get sick upon entering a crop circle. Nausea, headaches, and disorientation have also been reported. It is also unknown why these circles affect one person one way and another person another. Why these situations are not as openly discussed is not clear. It is ironic, however, because the oldest known official report of a crop circle—in 1678 in Hertfordshire, England—is associated with an illness that the farmer attributed to being inside the circle made by what he thought was the "Mower's Devil."

A trend in the formations is to utilize extremely complex fractal patterns, or sacred geometric patterns that reflect "changes of state," to convey intricate data. These formations, which often appear in 3D (including a full Mandelbrot Set—August 13, 1991, in Cambridge) or in images that follow the contour of the land but appear perfect from above (like the Silbury Hill formations—July 6 and 7, 2007, in Wiltshire, England) are becoming more common. Pentagonal (fivefold), hexagonal (sixfold), and heptagonal (ninefold) symmetries, all representative of human DNA and biology and hyper-dimensional mathematics, are frequent as well.

The circles have now appeared in twenty-six countries, represented by at least as many websites on the Internet. Curiously, however, England has garnered roughly 80 percent of them, with most appearing in southern England in the counties of Wiltshire and Hampshire. While there has not been a definitive answer as to why this is so, Silva suggests that it is because these areas sit on top of one of the world's largest chalk aquifers. This is significant, he says, because chalk is a good conductor of energy and water is an excellent way to store information.

In support of this, Silva pointed out at the Bay Area UFO Expo in 2006, that tests have shown that crop circle formations energetically imprint water left in bowls in the fields to levels up to 160 percent above the energetic imprinting of a bowl of water left in a normal field. In fact, he claims to have had the information for his now classic book "downloaded" to him after an experience in a circle. And, of course, the fact that humans are comprised of at least 70 percent water lends credence to the idea that crop circles can communicate information to human beings through the structure of water.

Colin Andrews and Pat Delgado pointed out—in one of their pioneering works, *Circular Evidence: A Detailed Investigation of the Flattened Swirled Crops Phenomena* (1989)—that many of these formations appear in close proximity to sacred sites, including Stonehenge, Glastonbury Tor, and Silbury Hill—all in Wiltshire County. This has prompted the question, Could both the sacred sites and crop circles in southern England have been situated to take advantage of the local geology and its electrical information-storage-and-transfer capabilities (the chalk aquifer)?

Andrews and Delgado coined the term "cereology" to describe the study of these landscape/circle relationships—their geographic placement, their alignments with one another, their alignments with sacred sites, their alignments with the four directions, and their alignments with stars and constellations, as well as the information embedded within the pictograms themselves.

The fact that these formations often appear in various alignments with sacred sites indicates to researchers that they must somehow be related to ley lines, which are parts of a larger energetic grid that spans the entire Earth. Because ley lines, sacred geometry, and sacred sites are all associated with mass consciousness programming and/or consciousness expansion, many researchers conclude that there is consciousness programming or downloading of information going on between the crop circle symbol and the masses who perceive it. Either that or the circles are programming the landscape via sacred sites, which in turn programs human consciousness. The specific alignments are thought to be incorporated into the designs to convey deeper levels of information. They can connect ideas and other details between the formations to create a kind of sentence structure that allows the encoding of more information.

Silva adheres to this notion of consciousness programming as a prime reason for the formation of the circles in conjunction with sacred sites. His book *Secrets in the Fields* (2002) is also a classic in crop circle research. He maintains that crop circles share the same technology as earthen mounds, stone circles, and other sacred sites around the world and that they are "the new temples." He maintains that the formations are meant to "wake up" these sacred sites, which in turn wakes up human mass consciousness.

Silva may be correct in asserting that the circles and the sacred sites share the same technology, because there are also key alignments over great distances. And these key alignments are not found just in southern England.

American researcher Jeff Wilson, director of the Independent Crop Circle Researchers Association (*www.iccra.org*) in Ohio, considers the mound structures in that state to be on par with those in Wiltshire, England. Why? Because of all the strategic alignments. The famous Serpent Mound of Ohio is in alignment not only with stellar, solar, lunar, and planetary astronomical positions and various local crop circle formations but also, apparently, with one of England's more famous crop circles, the Barbary Castle tetrahedron formation that appeared in Wiltshire in 1991. Some think that this particular alignment may possibly indicate that the Serpent Mound is a place of hyper-dimensional geometry and, hence, a place of consciousness transformation.

Wilson's group has documented a Huntingburg, Indiana, formation from 2006, noting its alignments to eight other formations, one up to 2,600 miles away in Santa Rosa, California. The alignments are so common that it has led Wilson to ponder whether these signs in the fields have "all been planned in advance to unfold across space and time."

Other key alignments occur with specific formations having to do with the Mayan calendar and its age-old prophecy. Like Silva, Barbara Hand Clow, author of *Alchemy of Nine Dimensions: The 2011/2012 Prophecies and Nine Dimensions of Consciousness* (2004), believes that crop circles activate human consciousness in the same way that sacred sites do. She asserts that specific formations like the Barbary Castle formation (exemplary of the dimensional structure of the Mayan prophecy of the nine dimensions of consciousness), the Ratchet circle in Hampshire, England (exemplary of the three speeds of light and how motion and spin activate matter out of geometric form), and the Cow Down symbol, also in Hampshire (exemplary of how electromagnetic forces are used in creating matter) are all pertinent to the revealing of the Mayan tradition of the nine dimensions of consciousness for which humanity is being prepared. "Crop circles are actually describing changes in the unfolding of the Galactic alignments," says Hand Clow. "We will be offered Galactic citizenship . . . provided that . . . we have attained multi-dimensional consciousness as a species."

Another good source for Mayan prophecies in relation to crop circles and their messages is the DVD *Mayan Prophecies and Crop Circles: An Extraordinary Connection* (2010). On August 2, 2004, the Mayan Long Count Calendar was metaphorically depicted in a crop circle; on August 9, 2005, the Tzolkin calendar itself (the actual Long Count) was displayed; and on August 15, 2006, the Mayan symbol for Venus was scribed—all in southern England. These all apparently indicate aspects of the Mayan prophecy of the "Nine Hells and Thirteen Heavens" leading up to the Shift of Ages.

But the Mayans are not the only ancient culture connected to crop circles. The ancient Sumerians were as well. The "DIN GIR" symbol—seen on a UFO described by Lonnie Zamora, the main witness and contactee in the Socorro, New Mexico, sighting/contact on April 24, 1964—was revealed in a crop circle in both 1992 and again in 1999 in southern England. "DIN GIR" translates as "people traveling on Celestial ships of fire," says Steve Canada, and he thinks he knows why this particular ancient symbol was used.

Canada has written thirty-five crop circle books, including *Bible Encoded Crop Circle Gods* (2006) and *Alien End of Days in 2010* (2009), and has nineteen websites, all dedicated to describing the various aspects of what he believes is the main message of the formations: that our Creators—the Nephilim of the Old Testament and the ones described by Zecharia Sitchin in *The 12th Planet* (1976) as the Anunnaki—are returning to Earth at their prescribed time as foretold in ancient texts like the Bible and the Torah and in crop circles. He also believes that these beings are returning for a very simple purpose: to replace humankind with a hybrid race that will not self-annihilate and destroy its environment. Canada told me in an interview, "Crop circles are only part of a puzzle presented to us in these crucial times, parts of which we need to integrate into the formulation of a policy of either welcoming or resisting the Return."

For more crop circle research, see *Crop Circles Revealed: Language of the Light Symbols* (2001) by Judith Moore and Barbara Lamb, *The Deepening Complexity of Crop Circles* (2001) by Eltjo H. Haselhoff, *The Hypnotic Power of Crop Circles* (2004) by Bert Jansen, *Crop Circles: Art in the Landscape* (2007) by Lucy Pringle, *The New Circlemakers: Insights into the Crop Circle Mystery* (2009) by Andrew Collins, *Government Circles* (2009) by Colin Andrews, and *Crop Circles: The Bones of God* (2000) by Michael Glickman.

EQUIPMENT/MATERIALS TIP: Geiger counters are devices that detect radioactivity, another term for ionizing radiation, the four major types of which include gamma, X-rays, beta, and alpha radiation. Virtually all Geiger counters detect gamma and X-rays, while some models detect alpha andbeta radiation as well. A typical Geiger counter consists of a Geiger-Müller tube, a visual readout, and an audio readout. The Geiger-Müller tube or detector is the heart of a Geiger counter. It is a type of ionization chamber that counts particles of radiation. That count is read by the user through a visual readout in the form of a traditional analog meter, or an electronic liquid crystal display (LCD) readout. These meters are available in different units, including mR/hr, or milliroentgens per hour (popular in the US and Israel), and µSv/hr, or micro-Sieverts per hour (popular in Canada and overseas). Most Geiger counters also have an audio readout that sounds one "click" for each particle count. These particles are emitted at random intervals, and a large number of particles produced in a short span of time sound almost like static from a radio. Geiger counters that have meter readouts in "counts" or "clicks" per minute (CPM) mimic the audible clicks in visual form. CPM is the unit normally used to measure alpha and beta radiation. Digital Geiger counters not only offer visual digital readouts on an LCD display, but they typically also have audio ports for external speakers, as well as data ports for readout on computers and data loggers.

WWW.GEIGERCOUNTERS.COM

Cryptozoology

This fringe branch of science is the study of unidentified animals that are hidden from normal awareness. This field includes such cryptids as the *chupacabra*, Bigfoot/Sasquatch, reptilians, the Mothman, giant sea creatures like squids and serpents, as well as mer-people (half-fish, half-human creatures), among a host of other mysterious creatures both large and small. For example, "rods" are a type of flying, tube-like creature that have been caught on film but have so far not been identified (see below). There are many uncategorized specimens and even ones thought to be not of this Earth. Lloyd Pye's "Starchild Skull" is a good example (see *www.lloydpye.com*).

Of the many cryptozoologists out there, arguably the most famous is Loren Coleman. He has written several books, including *The Field Guide to Bigfoot and Other Mysterious Primates* (1999); *Bigfoot! The True Story of Apes in America* (2003); *Cryptozoology from A to Z* (1999) with Jerome Clark; *Mysterious America* (2004); and *The Field Guide to Lake Monsters, Sea Serpents, and Other Denizens of the Deep* (2003) with Patrick Huyghe.

The emphasis in field work here is finding specimens for scientific scrutiny. Because specimens are so rare, very little opportunity exists for sightings and corollary photographs and videos. Says Coleman: "When gathering physical evidence of a cryptid, practice high-level techniques of scientific and forensic collection; use gloves and specimen sampling containers, etc." He also recommends having a camera or video camera with you at all times. "Listen, document, examine, investigate, and keep investigating," he continues. "You may learn much from the current investigation that may assist your understandings of the next one."

If you decide to hunt a specimen, know that you are forcing a possible life-and-death situation, and be prepared for any possible consequences. A cryptid, like any other wild animal, may attack if it feels threatened. You may want to consider the moral ramifications of such action.

> **INTERVIEW TIP:** Remember, an eyewitness account is only as good as the eyewitness. Be certain to obtain as much information on the person who is telling of the encounter as you gather about the incident itself. Gather psychosocial, personality, and community testimony about the individual witness. Avoid being distracted by the details of the event; {stay focused on} the physical evidence that is presented to you and/or the quality of the images given to you to investigate. Witnesses experience fear, wonder, and other emotions that may transform the known into the unknown. Their sharing with you demonstrates they are giving you a certain level of trust that you must not berate or betray.
>
> LOREN COLEMAN, PERSONAL INTERVIEW

Following are some other cryptozoological beings associated with UFOs.

Bigfoot

Bigfoot is the name given to the often large, hairy hominid beings sighted in North America. Called Sasquatch by Native Americans, Yeti in the Himalayas, Yowie in Australia, and Migyur in Bhutan, Bigfoot, or creatures resembling it, has been recorded in many ancient texts, and likenesses of it have been sighted on all seven continents. It is even claimed that some have been photographed on Mars.

There are basically two camps in "pro-Bigfoot" research, which assumes that there is some type of being that exists outside of scientific knowledge. The first camp believes that Bigfoot is an unidentified animal—a primate to be hunted, categorized, and dissected for the "benefit" of humankind in line with the rest of historical zoological research. That's the traditional approach.

The second camp prefers to view Bigfoot as "more" than an animal—as a creature that possesses high intelligence, emotional aspects, and some type of culture. So instead of hunting the legendary creature, researchers like Ida Kannenberg and Lee Trippett (*My Brother Is a Hairy Man* [2009]), contactees like White Song Eagle (*Teluke: A Bigfoot Account* [2008]), and researcher/contactees like Kewaunee Lapseritis (*The Psychic Sasquatch and Their UFO Connection* [1997] and *The Sasquatch People and Their Interdimensional Connections* [2010]) prefer to follow the examples set by anthropologists Dian Fossey (with gorillas) and Jane Goodall (with chimpanzees) by spending time with the creatures in the wild in their own natural habitat.

These researchers have found that Bigfoot is a different kind of human being that possesses advanced intelligence and psychic ability, and exists in multiple dimensions. Within the first camp of Bigfoot research, these kinds of conclusions are not generally taken seriously.

Yet more and more, as the "hunter types" get stymied with each hunting excursion, they are beginning to embrace what appears to be the larger reality of Bigfoot as an advanced being with special powers. Further, and possibly most astounding, we are discovering that the Bigfoot "people" have ties to UFOs and their occupants.

In the tip that follows, notice that the approach taken by Lapseritis is in contrast to the warning given above. While it has been reported several times that a Bigfoot has attacked a human, Lapseritis maintains that researchers can remain safe in the field by controlling their fear and propagating love. They are a different kind of people, he says, so if you treat them with respect, they will return it to you. These two approaches are a great example of how information in the often whacky field of UFO research can contradict itself.

INVESTIGATIVE TIP: Go camping alone, and leave your guns and cameras at home. Bring only unconditional love, not fear. This is what attracts the psychic Sasquatch.

> **Don t forget, they can read your mind, so you will never get any proof. This is what I discovered during my fifty-four years of research.**
>
> KEWAUNEE LAPSERITIS, PERSONAL INTERVIEW

Chupacabra

This creature first appeared in the late 1960s, surfacing again in Puerto Rico in 1995 in a wave of high-strangeness activity. Its name means "goat sucker" in Spanish. It is so called because the animal allegedly bites the necks of its victims—usually goats, chickens, and cattle—and drains them of their blood. No meat has ever been reported eaten or taken, other than in events that are perceived to be in association with cattle mutilations.

From Puerto Rico, the reports spread to Florida first and then to other parts of the United States—New Mexico and Texas predominantly, but also Oregon and Michigan, and as far north as Maine. The creature's identity is unknown partly because it so often gets reported as being something else. For example, chupacabras have been reported to resemble the New Jersey Devil, Bigfoot, a humanoid reptilian, a giant flying condor, a disfigured coyote, or a vicious kangaroo. They are most commonly described as "wild dogs."

Although descriptions vary, there are commonly reported characteristics: reptilian body, oval head, red eyes, fangs, long (often forked) tongue, and sharp quills that run down its back. It is sometimes reported to fly or to be able to leap great distances with powerful monkey-like legs. It can be three to four feet tall, walks upright, and has been known to attack human beings.

Not much has been written about chupacabras, but there are a handful of good discussions available, usually within books that deal with other mysterious phenomena. These include *Chupacabra and Other Mysteries* (1997) by Scott Corrales; *Cryptozoology from A to Z* (1999) by Loren

Coleman and Jerome Clark; *The Island of Paradise: Chupacabra, UFO Crash Retrievals, and Accelerated Evolution on the Island of Puerto Rico* (2008) by Jon Downes; and *Hidden Animals: A Field Guide to Batsquatch, Chupacabra, and Other Elusive Creatures* (2009) by Michael Newton.

EQUIPMENT TIP: When taking plaster casts of prints, use material that does not distort the original track, and when photographing tracks, use a ruler or some object for scale that has a standard size. When investigating at the location of the sighting, obtain pictures of the exact spot of the encounter with objects for scale placed within the framing of the photography.

LOREN COLEMAN

Reptilians

Researcher John Rhodes began writing articles about reptilians in 1994, when he published "The Human-Reptilian Connection." He developed the evolved reptilian-humanoid theory, which proposes that "a small group of reptiles or dinosaurs evolved intelligence and over time acquired a reptilian-humanoid form." The theory also suggests that these reptilian beings live underground and send "operatives" to the surface that appear as ETs. A group of these beings, he claims, are returning to their home planet, Earth, in the near future.

This provocative theory brought Rhodes and the subject a lot of attention throughout the 1990s in UFO and occult circles, paving the way for future researchers. Picking up on this thread, and fueled by Hollywood's fascination with the subject—during the 1980s, several movies appeared, including *The Last Starfighter* (1984), *Enemy Mine* (1985), and *They Live* (1988) starring "Rowdy" Roddy Piper—and British author/researcher David Icke's best-selling book *The Biggest Secret* (1999), interest in the subject was firmly established in the mainstream.

Icke's theory that reptilian alien beings constructed modern society as a prison has been accepted by several researchers. Icke's books are well researched and his lectures are well presented. His ability to defend his points against many of his critics helps him make a powerful case that these nefarious reptilian beings are the controllers of humanity.

Stewart Swerdlow, a Montauk Project survivor and mentalist, and Arizona Wilder, former psychic sex slave and high Satanic priestess, have told Icke that they have seen key political, military, research, and entertainment figures shape-shift into reptilian beings and then proceed to drink human blood. Their testimony is compelling. Icke, Swerdlow, and Wilder paint a grim picture about contact with, and subjugation by, these reptilian beings. For more information, see the original series *V* (1984–1985) and a new series of the same name begun in 2009 (*www.expansions.com*).

David Jacob's *Secret Life: Firsthand Documented Accounts of UFO Abductions* (1992) adds to the nefarious image of reptilians. It details a pattern of testimony describing the involvement of reptilian humanoids during reported abductions. These beings are usually reported as tall and in charge of other smaller beings—usually Grays, but also insectoids and hybrids of varying kinds. Says Jacobs:

> Reptilians almost always scare people . . . whereas the other ones might not scare them to the degree that the Reptilians do. So, because of the fear factor, there's always a kind of subjective judgment about the quality of the Reptilians' personality or essence.

Dr. Brenda Denzler, who earned her doctorate in religious studies at Duke University, adds:

> In the Judeo-Christian tradition at least . . . the image of the reptile has almost always been associated with Satanic and evil forces. And if you want to speak in terms of Jungian archetypes, certainly for the West, the image of the reptile is one of a dark

image, a shadow image. So that also gets folded into the whole conspiracy idea.

Sean Casteel, *UFO Magazine*

Despite this, Rhodes feels that the notion that these alleged beings are harmful and/or negative toward humans is a misrepresentation of the information. He finds that there is every indication that these "reptoids" may be both malevolent and benevolent—as human beings are—and a natural part of human history. He also argues that the true purpose of indigenous reptilian-humanoid beings on Earth is to assist humans in their evolutionary development. They are humanity's relatives, he says. To learn more, see *Our Haunted Planet* (1968) by John Keel, *UFO Abductors* (1988) by Brad Steiger, and *Solomon Island Mysteries: Accounts of Giants and UFOs in the Solomon Islands* (2009) by Marius Boirayon.

Rods

Researcher Jose Escamilla inadvertently discovered rods while taking photographs near Roswell/Midway, New Mexico, in 1994. Because the name Roswell was already famous for an alleged flying saucer crash, rods have been associated with UFOs ever since.

Escamilla is one of the only noted rods investigators. He has discovered that they can be as small as six inches or as large as one hundred feet in length. First thought to be some kind of UFO, they are now believed to be living creatures that are indigenous to Earth, a theory possibly akin to Trevor James Constable's theory that UFOs are really living plasma beings indigenous to Earth (see chapter 1). Rods are elusive and seem to be more transparent at some times than others. They are capable of extremely high speeds and have been filmed flying faster than tank projectiles. Not one specimen has ever been caught, nor has a dead body ever been found. Other than the interpretations of some ancient cave paintings—and the theory that rods are the descendants of the now extinct *Anomalocaris* (a type of ancient flying fish)—not much has been discovered about these creatures thus far.

Some of the best film was captured in Mexico in 1996 at the Cave of the Swallows, when a team of BASE jumpers (thrill-seekers who jump from buildings, antennae, spans, and geographical features) was being filmed free-jumping into the giant subterranean cave. When the film was inspected, rods were seen dodging the divers as they fell. According to Escamilla, the military has begun to show interest in rods because, apparently, they want to know how they propel themselves. Rods research is one of the more safe ufological pursuits.

INVESTIGATIVE TIP: Try to photograph or videotape rods using the "skyfishing technique," in which the camera is positioned in such a way that it can utilize the sun's light but not be hindered by glare. To do this, first point your camera at the sun, then move it away from it until there are no more glares.

JOSE ESCAMILLA

Inner Earth

Traditions of civilizations that reside inside Earth are found in cultures throughout the world. The legendary city of Agarttha is thought to reside inside a hollow Earth and is filled with beings who enjoy advanced technology, perfect health, and extremely long life running into the thousands of years. There are many compelling testimonials of the locations of these civilizations from ancient and modern history. Different versions place them inside a hollow Earth—an Earth with a vast empty space in the middle—as well as in subterranean spaces (see chapter 6).

One of the more popular stories, which comes from Richard S. Shaver, combines elements of both a hollow and a subterranean Earth. Shaver told of an ongoing battle between the Teros and the Deros, with surface humans caught in the middle. The story came complete with a new alphabet, new words, and ideas of death and mind-control rays aimed at humans from underground (see *Reality of the Inner Earth: Return to the Caverns with Richard Shaver* [2005], edited by Tim R. Swartz and *The Smoky God: A Utopian Hollow Earth Classic!* [2009] by Willis George Emerson).

A popular theory of the origin of UFOs is that they come from the inner Earth—the supposed home of the Ashtar Command, a fleet of silver disk-shaped craft charged with the defense of Earth from both alien intrusion and destruction by indigenous humans. These beings are thought to be associated with a Galactic Federation of planets in our Milky Way galaxy, as well as with a spiritual hierarchy of Ascended Masters. Underground alien bases are also thought to be home for some types of craft.

On the lighter side are the books of Dianne Robbins, including *Telos: Original Transmissions from the Subterranean City Beneath Mt. Shasta* (1996) and *Messages from the Hollow Earth* (2003). Robbins claims to channel the Ascended Master and high priest of Telos named Adama, who has described to her how humans can live in harmony with nature by changing the way they think.

There is scientific research to support a hollow Earth. The worldwide field excursions of Dr. Brooks Agnew and the North Pole Inner Earth Expedition (NPIEE) have led him to conclude that the North Polar entrance to the hollow Earth is located at the coordinates 84.4 degrees North by 41 degrees East, which is about 300 miles northwest of Ellesmere Island. The U.S. military has also dispatched missions to both poles to find out more about the many inner-Earth legends. For more on this research, see *Secret Land* (1948) narrated by Robert Montgomery, *The Hollow Earth: The Greatest Geographical Discovery in History* (1969) by Dr. Raymond Bernard, *Visitors to the Inner Earth: True Tales of Subterranean Journeys* (2011) by Professor Solomon and Steve Solomon, and *Journey to the Earth's Core* (2011) produced by the History Channel.

Ley Lines

Ley lines are theoretical lines that crisscross any part of the Earth and connect to form an energetic "Earth grid." They are known by many names, including ghost tracks, dragon lines, and the Earth's nervous system. Some say they are indicative of the knowledge of divine consciousness programming and refer to the core issues of what it means to be a human being. Others say they relate to spirituality, individual and mass consciousness, and the layout of entire civilizations.

Mathematician Rupert Sheldrake calls the Earth grid the Earth's "morphogenic field," a sort of hyper-dimensional consciousness of Earth expressed in the physical dimension as ley lines and their connecting "power points," or nodes or vortices, areas often thought to be portals to other dimensions. Some believe that the locations of sacred sites, burial sites, water sources, groves of trees, and other geographic features mark these lines and nodes.

Crop circle researcher Freddy Silva sees crop circles as extensions of these sacred sites. He claims that some force, whether ETs or a kind of God force, is waking up the Earth via crop circle mandalas (consciousness-altering symbols) and ley lines in order to evolve human consciousness. Author Richard Leviton agrees. He wrote *The Emerald Modem* (2004) to describe how humans were created to interact consciously with the consciousness of the Earth and galaxy through sacred sites. When all of the sites are activated, he says, the Earth's emerald-shaped light body becomes activated, allowing it and its many human consciousnesses to interact consciously with the galaxy. Says Leviton, in *The Emerald Modem*:

> But what's a modem got to do with the Earth? Nothing. It's a metaphor. A modem is how we connect to the Internet. It dials up and our computer is online for as long as we want to stay there. We're connected. The 85 features of the Earth's spiritual or energy body comprise a mechanism like a modem. They are organs and arteries, ganglia and cells in a living modem. We

have one; the Earth has one. The Emerald modem is how we get online with the myriad websites of the galaxy.

In *The Mayan Factor: Path Beyond Technology* (1987), Jose Arguelles makes the assertion that divine consciousness programming originates within our galaxy's central core—what science believes may be a massive black hole. According to the Mayans, it emanates a consciousness-programming beam called the "Hunab Ku" that rotates throughout the galaxy. This is represented by the central face with an extended tongue on the Tzolkin, or Long Count, Mayan calendar.

The Tzolkin is the artifact that shows the end date for the Mayan Fourth Age and the beginning of their Fifth Age. Arguelles describes how this beam, through other-dimensional channels, programs our sun, which in turn programs all of the planets in the solar system via the Earth and its ley lines. You could say that it's the spiritual sequence of divine consciousness programming, with ley lines and the Earth being the closet links in the chain to humanity. Arguelles was the first to point out the start of the great shift of this beam directly onto the Earth in 1987 with an event called the Harmonic Convergence. Soon, he argues, the shift will be complete, ushering in a new consciousness frequency (see *www.lawoftime.org*).

There are many theories about the significance of the Mayan prophecy. Many foresee apocalyptic Earth changes, World War III, or possibly a cosmic collision of some kind. Others believe the shift will mark the beginning of a new consciousness open to contact with an alien species or the return of Jesus. Others see a giant planet returning (see chapter 6). For more theories, search the Internet with these key words and/or phrases: "end of days," "Planet X," and "Mayan Calendar."

Dr. J. J. Hurtak, in *The Book of Knowledge: The Keys of Enoch* (1973), describes a chain, or mechanism similar to that of Arguelles, but goes on to add that there are alien races—like intelligences from the constellations Dracos, Ursa Major, and Ursa Minor—that influence human mass consciousness to their own ends through the Earth's grid and its many ley lines and nodes. These negative influences apparently stand in opposition to those of the Pleiades, the home from which many souls have incarnated on Earth. In *The Book of Knowledge*, we read: "The Big Dipper [Ursa Major] stands as the threshold that must be overcome by Man on this planet before he will be free of the consciousness image of the Bear which emanated thought-forms of war and destruction" (*www.affs.org*).

David Hatcher Childress describes what the ancients knew about ley lines, Earth's energy grid, and divine consciousness programming in *Anti-Gravity and the World Grid* (1987). He compiles the work of several occult researchers and their theories and details how it was Plato who first devised a system for predicting them.

Plato theorized that if you put the shapes known as the Platonic solids—an icosahedron (twenty sides), a dodecahedron (twelve sides), an octahedron (eight sides), a cube (six sides), and a tetrahedron (four sides)—within a sphere, the places where the shapes on the inside touch the inner surface of the sphere are where you were likely to find a ley line or power point. Then Childress and his associates entertain theories from several researchers and devise their own combination ley-line model called the UVG 120 Sphere. This is ancient knowledge that has been kept hidden away from mainstream society and preserved within many secret societies or brotherhoods worldwide. In my *UFO Magazine* article "There's Magic in This Kingdom" (May 2006), I discuss with scholar Jordan Maxwell the secret society/Druidic connection to Hollywood and the reasons why a faction of them chose the place they did to found the movie industry. Maxwell says that it is because there is a major ley line running through the city. The Druids did this, he says, so that they could use the magical energy of the line to enhance their magical works—magic over the people.

So I decided to cross Maxwell's Hollywood/ley-line theory with the research of New Zealander and former airline captain Bruce Cathie. He is a proponent of the theory that UFOs follow ley lines for guidance, or for energy, or for some other as yet unidentified reason. This theory was introduced by Tony Wedd in 1961 with his booklet *Skyways and Landmarks*, which built on information from Frenchman Aimé Michel's *Flying Saucers and the Straight-Line Mystery* (1958).

Cathie studied Michel and Wedd's work and was able to plot a global energy grid using witness reports to track the paths of UFOs over Aukland and then extending the pattern over the entire Earth. His books include a special mathematics dubbed "light harmonic math," which has led Cathie to develop three Unified Field theories in physics. His work suggests a connection between consciousness and ley lines, and to UFOs (see *The Harmonic Conquest of Space* [1998]). Cathie and Seattle, Washington, computer engineer Rod Maupin have designed a computer program to plot the grid anywhere on Earth (see *www.worldgrid.net*). Other works on the grid include *The Energy Grid* (1990) by Bruce Cathie; *Ley Lines: A Beginner's Guide* (1999) by Philip Heselton; and *The Ancient Secret of the Flower of Life*, volumes I and II (1999, 2000) by Drunvalo Melchizedek.

SPECIAL KNOWLEDGE/SKILLS TIP: The art of dowsing has been proven useful when trying to locate not only water (dowsers are often called "water witches") but also ley lines and vortices (inter-dimensional portals). These are often places of heightened UFO activity, among a host of other phenomena.

AMERICAN SOCIETY OF DOWSERS, *WWW.DOWSERS.ORG*

6

Associated
Phenomena, M-Z

Mars

NASA first photographed the surface of Mars and its now famous "face" during the *Mariner* 9 probe in the early 1970s. NASA supposedly did not notice the structure that came to be known as "the face" until the 1976 *Viking* mission—and even then, it was not considered relevant. Nor did NASA scientists see the structures surrounding the "face"— a city, including small mounds, five- and four-sided pyramids, and a structure later called a "fortress" in the Cydonia region of the Martian surface—that was shown on frame 35A72 of their photographs. They just archived it with the rest of the images.

It wasn't until 1979 that Dr. Vincent DiPietro rediscovered 35A72, along with frame 70A13, while researching in the Goddard Archives, part of the Goddard Space Flight Center in Greenbelt, Maryland. NASA vehemently denied that the image could be anything other than "tricks of light and shadow." So he and Lockheed computer scientist Greg Molenaar decided to carry out a private analysis—digitally enhancing the two frames and looking for other anomalies. Next, computer analyst Mark Carlotto, using "cubic spine interpolation" as well as other techniques, was able to enhance the contrast of the images and pick out increased detail. He discovered a headdress resembling the "nemes" headdresses famous in ancient Egypt, along with teeth and distinct eye features, including a teardrop falling out of the corner of one eye. These findings are now the stuff of legend.

Richard C. Hoagland has been instrumental in bringing what he calls an intentional cover-up of the real information NASA has about Mars to public attention. His book *The Monuments of Mars: A City on the Edge of Forever* (1987) and his DVD series *Hoagland's Mars*, volumes I–III are essential to understanding the mysterious structures and key "hyper-dimensional" mathematical clues imbedded in them. (See also *The Mars Mystery: The Secret Connection Between Earth and the Red Planet* [1998] by Graham Hancock.) Hoagland's scathing critique of NASA's policies, the alleged wrongdoings of its many and varied employees, and its controversial history and origin have all worked to make Hoagland NASA's number one critic.

Despite the agency's attempts to explain away the "face" and other distinct features, Hoagland makes a compelling case that NASA is hiding knowledge of a possible extraterrestrial origin for the human race. In an April 6, 2011, article posted at their official website, however, NASA still holds firm to its position that the "face" is a naturally formed feature (see *www.science.nasa.gov*). If there was an ancient civilization on Mars, what happened to it? Hancock states that Mars was bombarded by so many asteroids—and one giant one—that the red planet was literally "killed." He even writes that "'executed' would not be too strong a word." In fact, the planet today has a huge bulge on one side, allegedly due to the impact of the giant asteroid. Hancock concludes, in *The Mars Mystery: The Secret Connection between Earth and the Red Planet* (1998), that the same bombardment actively "stripped away the planet's formerly dense atmosphere so that liquid water could no longer survive anywhere upon it."

So it appears that this proposed ancient civilization on Mars was either destroyed in the catastrophe or fled underground or off-world for survival. But who could they have been? And where would they go if they left the planet?

Sitchin says that the Sumerians were told by their benefactors, the Anunnaki, that Mars was a kind of way station for those who came and went between Nibiru and Earth. So it is thought by some that the Martians/Anunnaki could have fled to Earth because their home planet was too far away in its 3,600-year orbit of the sun. Author DeAnna Emerson, in her book *Mars/Earth Enigma: A Sacred Message to Mankind* (1996), expresses this human/Martian connection in terms of a goddess religion of an alien culture shared by three planets: Earth, Mars, and Nibiru. This, she claims, explains the similarities of many monuments on Earth and ones now discovered on Mars: They display the same kind of symbols, are set facing the same directions, and incorporate the same advanced mathematics. These same symbols and mathematics, she says, are even being shown to humanity through the crop circle phenomenon (see chapter 5).

This intra-solar goddess tradition is represented on Earth by the Sumerian goddess Inana, known as the "Great Mother Goddess" and "Creator of all Mankind." She is also associated with the planet Venus (more on this later).

According to Emerson, this goddess tradition was usurped several thousand years ago to be replaced by the patriarchal and warlike religious theme dominant today. The sacred message being delivered to humanity with the rediscovery of the civilization on Mars and the recognition of crop circles—both of which came into public notice in the mid to late 1970s—is one of a return to a spiritual balance between male and female energies, a balance that will end all wars and the destruction of Earth and its many unique environments. It is a message that strikes at the very religious and spiritual center of what it means to be human.

Emerson writes:

[T]he Brookings Report noted the possibility that, should extraterrestrial life be discovered, "society might disintegrate"— or survive only by "paying the price of changes in values and attitudes and behavior . . ." To understand the reasons behind NASA's reluctance to share information regarding the Mars structures, it is imperative that we carefully scrutinize every aspect of religion.

Mars/Earth Enigma: A Sacred Message to Mankind

While it is clear that NASA's policy regarding this situation is to avoid political change and scientific upheaval, she argues, it is also intended to cover-up the "irrefutable alliance between politics and religion." David Flynn's book *Cydonia: The Secret Chronicle of Mars* (2002) explores these theories, as do *After the Martian Apocalypse: Extraterrestrial Artifacts and the Case for Exploration of Mars* (2004) by Mac Tonnies and *The NASA Conspiracies: The Truth Behind the Moon Landings, Censored Photos, and the Face on Mars* (2010) by Nick Redfern.

Men in Black

In popular culture, the term "Men in Black" (MiB) is used to describe men dressed in black suits, sometimes with glowing eyes or other monstrous features, who claim to be government agents and injure, scare, and harass UFO witnesses into silence. One of the most mysterious and allegedly dangerous aspects of UFO research and investigation is possible contact with one or more of these characters.

Gray Barker wrote one of the first accounts of the MiB phenomenon in association with secret knowledge (see chapter 2). In 1956, in *They Knew Too Much About Flying Saucers,* Barker reports several cases where witnesses were harassed on multiple levels: threats of violence (including harm to family members), as well as of bad publicity and rumors that could get them fired from their jobs or ostracized by their communities.

Albert K. Bender, author of *Flying Saucers and the Three Men* (1963), maintains that MiB female counterparts are "Women in White." MiB has apparently grown into a generic term that refers to any threatening or oddly behaved person encountered in conjunction with a UFO sighting or event. The encounter usually follows a pattern. After a sighting, witnesses are visited by a man or men who are often dressed in black suits. They assume that the men are government agents, because they commonly flash convincing badges and demand that the witnesses remain silent and/or hand over photographs and other physical evidence. If the witnesses refuse or question them, they are offered subtle, and sometimes overt, threats of varying consequences. MiBs are often reported as driving large, black, late-model cars, typically Cadillacs.

The number of witnesses who report MiB encounters is unknown and may be rather small. In fact, there really seems to be a rather small number of MiB cases of which there are any details available at all. For more information, see *The Truth Behind the Men in Black* (1997) by Jenny Randles, *Mystery of the Men in Black: The UFO Silencers* (1990) by Timothy Green Beckley, and *On the Trail of the Saucer Spies: UFOs and Government Surveillance* (2006) by Nick Redfern.

INVESTIGATIVE TIP: If you witness a UFO, it may be prudent to set up a hidden camera at home where you receive guests. This way, you may be able to photograph or video tape a MiB encounter at your residence. You would be the first!

Mind Control

What is mind control? There are many definitions of it and many ways to describe this subject. Basically, any time you are not in total control of your own thoughts, actions, and/or emotions, it can be argued that you are under the control and/or influence of another person's will. As psychologists, hypnotists, and magicians know, perception is a tricky thing. Magicians of old created the phrase "the hand is quicker than the eye" as a sort of disclaimer to their audiences that they can be fooled at any time—that their sight and other senses can, and will, not just betray them, but also be used against them.

In an ironic kind of cover for secret mind-control experiments, the subject itself went mainstream in the 1960s and 1970s, culminating in popular systems like the Silva Mind Control Method (see *Silva Mind Control Method* [1977] by Jose Silva and Philip Miele) and the protocols developed at the Monroe Institute (see *www.monroeinstitute.org*). Nowadays, there is a certain level of information about mind control that is commonly known.

For instance, hypnotist Keith Barry demonstrated the formerly esoteric technique of "instant induction" on an episode of the History Channel's *Deception with Keith Barry* (2011). In this three-step process, you first make contact with another individual, then redirect his or her focus, thus establishing confusion. With this method, Barry claims to be able to hypnotize most people at will to do his bidding. Barry is showing an international audience that human perception has certain blind spots that can be exploited by a knowledgeable practitioner. And he shows how his subjects—i.e., victims—don't know what happened to them until they are shown the video of their actions.

Here's another example. Count every F in the following text:

FINISHED FILES ARE THE RESULT OF YEARS OF SCIENTIFIC STUDY COMBINED WITH THE EXPERIENCE OF YEARS.

Did you count three? There are actually six. Read it again. The reason this is hard to perceive is that the brain does not process small connecting words like "of." Anyone who counts all six Fs on the first go is a genius. Three is normal; four is rare.

Knowledge of the ability to manipulate human perception— to exploit these blind spots and intentionally create illusions for the purpose of deception and influence and potential total control of an individual mind or a population of any size—has been known for thousands of years. And the time-tested techniques that were perfected in ancient times and harbored in secret societies to keep the knowledge away from the masses are alleged to be used today against those very masses. And some researchers say not just on individuals or societies, but on the entire population of Earth to some degree or another.

CAUTIONARY TIP: When dealing with mind-control aspects, one needs to determine which alter type is coming forward. Be careful in discerning "switches" in personalities during interrogatives of informants. You may be getting programmed information, instead of truth.

STEWART SWERDLOW, PERSONAL INTERVIEW

There are two general categories of mind control and/or programming: active and passive. Passive mind control usually happens via media—movies, television, and advertising of all kinds. You only have to think of how news organizations sometimes black out certain topics.

The array of experiments involving active programming, or programming that is forced on a target, took two main paths: internal programming methods that use psychology, trauma, sex, drugs, and sound to control behavior, and external programming that relies on technologies like microwaves, radio frequencies, scalar waves, and other forms of electromagnetic (EM) forces. Both kinds of active programming have produced successful results, and both avenues of research are pursued today.

As for the psychological, or internal, approach to mind control, most people know about the passive kinds of mind control that have become common in our society—the PR campaigns of Edward L. Bernays, the press magic of P. T. Barnum, and the way large corporations use advertising campaigns to influence the buying behavior of their consumers. And many are aware of the basic kinds of propaganda that have been employed on enemy targets during all wars since World War I—like dropping flyers on cities and/or enemy troops that tell them they are doomed, or publishing pro or con newspaper articles. George Creel, the chairman of the Committee on Public Information (the U.S. World War II propaganda machine) publicly called the use of propaganda necessary in the "fight for the minds of men." And there are researchers, contactees, and channelers who ascribe all of the above to alien perpetrators who have either subtly taken control of Earth's population through mind control or actually created society as we know it in order to keep control of humanity through mind control.

The idea of alien mind control of human beings is an old subject. In Hollywood, we can find many examples. In 1967, the film *Five Million Years to Earth* starring James Donald showed that insectoid Martians had enslaved humanity in the past. There is also the newer classic *They Live* (1988) starring Roddy Piper, in which reptilian aliens with holographic identity-concealing technology hide themselves from the world's populations as they constantly monitor and maintain their human societal prison. And let's not forget *The Arrival* (1996) starring Charlie Sheen. These insectoid-meet-reptilian aliens could also stay hidden. Sheen's character has to infiltrate their underground lair and expose the alien effort to terraform Earth. Abductees are reportedly hypnotized or targeted with beams of varying colors and intensities, and are only able to remember details under hypnotic regression, a technique used to retrieve memories from traumatized individuals (see chapter 5).

Some scholars—like Zecharia Sitchin, author of *The 12th Planet* (1976), William Bramley, author of *The Gods of Eden: A New Look at Human History* (1989), and Maximillien De Lafayette, author of *Anunnaki Chronology and Their Remnants on Earth From 1,250,000 B.C. to the Present Day* (2011)—adhere to the notion that aliens created modern society and monitor and/or control it today.

Finally, disinformation is probably the most prevalent type of passive mind control facing UFO investigators. This is where information is presented that is either totally or partially untrue. The best disinformation is false information leaked along with correct information. When documents are leaked, there is always a motive behind the leak. Is it good information that exposes some facet of the UFO cover-up? Or is it intentionally being planted to create confusion between researchers and/or the public? Or is the information merely wrong because of bad research?

While this commonly happens with documents supposedly leaked from government insiders—the December 1984 Jaime Shandera/MJ-12 documents, for example (see chapter 3)—it is even more common in movies and television. Take the historical moon landing, for example, which supposedly took place on June 20, 1969. Millions worldwide were captivated as they saw the live event unfold on television. Because of this, most believe that the event really took place on the moon. But this may not be the case.

Skeptics claim that there are numerous anomalies in the official footage—like an American flag blowing when there is no wind on the moon, or astronauts' footprints that were too perfect for an active walking track. Today, we can easily see how such an event could be faked with standard movie technology. Back in the late 1960s, however, because the technology was so new, audiences could easily be fooled. It has been argued that Stanley Kubrick was called in to shoot the first three moon landings. He was allegedly assassinated to cover up this fact, not because of *Eyes Wide Shut*. More than forty-three years later, the debate still rages on. (See *We Never Went to the Moon: America's Thirty Billion Dollar Swindle* [1974] by Bill Kaysing; *The Moon Landing Hoax: The Eagle That Never Landed* [2010] by Dr. Steven Thomas; and *The NASA Conspiracies: The Truth Behind the Moon Landings, Censored Photos, and the Face on Mars* [2010] by Nicholas Redfern.)

SPECIAL KNOWLEDGE/SKILLS TIP: It is the extroverts which are more easily hypnotized. You know Mr. Sunshine . . .; the one-season world, gung ho, go-get 'em guy, super successful? He goes under in two seconds flat. But it is the introvert that you cannot manipulate. . . . All those things; all those modalities, all those wonderful occult practices that have the ability to enlighten you, inspire you . . . to sharpen your reason; your critical ability, all of those things have the equal power, in the wrong hands, to do the opposite. It is the difference between sorcery and magic.

MICHAEL TSARION, *ARCHITECTS OF CONTROL*

The Moon

The moon is generally thought to have been formed out of a planetary collision between a theoretical planetoid dubbed "Orpheus" and the Earth. This theory was first brought forth in 1961 by NASA moon-mapper Bill Hartmann after it was determined that previous theories were not feasible. For example, it was found that the moon was too big to have been a captured satellite, and the physics for it having broken off from the Earth in primordial times were proved invalid.

However the moon came into being, science has recognized that, if it were not where it is today, life on Earth would be nonexistent. The moon naturally regulates the climate and spin of the Earth. It is also responsible for the tides of the oceans and the natural rhythm of aquatic life. The documentary *If We Had No Moon* (1999), which aired on the Science Channel, explores this topic. Entire human societies have based their calendars, and hence themselves, on the eight phases of the moon: new, waxing crescent, first quarter, waxing gibbous, full, waning gibbous, third quarter, and waning crescent. Women are influenced by the moon's gravity as well, as it regulates the female menstrual cycle by triggering ovulation and fertility.

NASA's *Clementine* spacecraft was launched in 1994 as part of a series of missions of the Deep Space Program Science Experiment (DSPSE). In the process of testing special equipment, the spacecraft orbited the moon for two months, during which time it is claimed to have taken 1.8 million images of the satellite's surface. The biggest discovery was the water found at the bottom of a crater near the South Pole (*www.nrl.navy.mil/clementine*).

Former fighter pilot John Lear is a proponent of the theory that the moon is inhabited. Lear, for example, has found evidence to suggest that the U.S. government has mining operations at various places on the dark side of the satellite (*www.thelivingmoon.com*). Others, like Richard C. Hoagland, have found evidence that there are artificial structures on the moon and Mars, and that NASA is actively covering up this information. He is in possession of NASA photographs that show what he thinks is likely a six-mile-high unnatural spire, as well as other seemingly man-made features. He, like Lear, typically uses NASA's own information to build his case for an information cover-up undertaken by the government agency (*www.enterprisemission.com*).

Swerdlow and Lear maintain that if you point an amply powered telescope toward any one of several craters on the light side of the moon and wait patiently, you will witness light reflections from vehicles moving on its surface. Filmmaker Jose Escamilla, in his critically acclaimed 2010 DVD *Moon Rising*, colorizes the surface of the Earth's satellite and finds startling detail. Escamilla shows evidence that the moon's true identity has been masked from Earth's view. He says that it is covered with forests, water, and communities. In fact, Swerdlow claims that the moon is really an artificial structure—a vehicle, more specifically—that was parked in its current place by reptilian aliens (see chapter 4). Authors Christopher Knight and Alan Butler offer well-researched support for Swerdlow's assertion.

In their book *Who Built the Moon?* (2005), the two authors postulate that, since there are so many weird mathematical and geophysical anomalies associated with the satellite, it could not possibly be a natural solar body. Some of the peculiarities include the fact that the moon is exactly 400 times smaller than the sun and precisely 400 times closer to the Earth. It has little to no heavy-metal composition, and it rings like a bell when struck, indicating that it is not only artificial but hollow as well.

Based on these observations and others, they have concluded that "an intelligent agency has constructed the moon to enable life to develop upon the planet we call Earth." Without saying exactly who the "they" is that did the building, they speculate that it could be human time travelers from the future. For more on this, see *We Discovered Alien Bases on the Moon: Documented with 125 NASA Photographs and Area Blowups* (1981) by Fred Steckling.

Planet X

The Term "Planet X" was first used by famous astronomer Percival Lowell (1855–1915) around the turn of the century. He derived it to describe the large, yet-to-be-indentified astronomical body that was theoretically causing the orbital perturbations—inconsistencies in a planet's orbit—of Uranus and later, as astronomer William Pickering (1858–1938) discovered, in Neptune's orbit as well.

When Pluto was discovered by Clyde Tombaugh while he was working at Lowell's observatory in Flagstaff, Arizona, in 1930, the late great researcher's Planet X hypothesis seemed to be confirmed posthumously. However, more orbital anomalies were detected in the 1970s that reawakened the Planet X theory. While critics pooh-poohed the idea of such a planet, crucial information came to light in *The Detroit News* on January 16, 1981, in an article by Hugh McCann entitled "10th Planet? Pluto's Orbit says 'yes.'"

U.S. Naval astronomer Thomas van Flandern, the proponent of the "Exploding Planet Hypothesis" (see *www.enterprisemission.com/hyper1. html*), gave a speech to the American Astronomical Society in which he suggested that there was still another unknown giant body whose gravitational pull was affecting the orbit of Pluto. The article included the work of Zecharia Sitchin, whose *12th Planet* (1976) was the first of seven books in the Earth Chronicles series that was written in support of van Flandern's new findings. Sitchin's work would prove to be foundational to the theory of a Planet X and the beings supposedly from that planet—the Anunnaki, the Bible's Nephilim (see below).

Public interest seemed to peak with a December 13, 1983, *Washington Post* article entitled "Mysterious Heavenly Body Discovered," by Thomas O'Toole. The article suggested that NASA's infrared astronomical satellite (IRAS) had detected a giant unidentified body headed toward Earth that was thought to be within our solar system. The article was used by many Planet X adherents to justify their claims that the unknown mass was actually a planet called Nibiru, the ancient Sumerian name for what they called the "12th planet" (in addition to the usual nine, plus the sun and the Earth's moon). Inconveniently, in 2006, the International Astronomical Union reclassified Pluto as a dwarf planet. No word yet from the Anunnaki about the miscount.

Upon further study, however, it was revealed that the perturbations detected by IRAS and used to detect the theoretical space body were caused by a miscalculation in Neptune's mass. This culminated in the consensual 1992 conclusion that Planet X did not exist. Ian O'Neil wrote:

> Although these IRAS observations were seeing mysterious objects, at this stage, there was no indication that there was an object . . . powering its way toward us. But the rumours had already begun to flow.
>
> "2012: No Planet X," *Universe Today*, May 25, 2008

Myles Standish makes a similar observation in "Planet X: No dynamical evidence in the optical observations" (*Astronomical Journal* 105 [July 16, 1992]).

At least part of the reason that the "rumors had already begun to flow" was the increasing popularity of Sitchin's work. As time went by, more and more scientific support suggested that Sitchin's theories needed further testing. A new field of research was born—Sitchin Studies—and a book was put together to chronicle the first-ever Sitchin Studies Day held in Denver, Colorado, on October 6, 1996. The conference was called Of Heaven and Earth: Essays Presented at the First Sitchin Studies Day; it featured scientists, philosophers, and members of the clergy.

Yes, the clergy. Apparently, the Vatican was very interested in Nibiru. ("Nibiru" is the term used in the Torah; it is called Olam in the Bible. Its other ancient names are Marduk and Ragnarok.) The Vatican's own Jesuit secret service, known as the Vatican Intelligence Service (SIV), organized and funded their own project to find out more. A secret probe called *Siloe* was launched that captured video footage of what Vatican officials think is Nibiru/Planet X. The probe sent the images to a remote abandoned oil refinery in Alaska in 1995 that had been secretly set up as a deep-space radio telescope. The telescope was then trained on the object's position and has been monitoring it ever since (see "Jesuit Footage and the 'Omega Secret' Code" by Luca Scantamburlo, *Nexus Magazine* [March/April 2007]).

Some think that Nibiru, today erroneously equated with Lowell's Planet X, could be a planet, a comet, an asteroid, or a brown dwarf—a sort of burned-out companion star of the sun. One researcher, the controversial Dr. Jaysen Q. Rand, believes that Nibiru/Planet X is the brown dwarf known as Wormwood in the Bible's Book of Revelation and that it is about to return (Rev 8:11). The Anunnaki are already here, he says, to help humanity through the anticipated catastrophic geologic upheavals via a kind of "rapture scenario" that will occur as Wormwood returns. He wrote a book describing this called *The Return of Planet-X: Wormwood and Its Effects on Mother Earth, a Natural Disaster Survivor's Manual* that is available at his website (*www.returnofplanetx.com*).

Of course, as we shall see with Sitchin, Rand is not without his detractors. Rob McConnell, host of Canada's *X-Zone* radio program and multimedia outfit, hired an American investigative team to verify some of Rand's biographical claims. Conclusion: Rand is not a doctor, never attended the universities that he claims, is not recognized as a successful producer in the music industry, and does not go by his real name, Paul Bondora (aka Cory Wade). A website was set up for the general public to make up their own minds (*www.2012hoax.org/jaysen-q-rand*).

Sitchin has been criticized as well. His work has been called "pseudoscience" by academicians and likened to *Harry Potter* scenarios by two curators of the prestigious British Museum, Dr. Irving Finkel and Christopher Walker. Yet Sitchin always said that he was simply relating information directly from the Sumerians themselves through his translations. He claimed that, without question, the Sumerians say that Nibiru is a giant planet many times larger than the Earth.

In its 3,600-year orbit of the sun, Nibiru rotates counter to the rest of the planets. Consequently, millions of years ago, reports Sitchin, the once-rogue planet became trapped by the sun's gravity and entered our solar system on a collision course with a watery giant called Tiamat, the "Watery Mother." Some believe that Tiamat was called Phaeton and was destroyed a mere 11,500 years ago (see *Cataclysm! Compelling Evidence of a Cosmic Catastrophe in 9500 B.C.* [1995] by D. S. Allen and J. B. Delair). From Sitchin's translations of the Sumerian account, the resulting collision supposedly destroyed Tiamat, creating the asteroid belt and the Earth, the largest remaining fragment of the Watery Mother.

Sitchin tells of a race of giant humanoids known as the Anunnaki who created humankind and civilization as we know it hundreds of thousands of years ago. These aliens sought gold from Earth to take back to Nibiru to suspend in their atmosphere and help bolster it. Nibiru apparently needed extra protection from the forces of open space.

Around 450,000 years ago, an Anunnaki expedition party landed and began to mine gold in South Africa. Today, there are mines in South Africa that researchers believe are at least 100,000 years old. But the workers got tired and rebelled. Some Anunnaki/Nephilim wanted to create new slave workers genetically using the DNA of an indigenous Earth hominid species and themselves. Others were morally against this. A schism developed and, according to the Sumerians, the drama that unfolded between rival family members over this issue has been at work shaping human history even today.

Many scholars have built on Sitchin's work. Neil Freer wrote two books, *Breaking the Godspell* (1987) and *God Games* (1998), in which he postulates, among other things, that the personalities of these Anunnaki still influence the regions over which they ruled. Israel, for example, is warlike, patriarchal, and politically aggressive, much like their ruler, Yahweh, who he claims is the Anunnaki leader of the Earth expedition known as Enlil.

In *The Gods of Eden* (1989), author William Bramley agrees with Sitchin about the arrival of alien beings from a giant planet with an extremely long orbit by Earth standards. But unlike Sitchin, Bramley refers to these beings as "Custodians" because, he says, either they never left Earth, or still maintain control of it through the dark dealings of secret societies like the Freemasons, one of many offshoots of what Bramley calls "the Brotherhood of the Snake." Not all of Nibiruan society is in control of Earth, he warns, only the "most brutal and despotic element of that society."

Bramley claims that "the network of Brotherhood organizations became the primary channel through which wars between human beings could be secretly and continuously generated by the Custodial society." He describes Earth and the physical dimension as a kind of prison for souls to be endlessly reborn in service to the Custodians.

Maximillien De Lafayette has yet another interpretation. He does not deduce that humans were created by the Anunnaki for work in the gold mines. Rather he interprets the Sumerian writings as describing work in agricultural fields. They were carrying baskets, he says, made for transporting food, not gold. There are many other such discrepancies between the two as well.

According to Lafayette, there are direct descendants of the Anunnaki living on Earth today. They are known as the Ulema culture, he says, and this Earthly race has evolved into multi-dimensional beings similar to what are described as Ascended Masters, or possibly the Sasquatch. They can and do live in the physical world but have great telepathic abilities and the power to dematerialize and materialize at will (see chapter 5). Lafayette described his theories in *460,000 Years of UFO: Extraterrestrials Biggest Events and Secrets from Phoenicia to the White House* (2008) and *Inside the Extraordinary World of the Anunnaki and the Anunnaki-Ulema* (2010).

Lafayette's theories seem to correspond to the story of the ancient goddess Innana as portrayed in the channeled tale by V. S. Ferguson called *Innana Returns* (1995). In it, Innana, a female Anunnaki who ruled over prehistoric India, has projected her consciousness in multiple forms to the present to try to affect change for the good of Earth and for humanity. She tells Ferguson that she is attempting to undo the damage caused by her cousin, Marduk, by the atrocities he has been perpetrating on humanity for hundreds of thousands of years.

Ufologist Ann Eller is another person who claims to have experienced psychic communion with the Anunnaki. She describes her experiences in her book *Dragon in the Sky: Prophecy from the Stars* (2009). She believes that it is her job to spread the message of the Anunnaki that humans are damaging their environment and that change is needed if they are to survive the coming Earth changes that will occur as Nibiru approaches.

Eller writes:

> When Planet X first appears it will look like a second Sun by day and a fiery dragon in the night sky. The gravitational pull will cause the Earth to wobble, lean away, and cause three days of darkness for the northern hemisphere. A series of natural disasters and Earth changes including earthquakes and tidal waves will occur causing worldwide panic. After three days of darkness, Earth will return to its upright position but will gradually slow and stop its rotation. The pole shift will then occur with the most traumatic catastrophes imaginable.
>
> *www.dragoninthesky.com*

Crop circle researcher Steve Canada is not necessarily as concerned about Earth changes as he is about the Anunnaki themselves. "Why do you think we went into Iraq?" he asked in an interview. "This is the location of ancient Sumeria, where the Anunnaki established the first human civilization. Current actions in southern Iraq are crucial to understanding what might be the Pentagon's policy and decision either to resist or welcome them."

One website, *www.theAnunnakiwillreturn.tumblr.com*, presents the idea that global warming is being used by the world powers to cover up the gravitational and hyper-dimensional influences of Nibiru on Earth as it approaches. Further, they see the recent trend of "cash for gold" around the world, the rising price of gold, and the removal of gold as a backing for real money systems as motivated by governments beefing up their gold stashes for bigger offerings of tribute to their ancient Anunnaki creators when they return to Earth.

Whether this information is true or not only time will tell. But it does buttress Canada's argument that it is the Anunnaki with which humanity should be concerned. Canada says that, because they do not like the fact that humanity has not taken better care of their planet, the Anunnaki have been slowly creating a hybrid race via abductions—a race that will be better caretakers of Earth and that will not be as self-destructive as modern humanity has proven to be (see chapter 5).

So, will Planet X return? Many think so. But while Sitchin stated that he did not believe that the planet's 3,600-year orbit would end until 2900 A.D., Canada hedges a little closer to the present, claiming the need to correct the calendar for the birth year of Jesus (see *www. Cropcirclebooks.com/tenalienmysteriessolved/*).

For more information, see *Dark Star: The Planet X Evidence* (2005) by Andy Lloyd, *Planet X Nibiru: Slow-Motion Doomsday* (2004) by Robertino Solarion, and *Mars/Earth Enigma: A Sacred Message to Mankind* (1996) by DeAnna Emerson. The movie *The Man From Planet X* (1951) starring Robert Clarke and the short films *Surviving 2012* and *Planet X* parts 1 through 5 are also of interest.

Psychic Abilities

Psychic abilities, known collectively as "extra-sensory perception," or (ESP), encompass a wide variety of paranormal human potentials. These abilities occur either between a consciousness and another consciousness, or between a consciousness and its environment. In terms of associations with UFOs, the general categories of telepathy, remote viewing, and channeling are most prominent in reports, testimony, and UFO lore.

As pagan folk knowledge began to coalesce into formalized practice in modern society, psychic abilities began to be expressed in terms of various movements. In the early 1800s, the Spiritists began employing mediums, a general term denoting any kind of energetic or spiritual human bridge between dimensions or consciousnesses. Spiritists maintain, however, that mediumship is a more specific discipline involving communicating with the dead in such a way as to connect with the past lives of reincarnated souls. It was popular in France and in Latin America.

Similar to, but separate from, the Spiritist movement was the Spiritualist movement. Mediums were employed here to contact the spirits of deceased persons as well. It is, however, considered to be a distinct religion that was popular in the 1930s and 1940s (see *The Weiser Field Guide to the Paranormal* [2011] by Judith Joyce).

In the early 1950s, reports of alien contacts began to attract attention (see chapters 2 and 5). Since those early days in UFO history, psychic abilities have become commonplace in ufology, and good UFO investigators should familiarize themselves with the basic psychic methods most often involved with UFO and contactee research. For more general information on these abilities, see *China's Super Psychics* (1997) by Paul Dong and Thomas Raffill and *The Parapsychology Revolution* (2008) by Dr. Robert Schoch and Logan Yonavjak.

Channeling

There is no standard definition for channeling, but it is widely accepted that channeling occurs when an entity takes over the motor skills, or some specific motor skill, of another human consciousness to relay information or to act out its own intentions. The phenomenon is similar to possession. Author Jon Klimo, in his book *Channeling: Investigations on Receiving Information from Paranormal Sources* (1987), devises his own definition: "Channeling is the process of receiving information from some level of reality other than the ordinary physical one and beyond the Self as we currently understand it." Automatic writing, speaking in tongues, and spirit possession are considered forms of channeling (see *www.channeling.net*).

Spirit possession is an example of the involuntary channeling of an entity. Barbara Marciniak, on the other hand, is a self-proclaimed intentional channel. In her popular book *Bringers of the Dawn: Teachings from the Pleiadians* (1992), Marciniak describes how a trip to the King's Chamber in the Great Pyramid of Giza in 1988 was her first opportunity to intentionally open herself as a channel for whatever was there to be channeled. "Within a few short minutes," she writes, "I felt the urge to speak, and as this urge began to express itself in a whispered voice dissimilar to my own, another portion of my mind—the rational, 'in-charge' version—began to question, with thought, the very voice that was speaking." Within an hour, the voice told her that it was "the Pleiadians."

Tom Kenyon, channeler of Mary Magdalene and Venusian/Sirians called "the Hathors," describes his experience in *The Great Shift: Co-Creating a New World for 2012 and Beyond* (2009). "It has to do with an aspect of our being called inter-dimensionality," he writes. "It is your attention to an event that brings it to your consciousness." He goes on to describe how, during "the time period of the communication, one is more or less detached and somehow suspended from one's normal ways of being in the world, including one's perception of perceived time. This is a direct result of changes in brain state (i.e., an increase in alpha and theta activity on the part of the channel)."

Kenyon warns interpreters of channeled information to be careful of how a channeler's own preconceived notions and biases can affect any incoming information. He admits that he's not sure why this happens, but that you should count on it to varying degrees, depending on the channel.

Many have claimed to channel extraterrestrials. Marshall Vian Summers, for example, has written a series of books, beginning with *The Allies of Humanity* (2001), in which he describes a voice that he hears and with which he communicates. He has made several recordings of this voice, of which copies can be purchased. The same basic messages are imparted in Summers's work that are given in most other channeled information—that humanity needs to change the way it thinks and lives if it is to survive coming changes.

Another popular UFO channeler is Nicholette Pavlevsky. She channels the ET "Baktar," who has dictated to her the book *Who's Who in UFOs and ETs: The Need for Discernment* (2003). She does not claim to know that everything she transcribes is accurate, but the material itself gives reason for consideration. For example, Baktar says that George Adamski was a "tool" put before the public to gauge their response. About *Star Trek* creator Gene Roddenberry, he tells Pavlevsky: "He received guidance from seven groups of ETs in creating *Star Trek*." About self-proclaimed Montauk Project survivor and *The Montauk Project* book series coauthor Peter Moon, Baktar says: "He is a disinformer who involves himself as an editor, cowriter, and publisher of Montauk Project books in order to control the information. His chosen last name 'Moon' reflects his secret society connection."

Baktar admits he is not always accurate. So, as always, you must try to corroborate the psychic information by cross-referencing other sources and by considering how it makes you feel. If any of the information does not feel right, it most likely is not right. Several documentaries have been made on this subject, including *UFOs and Channeling* (1998) starring Telly Savalas and the DVD *Channeling: The Highest Form of Communication* (2009).

Remote Viewing

Remote viewing is considered by some to be a form of telepathy. It occurs when a consciousness, presumably a human consciousness, uses directed visualization to tune in to any objects, places, or events throughout time and to retrieve pertinent information about them. This psychic technique was developed at the Stanford Research Institute by Harold E. Puthoff, Russell Targ, and Ingo Swann.

According to Joseph McMoneagle, the first military remote viewer in the Army's Stargate program based in Fort Meade, Maryland, remote viewing is a formalized discipline involving strict double-blind protocols in which a viewer knows nothing about the target. With knowledge of the intended target, a remote viewing *faux pas* known as "frontloading" can cloud viewer reception, because the viewer reflexively adds his or her own preconceived notions about the subject. In 1986, the Defense Intelligence Agency and SRI International published these protocols in the *Coordinate Remote Viewing Manual* (see *www.remoteviewed.com*).

McMoneagle likens remote viewing to a martial art. In *Remote Viewing Secrets* (2000), he writes:

> [Remote viewing is] a discipline, a science, and a technique containing certain principles that cannot, and should not, be diluted . . . one must not only learn those aspects that can be practiced through repetition under protocol, but also the more ephemeral realities which impact directly the fundamental rules of integrity that bind it all together.

McMoneagle also warns that if someone has a clear target of a UFO or alien, they take it with a grain of salt.

As you may have guessed, not all of the viewers and managers followed the protocols. Enter one Captain Ed Dames. From 1983 to 1988, Dames was known to task viewers with "anomaly" targets—like things on Mars, specific UFO events, and whether or not a Galactic Federation existed. Viewer Paul H. Smith writes that he was both disappointed in Dames for giving them targets that could not be verified afterward, as in a proper protocol, and because he "must grudgingly admit to some bit of admiration for the sheer chutzpah he showed, and the smattering of interesting results we produced thanks to his determination" ("UFOs and Remote Viewing: an Insider's Perspective" by Paul H. Smith in *UFO Magazine* [June/July 2005]). For more discussion of remote viewing, see *Captain of My Ship, Master of My*

Soul (2001) by F. Holmes Atwater; *The Stargate Chronicles* (2002) by Joseph McMoneagle; and *Reading the Enemy's Mind: Inside Stargate, America's Psychic Espionage Program* (2005) by Paul H. Smith.

Telepathy

Telepathy is the extra-sensory perceptive ability to send or receive psychic, or thought, communication intentionally between two living consciousnesses not necessarily in the same dimension, but operating in real time. Telepathic abilities include, but are not limited to, reading others' minds, mediumship, clairvoyance (the ability to see visions of the past, present, or future), clairaudience (the ability to hear information and/or communication from the past, present, or future), and psychokinesis (the ability to move physical objects with thought alone).

The Spiritualist movement sparked a popular trend in home psychic inquiry. K. E. Zener developed the Zener Cards for home telepathic testing. This card pack consisted of twenty-five cards in groups of five, each with a set of symbols: a circle, a square, a plus sign, a star, and three wavy lines. Testees tried to guess which card would next be flipped or which one was being displayed but kept from view.

Contactee Dana Howard and her series of books is an early example of claims of telepathic communication from beings from the planet Venus. Her books *My Flight to Venus* (1954), *Diane: She Came from Venus* (1956), *Over the Threshold* (1957), and *Vesta: The Earthborn Venusian* (1959) are all classics on the subject. Howard first met a physical Diane in 1939. Then, after sixteen years of telepathic communication between Howard and the Venusian, during which knowledge of spiritual growth and advancement were imparted to Howard, Diane manifested in front of twenty-seven witnesses, including Howard, at a Church of Divine Light séance in Los Angeles conducted by nationally recognized medium Reverend Bertie Lillie Candler.

Solar System

A solar system usually consists of a star and its orbiting satellites. About 300 solar systems have been discovered in the Milky Way galaxy and beyond. A few of these have been discovered to have planets that may possibly be able to support life as we know it. Multiple collisions characterize young systems, which settle down over time, although never totally. Our own solar system is a great example.

With the exception of highly volcanic solar bodies like Saturn's moon, Io, most of the bodies in our system are pockmarked with thousands of craters. This means that the arrangement of them today is the result of a history of violent impacts, collisions, and possibly explosions of entire planets (see "Alien Solar Systems," an episode of *How the Universe Works*, a Science Channel series). In our own solar system, we have eight planets (Mercury, Venus, Earth, Mars, Saturn, Jupiter, Uranus, and Neptune), many with their own satellites and encompassed by an "Oort cloud"—named after Dutch physicist Jan Oort, who suggested the possibility of this perimeter in 1950.

The Oort cloud is a storage house for a variety of frozen debris, mostly ice and dust. It is so far away from the sun that it takes light a full year to reach it. Still, it is thought that objects from this region can break free and travel inward toward the planets and the sun. Comets like Halley's Comet (seventy-six-year orbit, last appeared in 1986), the Hale Bopp comet (2,500-year orbit, last appeared in 1997), and Comet Shoemaker-Levy 9, whose fragments peppered Jupiter in 1994, are thought to originate from within this mysterious region of space (see *www.jpl.nasa.gov*).

Moving inward toward the sun, we find the Kuiper Belt, another orbiting ring of frozen debris of various sizes, orbiting just beyond the last planet, Neptune. Pluto—considered a planet until 2006, when the International Astronomical Union reclassified it as a "dwarf planet"—is now thought to be a member of the Kuiper Belt. Objects from here sometimes break out of their orbits and may collide with other inner solar system bodies. Between the orbits of Mars and Jupiter is the asteroid belt, another ring of rocky debris thought to be the remnants of an exploded planet or of a planet that was involved in a massive ancient collision. The inner workings of the solar system have been likened to a piece of intricate machinery, like a clock. Others, like the famous Greek Pythagoras, see the precise movements of the solar system as a kind of music—what he called the "music of the spheres." This machinery is the basis of the occult practice of astrology, a system focused on how the movements and positioning of the bodies of the solar system and the stars affect an individual's physical body and spiritual self.

Researchers suspect that there is life in other places in the solar system besides the Earth. Mars is thought to have been suitable for human life once, as evidenced by what is thought to be a microscopic form of life photographed in meteors from it (see *Apod.nasa.gov/apod/ap960807.html*).

Astronomer Carl Sagan also considered Saturn's moon Titan to be a candidate for possible primitive cellular life (see chapter 2). However, information and testimony from contactees, abductees, psychics, and time travelers say that life exists virtually everywhere in our solar system. And it is from these same sources that information about extra-solar planets has come to light. The work of Wendelle C. Stevens accounts for much of this testimony. Planets like Ummo, Acart, and Alcyon are but a few of the extra-solar planets that have been identified by researchers. Kelvin Rowe's book *A Call at Dawn: A Message from Our Brothers from the Planets Pluto and Jupiter* (1958) discusses these possibilities.

Of all the literature about life on other plants, especially in our solar system, more information has been brought forth about Earth's moon, Mars, and Venus than about any other bodies because information about these relatively closer bodies is more accessible to independent researchers, and telescopes are able to reveal more detail. These sources can then be cross-referenced with the evidence and testimony from other researchers.

Time Travel

What is time? Most scientists see time as a fourth dimension, along with height, length, and width. It is commonly thought to flow uniformly in one direction—from the past or present into the future. This is known as the "arrow of time." However, physicist Albert Einstein proved that time passes, or flows by, like a river, at different rates depending on the influence of gravity. If we could travel at or near the speed of light (generally accepted as 186,282 miles per second), Einstein claimed that we could move along that river, traveling with its flow. Einstein predicted time travel to the future, but not to the past.

Einstein's two famous theories—special relativity (1905) and general relativity (1915)—postulated that time is fused with space in a symbiotic relationship known as "space-time" or "time-space." This paved the way for quantum mechanics (QM), which embodies ideas like the Heisenberg principle—the theory that light can be both a particle and a wave, depending on the observer—and of "nonlocality"—the mysterious phenomena connecting subatomic particles over time and space. QM has led to theories about black holes (or wormholes), singularities, and cosmic strings.

String theory states that the particles observed in a particle accelerator (aka an atom smasher) are viewed as if they were notes on a guitar string that stack together at the micro level to form the universe. These are what are known as "cosmic strings" (see *www.superstringtheory.com*).

If relativity is a description of the macro-universe and QM is a description of the micro-universe, then string theory can be seen as an attempt to reconcile them into one unified equation—a theory that can explain the entire universe. Morgan Freeman explores this possibility in "Is Time Travel Possible?" an episode of *Through the Wormhole* that appeared on the Science Channel in 2010.

Mainstream quantum physicists like Michio Kaku (*Physics of the Impossible: A Scientific Exploration into the World of Phasers, Force Fields, Teleportation, and Time Travel* [2008]) and string theory physicist

Brian Greene (*The Fabric of the Cosmos: Space, Time, and the Texture of Reality* [2005]) disagree with Einstein and don't believe that time travel is possible. Greene, for example, says that all time-travel theories operate at the edge of known physics and, consequently, are unlikely to work. And even with a unified equation, he says, time travel to the past, while mathematically possible, is not physically possible. However, he does tell us how time travel to the future may be possible:

> If you want to know what the Earth is like one million years from now, I'll tell you how to do that. Build a spaceship and go near the speed of light for a length of time. . . . Come back to Earth, and when you step out of your ship you will have aged perhaps one year while the Earth would have aged one million years. You would have traveled to Earth's future.
>
> *www.livescience.com*

This is what is known as "time dilation." In other words, the faster you go, the slower time goes.

Despite these arguments, however, other mainstream university researchers claim to have built stargate-like portals, or wormholes, for inter-dimensional and/or time travel. So why not time travel to the past? Three main reasons are given against this: paradoxes, constraints, and limited technology.

Paradoxes arise when time travel would result in some type of logical inconsistency. The most famous of these is known as the "grandfather paradox," in which a time traveler travels back to the past and kills his grandfather, thereby ensuring that the traveler would never be born or ever able to have gone back in time. The "twin paradox" posits one twin who goes faster than the speed of light and is thus younger than the second twin when he or she returns. Another is the "faster than light paradox," in which a time traveler could return from a trip before even setting out. (For several more examples, go to *www.science. howstuffworks.com.*) These paradoxes create constraints, such as when a person traveling back in time takes a particular action that creates alternate realities different from the ones that have already occurred (see *Plato.stanford.edu/entries/time-travel-phys/#10*).

Of course, others, like Dr. Igor Novikov, think that the universe is somehow self-correcting and would not allow such paradoxes. He has devised the Novikov self-consistency principle to describe this. Another theory is that there are "multiple universes" or "many worlds," a theory first proposed by Hugh Everett III in 1957. This theory suggests that, by traveling into the past, we actually travel into a parallel universe. From the moment we arrive, the universes start diverging, becoming different branches of the original time line that are each valid in and of themselves. Whether the universes split or whether they always existed in some other dimension is not known. This phenomenon is explored in *Sliders* (1995–2000) starring Jerry O'Connell, *The One* (2001) starring Jet Li, and *Jumper* (2008) starring Hayden Christensen.

The other chief objection to time travel to the past is the incomprehensible amounts of energy required to punch a hole in space-time, or stabilize a wormhole, or engineer a double cosmic-string ring capable of bending space enough to let us make the journey. According to the theory of relativity, to punch a hole in the fabric of space-time would require either the energy of a star or theoretical negative energy, an exotic energy with a value of less than zero, says Kaku. Quantum mechanics tells us that we would need enough power to move a wormhole's "mouth A," or a black hole in this universe, to be close to its other end at "mouth B," either another black hole in this universe or a theoretical "white hole" opening in a parallel universe.

"Wormholes are the future, wormholes are the past," said Kaku. "But we have to be very careful. The gasoline necessary to energize a time machine is far beyond anything that we can assemble with today's technology" (*www.livescience.com/1339-travel-time-scientists.htm*).

Not-so-mainstream work in the field of time travel has supposedly been conducted by several of the world's governments, including Russia and the United States. The controversial Bob Lazar claimed that Project Looking Glass was a U.S. military time-travel project conducted at Area 51 (see chapter 4). Some claim that the U.S. Defense Advanced Research Projects Agency, or DARPA, a division of the Department of Defense (DoD), undertook time travel experiments between 1968 and 1972 under the moniker Project Pegasus. The first place they went, according to self-proclaimed military time traveler Andrew Basiagio, was Mars (see "Time Traveling for the U.S. Military" by Len Kasten, *Atlantis Rising* 82 [July/August 2010]).

In 2003, the U.S. Air Force Research Lab also issued an eighty-eight-page report entitled *The Teleportation Physics Report*, which described a range of concepts and experiments in time travel. The author of the report, Eric Davis, stated that moving from location to location was "quite real and can be controlled" (*www.fas.org/sgp/eprint/teleport.pdf*).

We can supposedly move in the physical, mental/quantum, or astral/spiritual levels of consciousness, depending on what techniques we employ. Survivors of the Montauk Project have been claiming for decades that time travel is a reality; moreover, they claim that it has been going on since the early 1940s using Nikola Tesla's technology (see chapter 5). If this is true, the time traveler ET theory is more plausible. This is also known as the terrestrial extra theory (TET), which postulates that Earth humans from the future are traveling in UFOs to various points in their past (including our present) for a variety of reasons. TET challenges the idea that reported alien sightings are sightings of beings not of this Earth. The probability that they have traveled light years to get to Earth and reportedly look human is not as likely, some say, as the theory that these beings are native to Earth, but are from the future (*www.terrestrialextras.com*). *Visitors from Time: The Secret of the UFOs* (1992) by Marc Davenport explores this thesis, as does *Who Built the Moon?* (2005) by Christopher Knight and Alan Butler.

Still, ever since H. G. Wells wrote the now legendary *The Time Machine* in 1895, the idea of building our own time machines and traveling to the future has sparked countless imaginations. Wells tells how a man built a time machine and traveled millions of years into Earth's future. He encounters the Eloi, a new race of humans who are fragile yet playful. This future society has no bugs, weeds, disease, or violence. However, they cohabit with the Morlocks, a race of disfigured albino creatures that emerge from their underground lairs at night and roam the hills to feast on the flesh of the Eloi. Will our traveler survive? Will he make it back to his own time? What an adventure!

Because of Wells's inspirational story, there is a host of independent inventors who have followed his archetype and claim to have built time-traveling machines for both physical and mental travel—both forward and backward in time. For example, at his Time Travel Research Center in Long Island, Dr. David Lewis Anderson claims to have expanded his "time-warp field theory," continuing the work he began for the Air Force back in the 1960s. He claims to have developed a third-generation time-warp generator and has set out ten types of time-control technologies and methods, along with a feasibility analysis of each method. Among these technologies are quantum tunneling, time-warp fields, and wormholes (see *www.andersoninstitute.com*).

Self-proclaimed time traveler and adventurer Steven L. Gibbs claimed to have invented the first commercial time machine in 1985. He called it the Hyper Dimensional Resonator (HDR), which, according to him, can send people physically through time. He tells of an incident in which two time travelers gave him the plans to create his very own time machine.

The bibliography on time travel is extensive. Some of its best offerings include *Stranger Than Fiction: The True Time Travel Adventures of Steven L. Gibbs—The Rainman of Time Travel* (2001) and *Why I Believe the HDR Unit Works and Time-Travel Is Possible!* (2010) both by Patricia Griffin Ress (2010); *The Time Travel Handbook: A Manual of Practice Teleportation and Time Travel* (1999) by David Hatcher Childress; *The Music of Time* (2000) by Preston Nichols and Peter Moon; *Time Travel: A How-To Insiders Guide* (2001) by Commander X and Tim Swartz; *A Course in Time Travel: A Handbook for*

Multidimensional Consciousness, an eBook by Curtis Jackson at *www. timetravelers.org; Breaking the Time Barrier: The Race to Build the First Time Machine* (2005) by Jenny Randles; *Time Travel Now* (2005) by William F. Hamilton III; and *Uninvited Future Observers* (2010) by David Robinson Fair. Media presentations are found in *Doctor Who* (1963–1989), *The Time Travelers* (1964) starring Preston Foster, *Time Bandits* (1981) starring John Cleese, *Star Trek IV: The Voyage Home* (1986) starring William Shatner, *Quantum Leap* (1989–1993) starring Scott Bakula and long-time sci-fi actor Dean Stockwell, and *UFO: Secrets of the Third Reich,* part IV (2000).

Underground and Undersea Bases

Natural underground caves honeycomb the Earth. Dr. Richard Sauder, author of *Underground Bases and Tunnels: What is the Government Trying to Hide?* (1995) and *Underwater and Underground Bases: Surprising Facts the Government Does Not Want You to Know!* (2001), asserts that many of the world's governments, especially that of the United States and its military affiliates, have done extensive tunneling on their own for the purpose of creating secret facilities known as Deep Underground Military Bases, or DUMBs. In his latest work, *Hidden in Plain Sight: Beyond the X Files* (2010), he continues to build his case that many of the world's governments use natural and man-made caves as underground and underwater facilities.

Sauder does not claim that these bases are made or used by aliens, just that many of the world's governments are busy building these secret structures for some unpublicized reason or reasons. His work exposes information that has been available to the public but kept out of the mainstream media. Sauder's efforts demonstrate that the U.S. government can often provide valuable data about itself—its activities and conduct—if you are diligent enough to do the work to find it. It's just good, old-fashioned research, he says.

Sauder said that he "began a lengthy federal document search by filing Freedom of Information Act (FOIA) requests, riffled through card catalogues, electronic data bases and military publications." He cross-checked this data with corporate records from giants like Bechtel and Morrison-Knudsen Company, Inc., two of the United States' biggest underground tunneling and construction companies, along with several other members of the American Underground-Construction Association (AUA), in order to verify his information.

Using largely governmental information has both its advantages and disadvantages. One advantage is that this kind of information is usually considered highly credible; consequently, it can protect you and your research from public ridicule. But the downside, which will be made apparent shortly, is that it may be unreliable information, or disinformation, so it must be cross-checked with other databases. Also, it could draw the attention of the government, which has many ways of harassing witnesses and those in possession of "sensitive" or "top secret" information.

Underground bases were originally built in North America to protect the continent from Soviet attack. This is evidenced by the formulation of the North American Aerospace Defense Command (NORAD), established during the height of the Cold War by the United States and Canada to protect their respective countries from land, sea, or air strikes. The command has three subordinate regional headquarters: the Alaskan NORAD Region at Elmendorf Air Force Base, Alaska; the Canadian NORAD 1 Canadian Air Division in Winnipeg, Manitoba; and the Continental NORAD region home-based at Cheyenne Mountain Air Force Station, Colorado.

Cheyenne Mountain is an example of a known U.S. military underground base. The Cheyenne Mountain facility became the NORAD Combat Operations Center on April 20, 1966. Today, the Cheyenne Mountain complex serves as NORAD and USNORTH-COM's Alternate Command Center. Daily operations for these divisions typically take place at nearby Peterson Air Force Base in Colorado Springs, Colorado.

The installation claims to be responsible for monitoring all incoming craft toward U.S. and Canadian land, sea, or air space while remaining securely nestled within the mountain. The official NORAD website touts their many exploits. For example, an article titled "NORAD jets respond to aircraft in National Capital Region, April 18, 2011" describes how two F-16 fighters were scrambled to escort an unauthorized aircraft from the restricted area. There are several articles with similar stories.

Of course, it has also been alleged that some of these bases are the settings for interaction between humans and aliens. The most famous of these is the secret underground facility at Dulce, New Mexico. According to author Timothy Green Beckley, rumors began to surface about an underground laboratory underneath Dulce in the 1970s with the testimony of contactee Paul Bennewitz.

Bennewitz claims that he was contacted by aliens at the underground lab via his radio receiver; they told him to go to Dulce. Once there, he began monitoring the area and taking photographs of UFOs flying into and out of openings in the mountain. In the end, Bennewitz was harassed by unknown forces, institutionalized, and "pushed over the edge never to return to sanity" (*Project Beta: The Story of Paul Bennewitz, National Security, and the Creation of the Modern UFO Myth* [2005] by Greg Bishop).

Some also claim that, in 1979, there was a human versus alien skirmish inside the base that left few survivors. Beckley states:

> One individual in the US military who was involved in the early stages of this investigation claims he engaged in hand to hand combat with ETs who had taken over level seven of the Dulce Base after a conflict with our soldiers. Another person involved in this epic committed "suicide"—or was it murder?—shortly after the Dulce affair was made public.

> Timothy Green Beckley and Christa Tilton,
> *Underground Alien Bio Lab at Dulce*

Beckley is referring to government whistle-blower Philip "Phil" Schneider. In a lecture videotaped in May 1996, Schneider claimed that, not only had his father, Captain Oscar Schneider, been involved with the infamous Philadelphia Experiment, but that he also worked on secret government projects as a government structural engineer/geologist who was, among other things, involved in building underground military bases around the country. Schneider also claimed to be one of only three people to survive a 1979 incident between the alien Grays and U.S. military forces at the underground base.

During that year, Schneider was employed by Morrison-Knudsen, Inc. where he was involved in building an addition to the deep underground military base at Dulce. The project entailed drilling four holes in the desert that were to be linked by tunnels. His job was to go down the holes, check the geology, and recommend the necessary explosives to deal with the situation. In the process, the workers accidentally opened a large artificial cavern. Unfortunately, it was a hostile Gray alien base.

In the panic that ensued, sixty-six workers and military personnel were killed, with Schneider being one of only three people to survive. He claimed that scars on his chest were caused by his being struck by an alien beam weapon, which later resulted in cancer. Schneider's body was found on January 17, 1996, in his Oregon apartment. Officials estimated that he had been dead five to seven days and he reportedly had a rubber hose wrapped three times around his neck. Nonetheless, the death has been officially ruled a suicide. Many believe that he was murdered to silence him.

Schneider's ex-wife, Cynthia Drayer, believes that Phil was murdered because he publicly revealed the truth about the U.S. government's involvement with UFOs. Not much is known about secret underwater government, or alien, bases, because the cost of funding inquiries into these facilities is beyond the reach of most independent researchers. Also, what is thought to be known about them is derived largely from testimony from witnesses. Still, speculation is rampant about underwater bases in areas of water where there are histories of UFO sightings.

A case in point is the work of Preston Dennett. Dennett has concluded that there is an undersea base off the coast of California near Santa Barbara/Catalina Island. He bases his claim on the area's history of UFO activity and on corollary testimony. Dennett's theories were featured on a 2006 episode of the History Channel series *UFO Files* entitled "Deep Sea UFOs: Red Alert." Other alien undersea bases are thought to be located off the east coast of Puerto Rico, in the Dragon's Triangle off the southeast coast of Japan, and in places where nuclear bombs have been tested.

Schneider also claims that many nuclear tests, including at Bikini Atoll, were secretly carried out to attack and destroy underwater alien bases. He urges researchers to take a close look at photographs of the blasts at Bikini Atoll and other oceanic test sites, claiming they will see UFOs leaving the area.

Andros Island, situated north of Cuba in the Caribbean Sea, is not just a known UFO hot spot. There is speculation, based on testimony of former employees and eyewitness accounts, that the U.S. Naval Base there, the Atlantic Undersea Test and Evaluation Center (AUTEC), is a jointly run human military and alien space base. Witnesses report that UFOs and USOs (unidentified submerged objects) come and go regularly. The *UFO Hunters* television series did a segment on the base that revealed an underwater pipeline that extends into the deep unknown. They found no UFOs, however.

The bibliography on these bases is extensive. It includes *UFO Contact from Undersea* (1982) by Dr. Virgilio Sanchez-Ocejo and Wendelle C. Stevens, *The Dulce Wars: Underground Alien Bases and the Battle for Planet Earth* (1999) by BRANTON, *UFOs Over California: A True History of Extraterrestrial Encounters* (2004) by Preston Dennett, *Entrances to Subterranean Tunnels: Underground Alien Bases* (1990) by Sherry Shriner, *Underground Alien Bio Lab at Dulce—Bennewitz UFO Papers* (2009) by Timothy Green Beckley, *UFOs and Water: Physical Effects of UFOs on Water Through Accounts by Eyewitnesses* (2010) by Carl W. Feindt, and *Alice in Wonderland and the World Trade Center Disaster: Why the Official Story of 9/11 Is a Monumental Lie* (2002) by David Icke.

RESEARCH/RESOURCE TIP: Every serious researcher maps their local sightings so they can get a better overview of the phenomena they are studying. I suggest using the free program Google Earth. The downloadable version allows you to create a pushpin database that you can share with your friends or publish online. This electronic capability in mapping has changed the face of many fields of research, especially ufology. Make sure you get a VFR and IFR aviation map from your local airport. These maps contain the flight paths of general aircraft and commercial airliners and the locations of military operating areas (MOAs). This will help you determine if the UFO could have been a misidentified aircraft, and if there exists the possibility of military involvement in the activity.

JOHN RHODES, PERSONAL INTERVIEW

Venus

This mysterious planet has been associated with goddess traditions for thousands of years. The rising and setting of Venus is the central theme of one of the few surviving texts of the goddess-worshipping Mayans known as the Dresden Codex. This ancient culture used observations of Venus to formulate its well-known calendar, the Tzolkin. The planet was revered by the ancient Egyptians and Sumerians as well. It is known by many female names, chief among them the Sumerian "Innana."

In contradiction to this, and to the work of Emerson above, author Dr. Larry Brian Radka, in his book *Astronomical Revelations on 666: A Scientific and Historical Study of Asteroids and Comets with Respect to the Apocalypse* (1997), maintains that it was the later dark Babylonian priests who "blasphemed" by changing Venus from a male to a female deity. They did this, he argues, to deny the existence of the male god.

How the worshipping of a planet as female instead of as male is blasphemous Radke does not say—especially in a tradition that propagates peace, individual experience, and growth. But he does make a strong case that a planet known in antiquity as Zion—or Rahab, or simply Heaven—was split in two by the Great Red Dragon (four large stars or moons that formed into a commentary body) and expelled from an outer planet. The smaller half became the son of the Mother Zion, Venus—in this tradition, associated with Jesus, a male deity known as "the bright and morning star."

The larger half became known as the Daughter of Zion, or Earth. However, the first Earth was struck by another projectile creating Mercury, Mars, Earth's Moon, and the Earth as we know it today. The entire account, says Radke, is described in the biblical Book of Revelation.

All male and female arguments aside (see *Men Are from Mars, Women Are from Venus: A Practical Guide for Improving Communication and Getting What You Want in Relationships* [1993] by John Gray), several contactees have claimed affiliation with Venus. Wendelle Stevens and Edward James's *UFO Contact from Planet Venus* is a classic in the field and chronicles the story of valiant Thor, the man from Venus. Frank Stranges, in his book *Stranger at the Pentagon* (1972), also describes the mysterious Thor after having met with the Venusian at the Pentagon along with U.S. military officials in 1959. Thor's message was one of peace and antinuclear proliferation. He claimed that nuclear explosions affected dimensions other than the material plane, including the dimensions on Venus. He is said to have kept his ship, with a compliment of 200 Venusians, safe underneath the waters of Lake Mead on the Nevada/Arizona border. Stranges says that Thor offered the United States and planet Earth long life and advanced technology, but was rejected. So he and his cohorts reportedly left the planet in 1960.

Other Venusians or Venusian contactees include George van Tassel, Howard Menger, and George Adamski (see chapter 2). Another individual who claims that she is physically from Venus is Omnec Onec (her Venusian name), also known as Sheila Gipson and Sheila Shultz. She says she came to Earth in 1955, arriving in Tibet on a UFO with her uncle after she chose to incarnate in a material body. She did this for two reasons. First, it gave her the opportunity to come to Earth and work out her Earthly karma. Second, she was to function as an ambassador from Venus to Earth to spread the messages of peace, love, and the responsible use of technology.

Omnec Onec: Ambassador from Venus (1990), published with the help of Wendelle C. Stevens (back in print in 2008; see *www. conspiracyjournal.com*), outlines her journey to attempt to instill values on Earth that would lead to nonaggression, a clean environment, and an emotional atmosphere not predicated on fear. Appearing on the *Jerry Springer Show* in the early 1990s, Onec described how she lived on Venus in another dimension without a physical body. People lived in domed cities, she said, that protected them from the tremendous heat and natural forces on the surface—forces that still affected them on this other plane of existence.

On top of host Springer's giggling remarks, a professor from Loyola University began to ridicule her snidely about how NASA had already mapped the entire surface of Venus and how there couldn't possibly be domed cities that would escape detection. Onec kept her composure through the snickers and sneers, giving the appearance that she was telling the truth as she knew it. Viewers were left to decide on their own what to make of Onec's story.

About the same time, the NASA *Magellan* probe, launched by the space shuttle *Atlantis* on May 4, 1989, was sending back curious data about the surface of Venus. A *US News & World Report* article on May 13, 1991 quoted MIT's Gordon Pettingill:

> Under Magellan's radar glare, mountaintops shine almost as if they were coated with metal ... surprisingly, some of the domes are translucent to radar, suggesting that they are composed of light glassy material ...

Could Onec's claims be proven correct by the *Magellan* data? Does this lend more credence to the claims that NASA is, indeed, suppressing much evidence from throughout our solar system that indicates we are not alone? Does the fact that, as time goes on, more and more people are coming out with their own contact experiences of all kinds, including those with Venus, indicate that there is a real phenomena behind these encounters? Or does it mean that there are just that many more liars?

Even the Japanese First Lady has claimed to have flown to Venus in a UFO. In a September 2, 2009, Reuters news article, the Premiere's wife, Miyuki Hatoyama, is quoted from a book called *Very Strange Things I've Encountered* (2008). She said in the book: "While my body was asleep, I think my soul rode on a triangular-shaped UFO and went to Venus. It was a very beautiful place and it was really green."

For more on Venus, see *My Flight to Venus* (1954) by Dana Howard; *My Trip to Mars, the Moon, and Venus* (1959) by Buck Nelson; and *Pioneers of Space—The Long Lost Book of George Adamski: A Trip to the Moon, Mars and Venus* (2010) by George Adamski.

EQUIPMENT TIP: Get a capable telescope. Celestron, Meade, and Sky-Watcher are reputable brands. An excellent source for telescopes for users of all ages and experience is *www.telescopes.com*. When you're there, pick up a copy of *Celestron Sky Maps* and *Luminous Star Finder* to help you locate objects in the night sky.

Protocols
for Contact

Contact with extraterrestrial species has apparently taken place in a number of cultures throughout recorded history. Because of this, it is difficult to point to an "official" beginning of the phenomenon in modern times. Researcher Timothy Green Beckley, for instance, is reported to have flashed lights at a UFO when he was a young man in the 1950s and gotten a response. Today, the simple practice of flashing a spot beam three times for a response from a UFO is repeated with success at James Gilliland's ranch in southern Washington State on a weekly basis. It is an old shamanic technique known to anthropologists as "call and response."

Practitioners of Western magic or indigenous traditions know that repeating words, phrases, and/or actions three times is a symbol for initiation or consecration. But who was the first person, and what was the first culture, to do this?

In fact, the more we study the subject, the more we realize that it could be a totally natural thing for humans to interact with off-world beings and cultures, as is evidenced in *Star Ancestors* (2000) by Nancy Red Star. Indigenous cultures have developed and refined time-tested ceremonial protocols for invoking, inducing, and/or initiating contact with both extraterrestrial and ultraterrestrial beings and cultures. In mainstream society today, however, we have apparently lost this knowledge—outside of call and response.

This knowledge has been preserved outside of the mainstream, however, by various indigenous tribes around the world and by various secret societies in the East and West. These mystery schools teach techniques that involve what is broadly termed "magic," or the combination of intention, symbolism, and ritual in any form (see my DVD, *The Magical Mystical Contract* [2008] and a lecture at the Bay Area UFO Expo).

Exopolitics

Exopolitics is generally considered to have begun formally at the Stanford Research Institute in Menlo Park, California, in 1977 when Alfred L. Webre led an investigation into the possibility of civilian contact with an extraterrestrial species while working under the auspices of the Center for the Study of Social Policy. Webre's civilian academic group worked in conjunction with President Jimmy Carter's domestic policy staff at the White House from the spring to the fall of 1977, when the program was abruptly discontinued. Webre has relied on information gleaned from the practice of "remote viewing," which was also pioneered at Stanford in the 1970s by Harold Puthoff and Russell Targ (see chapter 6).

Despite the "official" beginning of the study of exopolitics in a formalized, academic format, however, it can be argued that UFO abductees/contactees acted as some of the first exopoliticians, or ambassadors, for Earth (see *www.exopolitics.com*). The themes of nonviolence, nonproliferation of nuclear weapons (especially in space), and tolerance have been espoused by contactees since the late 1940s, allegedly in an effort to get humanity to stop killing itself with war, pollution, and greed, and endangering a well-populated Galactic community on inter-dimensional levels. Lisette Larkins's *Talking to Extraterrestrials: Communicating with Enlightened Beings* (2002) and Jim Moroney's *The Extraterrestrial Answer Book: UFOs, Alien Abductions, and the Coming ET Presence* (2009) both explore this interpretation.

It can also be argued that many ancient personalities were the first exopoliticians because of their supposed relationships with extraterrestrials. Farah Yurdozu, for example, makes the case that Turkey's legendary founder Mustafa Kemal Ataturk was the first exopolitician. The Bible's Enoch, Ezekiel, and Moses are other examples of this, and there are many more.

However, no overview of the body of exopolitical knowledge is complete without the mention of one of the pioneers in the field, researcher Wendelle C. Stevens, who was approached by a man in the early 1980s at the first International UFO Congress held in Laughlin, Nevada. Stevens's untiring work with many abduction cases apparently gave him the credentials as a person who could facilitate an as yet unfinished project called the Interplanetary Cultural Center. The man who approached Stevens, who is thought to have been a humanoid extraterrestrial, told him that he wanted his help to start the diplomatic institution. The problem was, and is, says Stevens, that there is no one who can speak for the Earth as a single body.

The idea that Russian leader Mikhail Gorbachev was prepared by an extraterrestrial race to be a world leader to fulfill this function as spokesperson for the Earth was explored by Stevens in his future work, which presents exopolitical scenarios and information. Since his passing in September 2010, however, the rights to Stevens's work have been purchased by *Open Minds* magazine, which plans to present aspects of it in the future (see *www.openminds.tv/magazine*).

A rare classic in what is now considered to be the field of exopolitics is *The Cosmic Blueprint for After* (1989) by Dr. Jaysen Q. Rand (aka

Paul Bondora, Cory Wade). It presents a complete outline of society after first contact, as channeled to Andrews by a "Fourth Racer" named Aalon (see chapter 6). Perhaps the first official exopolitics book—a book that has opened the doors to a handful of others—was published in 2004 by Dr. Michael E. Salla. Below you will find brief descriptions of many of the players, institutions, and documents that make up today's exopolitical scene.

Alfred L. Webre

Alfred Webre directed the 1977 ET communication study commissioned by President Jimmy Carter. He is also international director of the Institute for Cooperation in Space (ICIS), founder of the No Weapons in Space Campaign (NOWIS), a Canadian coalition to prevent the weaponization of space, and author of *Exopolitics: Politics, Government, and Law in the Universe* (2005, eBook first edition 2000).

Webre offers several descriptions of exopolitics. It is, he says, "a discipline for understanding 'Universe' through its politics and government," as well as "a political, governmental, and legal process by which the interests of human society—its individuals, institutions, and nations—can reach out to, interact with, and create a cooperative future with off-planet cultures." He also calls it "a structural process by which the evolutionary and social needs of life-bearing planets are determined and mediated"—or, very simply, "the study of the political process of governance in interstellar society."

In Webre's view, the universe is home to a diverse pantheon of life forms, both extraterrestrial and inter-dimensional. He believes that Earth has been quarantined from the rest of the universe because of an ancient war. Basing his argument on remote-viewing information and techniques (pioneered at Stanford), Webre cites the *Urantia Book* as an exopolitical document as well (see *www.urantia.org*).

Michael Salla

Dr. Michael Salla founded the Exopolitics Institute in 2005 (see *www. exopoliticsinstitute.org*). He is currently its director. He is also the author of the first book on the subject, *Exopolitics: Political Implications of the Extraterrestrial Presence* (2004) and of the more recent *Exposing US Government Policies on Extraterrestrial Life* (2009).

The Exopolitics Institute is an organization dedicated to the study, promotion, and support of exopolitics. It publishes the *Exopolitics Journal*, runs a news service called ExoNews, and offers several courses in various aspects of the subject. The institute's website is also home to a good list of exopolitical Internet links, demonstrating the global sweep of the influence of the emerging field.

The institute defines exopolitics as "an interdisciplinary scientific field, with its roots in the political sciences, that focuses on research, education, and public policy with regard to the actors, institutions, and processes associated with extraterrestrial life, as well as the wide range of implications this entails through public advocacy and newly emerging paradigms."

Salla makes the case that global politics since the 1930s has proceeded in response to the extraterrestrial presence on Earth, including the war in Iraq—which, Salla maintains, the United States wages in order to gain control of certain ET artifacts like a stargate.

Salla, along with psychic Angelika Whitecliff, founded and hosts the Galactic Diplomacy website (*www.galacticdiplomacy.com*), which is dedicated to guiding extraterrestrial contact. Salla's latest book, *Exposing US Government Policies on Extraterrestrial Life* (2010), details the most recent exopolitical developments.

Richard Boylan

Richard Boylan is president of the Academy of Clinical Close Encounter Therapists (ACET), a nonprofit educational and research organization. He is also a member of the National Board of Hypnotherapy and

Hypnotic Anesthesiology and a behavioral scientist and certified clinical hypnotherapist who provides "hypnotherapy for recalling full details of partially remembered close encounters with the Star Visitors, stored in subconscious memory."

Since 1989, Boylan has conducted research into human encounters with what he calls the Star Visitors, which has led to his current focus on and creation of the Star Kids Project. Here, he is a consultant to Star Kids and Star Seeds, otherwise known as "indigo children," seeking to understand their origin, identity, and mission better, so they can achieve full awareness of and clarity about their identity, inner growth, spiritual development, and future path.

Boylan is the author of four books: *Close Extraterrestrial Encounters* (1994), *Labored Journey to the Stars* (1996), *Project Epiphany* (1997), and *Star Kids: The Emerging Cosmic Generation* (2005), a free eBook available at his website (see *www.drboylan.com*). He is currently working on a fifth book, *The Star Nations–Human Connection*.

Paola Harris

Paola Harris is founder and director of Starworks Italia, which is dedicated to full disclosure of the extraterrestrial presence on Earth, the international exchange of information, and the promotion of exopolitical discourse worldwide. Harris attempts to bring the study of exopolitics into the mainstream and out of the "conspiracy" realm, because she feels that the combination of the two tends to turn people off on the subject.

Harris also teaches exopolitical classes at the Exopolitics Institute and acts as the organization's international liaison director. Her website (*www.paolaharris.com*) is a portal for up-to-date reports, stories, and events and is available in five languages. Harris is the author of *Exopolitics: How Does One Speak to a Ball of Light* (2007) and *Exopolitics: All the Above* (2009).

Formal Communications

Arguably the first sets of protocols for communicating with other-worldly beings was developed in ancient times, possibly taught by the ETs themselves and preserved by Earth's many indigenous cultures. These beings impart wisdom, prophecy, and healings of all kinds, says Red Star. And there is a special relationship between ETs, the native peoples, and corn, which is preserved in many ritualistic forms (see chapter 3). Resources on this subject include *Legends of the Star Ancestors: Stories of Extraterrestrial Contact from Wisdomkeepers around the World* (2002) by Nancy Red Star; *The American Indian UFO–Starseed Connection* (1992) by Timothy Green Beckley; and *Golden UFOs: The Indian Poems* (1992) by Ernesto Cardenal.

Western Magic

Secret societies like the Golden Dawn, the Ordo Templi Orientis (OTO), and the Rosicrucians are just a few of the many organizations that research, practice, and teach various forms of ritual magic as a way to contact non-terrestrial beings. Many of these groups are offshoots of what is probably the largest one, the Freemasons. The Golden Dawn, the OTO, and the Rosicrucians are all said to be of Masonic origin.

At Camp Hero Army Base at the tip of Long Island, New York, many kinds of magical rituals were performed to invoke beings, energies, and UFOs. The legendary Western occult figure Aleister Crowley is said to have opened a portal in 1918 through a ritual at or near the base. Known as the Amalantrah Working, the ritual fostered contact with Lam, among other beings, an alien entity resembling a Gray. Crowley's act may have allowed UFOs, among other things, to travel to this dimension. It was also an attempt to invoke a mother Goddess known as Babalon in order to infuse a "Scarlet Woman," who would then be impregnated to bring forth a "Moonchild" who would usher in a new age of enlightenment. Crowley wrote about this in his 1917 novel *Moonchild,* saying, "the wish has always been for a Messiah, or Superman."

Crowley inspired many future magicians to try their hand at ritual manifestations of all kinds. He was known to have influenced Navy Intelligence Officer L. Ron Hubbard and rocketry pioneer Jack Parsons. In 1946, they attempted to invoke the same "goddess" energy in an act known as the Babalon Working. However, legend has it that Parsons and Hubbard were not successful, as Crowley was, in closing the portal they had opened. Crowley criticized Parsons, who was likely being manipulated and spied on by Hubbard. For more on this, see *Sex and Rockets: The Occult World of Jack Parsons* (2004) by John Carter and *The Montauk Book of the Dead* (2005) by Peter Moon. Crowley's Moonchild philosophy was also an inspiration to Hitler. (See *Secret Agent 666: Aleister Crowley, British Intelligence and the Occult* [2008] by Richard Spence).

Nazi Occultism

Hitler, with inspiration from Crowley, used two Freemasonic "psychic" societies, the Vril Society and the Thule Society, to contact extraterrestrial beings as early as the late 1920s. The infamous world leader is said to have had a meeting with an alien in 1933, the same year President Roosevelt is alleged to have had one. Controversial author BRANTON, in his classic *The Omega Files: Secret Nazi UFO Bases Revealed* (2000), says,

> Remember that the German secret societies of Bavaria, which had helped to precipitate the first and second world wars, date back to ancient times when—following the occupation of Egypt—the [un]Holy Roman Empire military forces based in Germany, the seat of government for the H.O.R.E, brought back from Egypt the black Gnostic "serpent cults" which later gave rise to the Bavarian Illuminati, the Bavarian Thule Society and a host of other lesser known satanic racist cults which gravitated around these. Could the occultist spies who sabo-

taged the Polaris expedition have been attempting to protect a secret hidden deep within the polar regions? Could this secret have had something to do with an ancient collaboration between Bavarian satanic cults and reptilian-based aliens? Yet, what about the military and strategic option achieved by this strike? Was it wasted resources so far? Today, all historians agree that World War II was not accidentally started but pretty well-planned from at least the early '30s. At least since 1933, incidentally the same year when one of the first "official" treaties between the Grays and Bavarian Intelligence was initiated, no doubt with more than a little help from the secret societies operating there.

The Nazis were reputedly then able to glean pertinent information from their occult rituals that allowed them to build several models of disk-shaped craft. They were supposedly told how to make the advanced flying machines by aliens from the planet Aldebarran.

Hitler is also alleged to have met beings from the inner Earth personally—beings who lived under Tibet. Liaisons from this underground culture moved to Berlin to consult with Hitler about Germany's plans for world domination. These liaisons were known as the Green Society (see "The War for Planet Earth" by Len Kasten, *Atlantis Rising* [November/December 2007]). The movie *Hellboy* (2004) starring Ron Perlman portrays these events.

Alien Energy: UFOs, Ritual Landscapes and the Human Mind (1994) by Andrew Collins (*www.andrewcollins.net*) is the seminal volume of attempts at contact in a variety of situations and settings in Western culture. In many ways, it is comparable to Red Star's *Star Ancestors* (2000), in that it puts forth the idea that

unknown aerial phenomena and other sustained life forms are the outer manifestations of a more primary energy. . . . quantum physicists recognize this energy as the multi-dimensional superforce, or the Unified Field. These atmospheric and ground-based energy forms appear to possess an independent consciousness and intelligence interacting with human mind through archetypal intervention and symbols.

From the data gained from several meditative, ritualistic, and indigenous ceremonies used as a setting for "thought experiments," Collins concludes that these energy forms are connected to ceremonial landscapes, sacred sites, and many of the crop circles studied at Avebury and Silbury Hill in England. Collins has shown conclusively that a human consciousness can interact with these alien life forms by use of their intention—something indigenous peoples around the world have known since time immemorial (see chapter 5).

SETI

The Search for Extraterrestrial Intelligence, or SETI Institute (*www. seti.org*), is a research and education organization whose method of searching for extraterrestrial life is to scan Earth's skies for radio signals, especially in the microwave band, which are thought to be detectable from extraterrestrial civilizations if someone is looking for them.

SETI experiments with radio signals have taken place in several countries since the idea gained momentum in the 1960s—some short-term, some spanning many years. Organizations like NASA's Ames Research Center, NASA Headquarters, the National Science Foundation, the Department of Energy, the U.S. Geological Survey, and the Jet Propulsion Laboratory (JPL) have sponsored projects. "We believe we are conducting the most profound search in human history—to know our beginnings and our place among the stars," says the institute's website. However, the organization has its detractors. Researcher Stanton Friedman is well-known for his media exchanges with SETI senior astronomer Seth Shostak. He calls the organization "the Silly Effort To Investigate."

On the other hand, Alfred Webre notes:

Programs like SETI are starting points for interactive exopolitics....[Its] very existence is a plus for Earth. SETI proves that humanity is at a developmental stage where it can acknowledge interaction with other intelligent civilizations. SETI embodies our first institutional steps to reach out to fellow civilizations in the Universe. These civilizations already know, of course, that we are in enforced isolation. SETI's true significance is that humanity can exhibit rational behavior in outer space.

www.seti.org

CSETI

The Center for the Study of Extraterrestrial Intelligence, or CSETI (*www.cseti.com*), is "dedicated to the furtherance of the understanding of extraterrestrial intelligence." Dr. Steven Greer is its international director and oversees two foundational projects: the Disclosure Project, which has encouraged hundreds of former military, government, and corporate whistle-blowers to come forward to give official testimony to the secret knowledge of the ET presence; and the C5-Initiative, in which formal contact scenarios are cultivated in order to test the possibilities.

CSETI offers training, lectures, and workshops in various methods for contact preparation. Greer has written several books, including *Extraterrestrial Contact: The Evidence and Implications* (1999), *Disclosure: Military and Government Witnesses Reveal the Greatest Secrets in Modern History* (2001), and *Hidden Truth: Forbidden Knowledge* (2006).

ECETI

Enlightened Contact with Extraterrestrial Intelligence, or ECETI (*www.eceti.org*), is a team of paranormal investigators based at James Gilliland's ECETI Ranch in Trout Lake, Washington. The team, including Gilliland, has documented many kinds of ET contact at the ranch. The video archive at the website is immense, chronicling over ten years of video evidence of a variety of sightings, orbs, and other contact experiences.

Among the many techniques taught at the Sattva Sanctuary, also located at the ranch, are Kunlun Nei Gung, Ye Gong, and many other self-mastery techniques geared to prepare people for possible contact. Visitors are welcome on site, with camping and lodging accommodations available, to confirm or deny ECETI's many findings.

Cosmic Contracts

Cosmic contracts are protocols or agreements developed between the inhabitants of Earth and off-planet beings. These agreements, like the ones given below, are meant to regulate the relationships that will result from possible contact.

The Abductee Manifesto and the Declaration of Adherence to Cosmic Law

These documents are both presented in the book *Exopolitics: A Comprehensive Briefing* (2008) by Ed Komarek, a free eBook available at *www.authors.exopaedia.org*. This book is possibly the most complete single-volume work on the subject to date. Komarek offers formalized exopolitical documents like the two mentioned above, as well as a wealth of other information.

The Declaration of Human Sovereignty

This document was developed by the Human Sovereignty Working Group, a network of people committed to humanity's survival and the advancement of human sovereignty, freedom, and self-determination as humanity emerges into the Greater Community of intelligent life. It formally establishes the human race's right to be free from interference from extraterrestrial nations (see *www.humansovereignty.org* and *www.alliesofhumanity.com*).

The Greada Treaty

The Greada Treaty (1954) between Unites States and the Grays was signed by President Eisenhower after he secretly met with extraterrestrials at Edwards Air Force Base using a dental exam as a media cover while on a trip to Palm Springs, California. (See *Omega Files* [2000] by BRANTON and "Origin, Identity and Purpose of MJ-12" by William Cooper.)

Outer Space Security and Development Treaty

The Outer Space Security and Development Treaty of 2011 establishes a framework and procedures to assure that space will be a neutral realm from which all classes of weapons are banned, and from which no hostile action shall be taken toward Earth or the surrounding cosmos. This treaty invites nations to become signatories and invites all parties—including nation states, indigenous nations, and cosmic cultures—to commit to assure and verify that space remains neutral and at peace (see *www.peaceinspace.com*).

Space Law Treaty (UN 1967)

This international treaty binds the United States and the Soviet Union to use outer space only for peaceful purposes. In June 1966, both countries submitted draft treaties on the uses of space to the United Nations. "These were reconciled during several months of negotiation in the Legal Subcommittee of the UN Committee on the Peaceful Uses of Outer Space, and the resulting document was endorsed by the UN General Assembly on December 19, 1966" (*www.oosa.unvienna.org/oosa/SpaceLaw*).

United Nations Decade of Contact Resolution

Advocated by Alfred Webre, this global initiative seeks to establish full disclosure of the ET presence, the implementation of educational programs geared toward contact and awareness, the disarmament of space-based weapons and war in space in general, and diplomacy to act ethically toward ETs already visiting Earth. See Webre's *Towards a Decade of Contact* (2000), an eBook available at *www.exopolitics.com*.

How to Protect Yourself

Most UFO investigators offer practical advice for protection: watching your back, using your rearview mirror, always backing up your documents and other research, developing more than one contingency plan in any given situation, and videotaping your private spaces. I asked James Gilliland if he thought a gun was a good idea for protection and he said, "I don't foresee having to use my shotgun. But it sure feels nice to know that I have one."

It is always smart to know the law as well—know your rights as an individual and be familiar with what authorities can and cannot do lawfully. For example, do the military have the right to shoot trespassers on Area 51 when it is widely known that there are secret operations based there that may have health, economic, and spiritual ramifications for the entire world?

The need for protection can be broken down into five categories: physical, legal/lawful, emotional, mental, and spiritual. Many of you will have your own ideas about how to protect yourselves in these areas. For those who do not, here are a few suggestions.

Physically

Training in some type of martial arts is appropriate if you are investigating UFO phenomena. You don't have to become a master of any specific discipline, but knowing one or two good moves to either subdue or escape from an attacker is important. A basic understanding of punching, kicking, and blocking techniques is useful as well, and at least a familiarity with hand weapons can help get you through many situations. Maintaining your fitness through regular exercise and stretching helps ensure the proper and successful execution of any techniques for self-defense.

Those of you who feel as if you need to carry a gun during an investigation (if you are licensed to carry one) are most probably already aware of the proper use and safety protocols for the firearm of your choice. For those who do not know much about guns and want to learn, check out Appendix E at at the end of this book to get you going.

Legally/Lawfully

Knowing the laws of the land in which you are investigating is very important. In the United States, the language of law is distinctly different from day-to-day usage. The same is true in other countries. If you plan on doing an investigation in a foreign country, always study the common language and the language of that country's legal establishment. Or bring a knowledgeable guide!

Of course, the universal language of law is the language of contracts. And as anyone who has been to a foreign market (or flea market in the United States) can tell you, anything is negotiable. Money talks, as a rule. But a keen understanding of what you want and what the other side needs can be of paramount importance. The negotiation of a contract is truly an art form. For guidance on this, see Brian Blum's *Contracts: Examples and Explanations* (2007), James Allen's *As a Man Thinketh* (1902/2011), and *Uniform Commercial Code in a Nutshell* (2008) by Bradford Stone and Kristen David Adams.

Emotionally

Keeping emotionally centered and knowing that you are emotionally centered at any given time are key skills when doing any investigation.

Handling stress under pressure is not an easy thing to do. Many have found that the varied practices of yoga can help cultivate a calm sense of confidence and well-being. It usually takes months of training for police officers, firefighters, emergency medical technicians (EMTs), and soldiers to learn to move quickly and still be able to think in a calm fashion. The more you train now, the more likely you will be to operate calmly "under fire" later.

Meditation can also help cultivate an acute sensitivity to your internal organs and your body in general. This can be important if you think you may be the target of some type of external bombardment. If you notice subtle changes in your emotions or wild mood swings, these may not be your own. In this case, see *www.us-government-torture.com*.

Mentally

Careful planning and preparation are traits of successful strategists. Staying mentally sharp and realizing if or when you are being lied to, stolen from, or swindled can keep you safe and help you avoid a lot of tricky situations—especially in foreign countries. If you methodically plan each step of an investigation ahead of time, you will be able to imagine possible roadblocks and prepare for them. This is important in foreign countries, where you will have to account for language issues when getting food or fuel, exchanging currency, using the restroom, talking with police officers, or presenting your proper paperwork. It is also important when talking to interviewees. Make a list and check it twice!

Spiritually

Having a thorough understanding of the forces that may affect you or your loved ones or colleagues during an investigation will enable you to prepare properly for any kind of spiritual attack. Stones, power artifacts, talismans, charms, amulets, drawn energetic protective shapes, antidotes, symbols, elements, magical words and phrases, and mantras can all be helpful, depending on the situation and the knowledge and skill of the practitioner.

From a magical standpoint, things like sage, sea salt, and white garments can offer protection from malevolent beings and/or entities. Certain kinds of stones—hematite, black tourmaline, lapis lazuli—are thought to impede negative energy. In terms of your ritualistic technique, it is always proper to follow protocol. Always erect a protective shape—most commonly a circle—especially in the event of an intentional contact by an entity. *Celtic Traditions: Druids, Faeries and Wiccan Rituals* (2000) by Sirona Knight gives a wide variety of ritual magical lore.

Appendix A:
The Field
Investigator's Kit

Adapted from Raymond Fowler and Chuck Reever's MUFON *Field Investigator's Manual*. Reprinted courtesy of MUFON.

MUFON divides its field kit into three equipment categories: necessary, desirable, and optional.

Necessary Items

- MUFON photo identification card (not expired)
- MUFON *Field Investigator's Manual*
- MUFON questionnaire forms
- sample containers (plastic zip-lock bags)
- tape measure (100 foot) and ruler

- compass

- flashlight (with extra batteries)

- headlamp

- clipboard or three-ring notebook

- pencils, pens, or permanent markers

- tweezers

- area maps or computer mapping capability

- magnifying glass

- string

- tarp, tent, and stakes

- knife/Leatherman (multi-purpose tool)

- star finder or computer astronomy program

- small garden trowel, shovel

- digital and film cameras

- calculator

- digital audio recorder

- binoculars (with image stabilization)

- disposable polyethylene gloves

- color chart

- first aid kit

- inclinometer or plastic protractor

- insect repellent

Desirable Items

- video camera (hi-def if possible)
- digital camera (6 megapixels or higher)
- several 100-foot chalk lines
- camera tripod/monopod
- paraffin or plaster of Paris
- laptop computer
- personal business or MUFON calling cards
- GPS unit
- FRS/GMRS radios
- cell phone

Optional Items

- Geiger counter
- magnetometer
- police-radio monitor, where legally permitted
- camera light meter
- laser range finder
- ground penetrometer
- pocket weather meter
- night-vision goggles/binoculars

Guidelines for Choosing
and Maintaining Your Equipment

- Equipment should fit into one large or two small carrying bags.

- Some equipment is multi-functional; for example, a GMRS radio can also function as a GPS. Avoid duplication.

- A compass may be useful for detecting magnetic fields. Some compasses have an inclinometer or clinometer (to measure angles of slope, elevation, or depression with respect to gravity) built into the unit. A magnetometer is more sensitive, but it is also more expensive.

- Cameras and computers must be carefully packed for transport.

- If you are traveling by air, only pack the essentials. Contact your state director (or other state director, if you are out of state) to acquire the rest of the equipment you need.

See *The UFO Investigator's Handbook: The Practical Guide to Researching, Identifying, and Documenting Unexplained Sightings* (1999) by Craig Glenday for more tips on proper equipment for investigations, as well as *The UFO Handbook: A Guide to Investigating, Evaluating, and Reporting UFO Sightings* by Allan Hendry.

Appendix B:
Characteristics
of an Abductee

There are many personality and behavior traits which can indi-cate that a person has possibly been abducted by aliens. In 1984, researchers Wendelle C. Stevens and A. J. Gevaerd made an early attempt to catalogue the basic personality traits common among alleged UFO abductees/contactees in their book, *UFO Abduction at Maringa*. This short list of seven traits—which includes such attributes as being honest, humble, a dedicated worker, family-oriented, not particularly religious, not formally educated, and seeing themselves as a part of nature—was expanded to include a trait-comparison chart in Rodolfo R. Casellato, Joao Valeria da Silva, and Wendelle Stevens's 1985 book, *UFO Abduction at Botucatu.*

A major evolution in the traits list came in 2002 when the Sci-Fi Channel (today the Syfy Channel) initiated a Roper UFO Poll. As a part of the poll, researcher/contactee Melinda Leslie compiled a much more detailed list of abductee traits. Richard D. Butler's Abduction Classification System was also included as a part of this poll. Leslie's revised and expanded abductee traits list and Butler's classification system together make for a valuable cache of knowledge for the researcher/investigator.

But Leslie admitted that there was another contactee/abductee questionnaire even more comprehensive than hers. As of July of 2012, Leslie said that contactee Nadine Lalich's "Questionnaire to Evaluate Possible ET Contact," located at her alien abduction self-help website *www.alienexperiences.com*, is the most up-to-date list available.

Below you will find three seminal contributions to the study of abductee research:

- Wendelle C. Stevens and A. J. Gevaerd's Abductee Profile

- Richard D. Butler's Abduction Classification System

- Nadine Lalich's "Questionnaire to Evaluate Possible ET Contact"

Wendelle C. Stevens and A. J. Gevaerd's Abductee Profile[1]

In 1984, Wendelle C. Stevens and A. J. Gevaerd compiled this list of traits of an abductee. It is one of the earlier known attempts to make sense of the alien abduction phenomena.

1. He is usually honest and sincere, both with himself and his friends. He is very trustworthy and reliable in all respects.

2. He is a dedicated worker but seeks no recognition for himself. He seeks no honors or prestige in his society.

---

1 Excerpted from *UFO Abduction at Maringa: The AGRIPO Experiment* by A. J. Gevaerd and Wendelle C. Stevens (196–197). Reprinted courtesy of UFO Photo Archives Publishing, *www.UFOPhotoArchives.com*.

3. He is a good and reliable family man and usually quite patriotic to his community and country, having high ideals about the future of his society.

4. He is not particularly religious in a secular sense but is especially devoted to his Creator and nature inside of himself. He respects all existence at all levels and does not take the life of lesser creatures without good reason.

5. He is not highly educated in a formal sense, leaving less to be "trained back out" of his mind when he is awakened to the greater realities, but he does have an excellent practical mind and is basically "self-taught."

6. He lives at a humble station in life, preferring to work hard for his sustenance rather than leaching off of his society without proper contribution to it. He never cheats at anything, realizing that such acts are really cheating self.

7. He sees himself in every aspect of nature and creation and seeks to contribute to it.

Richard D. Butler's Abduction Experience Classification

Richard D. Butler devised the following system to provide a standard of classification in abduction research.

[AE-1] Lucid Dream

This is a lucid dream experience generated internally by the subject's subconscious. There is no human/ET interaction at any level. They are usually grandiose in nature and lack a logical progression.

[AE-2] Techno/Telepathic Lucid Dream

This is a lucid dream experience, internally generated by external forces. It is ET in origin and accomplished by technologically enhanced psychic intrusion of the subject's subconscious. The subject reports the disassociation, or collapse, of a normal dream and the insertion of a scenario or message that enhances certain ideals or beliefs. If the subject awakens immediately after, they report a circle of glowing whitish colored energy on the ceiling, approximately 2 to 3 feet in diameter, with a shaft of the same energy slowly retracting back into the circle. This shaft is approximately 3 to 6 inches in diameter and 2.5 to 4 feet long.

[AE-3] Psy/Bio Energy Field Extraction

This experience involves the extraction of a conscious energy field from the subject's body. It should not be confused with naturally occurring OOBE phenomena, as separation is externally induced. The technology employs the use of a white or bluish-white colored extraction beam. Subjects describe a feeling of deep penetration of this beam throughout their body, followed by the sensation of an irresistible or attractive force. The extracted field maintains cohesion, and is capable of perceiving stimuli at a greatly enhanced level. Perceptions include 360-degree sight and sensory feedback at the molecular, and even atomic, level. Experiences seem to focus around communications and reinsertion of the bio-field into a humanoid body other than the original. It is this type of abduction that accounts for the severe missing-time memory failure in some cases.

Since the subject's brain is not physically present, the memories are not hard-written. There does appear to be a shadow memory effect that can retain the memories of the events in some type of energy memory matrix, within the subject's bio-field. Full understanding of this process could lead to breakthroughs in education and learning technologies.

[AE-4] Physical Abduction

This is the physical removal of a subject from their environment to an ET environment. The subject is first tranquilized to reduce possible injury to either side. These abductions follow a very strict military-like protocol. Subjects are transported via a small shuttle, lifting beam, or direct transfer. Direct transfer utilizes a hyper-dimensional tunnel. It will appear as a large brilliant white energy gate. The subject steps through the gate and is instantly aboard the craft. Also reported is the nullification of the nuclear repulsive forces in solid objects. This allows the subject to pass through solid objects physically. Once onboard, the person is subjected to various physical tests and procedures. The main thrust is in the genetic experimentation area. Reports of sperm and ovum extraction are quite common. After these procedures are performed, the subject is returned unharmed to their original location. A screen memory is then inserted into the subject's subconscious. This slightly shifts the reality recalled by the abductee, but never erases the event entirely. This distinguishes them from [AE-3].

[AE-5] Past Life Recall

These experiences are the least reported and the most interesting, in terms of their implications. They appear to represent events in the experience of an ET life form. Subjects relate being in an underground military facility, sometimes on Mars or the moon, and even under the Earth's oceans.

Memories of being onboard a spacecraft and other ET environments are also recalled. What is so interesting is that the subject views this, not from an Earth human perspective, but from that of an ET. This suggests two very interesting possibilities: (a) During telepathic communication some memories are subconsciously transferred; (b) The subject is recalling actual past life memories of their own. This second possibility opens the door to much speculation. It suggests that part of the abduction phenomena may be a massive and covert reconnaissance operation. It may also explain why the Grays have said they have the right to do what they do. If abductees are souls that have been transferred from the ET environment to Earth, then technically they are not abducting human beings but volunteer ETs.

Nadine Lalich's "Questionnaire to Evaluate Possible ET Contact"[2]

1. Do you secretly feel you are special or chosen?

2. Do you have a strong sense of having a mission or important task to perform, without knowing where this compulsion comes from?

3. Do you have a cosmic awareness, an interest in the environment and the issues affecting the Earth and all life forms, in becoming a vegetarian, or have you become very socially conscious?

4. Do you frequently think about or dream about disasters or Earth changes such as quakes or floods, with the conviction that they will happen?

5. Do you have dreams where superior beings, angels, or aliens are educating you about humanity, the universe, global changes or future events?

Fears

1. Do you secretly fear being accosted or kidnapped if you do not constantly monitor your surroundings?

---

2 Reprinted from *www.alienexperiences.com* with permission from Nadine Lalich.

2. Are you now or have you ever been afraid of your closet, and what might come out of it?

3. Have you frequently found yourself repeatedly checking throughout your home before you go to bed at night?

4. Have you installed or seriously considered installing a security system for your home, even if there was no justification?

5. Do you have an abnormal fear of the dark?

6. Do you feel fear or anxiety over the subject of aliens or UFOs?

7. Do you feel as if you are being watched frequently, especially at night?

8. As a child or adult, have you seen faces or beings near you while in bed that were not explainable?

9. Do you have a fear of looking into the eyes of animals, or have you ever dreamed of looking closely into the eyes of animals, such as owls or deer?

10. Do you have strong reactions to discussions about or pictures of aliens?

11. Do you have inexplicably strong phobias of particular sights or sounds, heights, insects, bright lights, your personal security, or being alone?

12. Do you have the feeling that you are not supposed to talk about encounters with alien beings, or that you should not talk about the beings themselves?

13. Do you have trouble sleeping through the night for reasons you cannot explain?

14. Do you wake up frequently at the same time each night?

15. Do you have a sleep disorder or suffer from insomnia?

16. Have you ever awoken in the middle of the night startled, feeling as though you have just dropped onto your bed?

17. Do you feel you have to sleep with your bed against a wall in order to feel safe, or sleep in some other peculiar manner to be comfortable?

18. Do you wake up by hearing a loud noise, but fail to get up to investigate and, instead, fall back into a deep sleep?

19. Do you ever hear popping or buzzing sounds, or any other unusual sounds or physical sensations, upon waking or going to sleep?

20. Have you seen a hooded figure in or near your home or next to your bed at night?

21. Have you experienced a sudden, overwhelming desire to go to sleep when you had not planned to?

22. Have you awoken in the morning or in the middle of the night to find yourself in a different location in your home, in a different position in your bed, or wearing different clothing from when you went to sleep?

Memory and Dreams

23. Do you have a conscious memory or a dream of flying through the air or being outside your body?

24. Do you dream about seeing UFOs, being inside a spaceship, or interacting with UFO occupants?

25. As a child or teenager, was there a special place you secretly believed held a spiritual meaning just for you?

26. Do you have dreams of being chased by animals?

27. Do you have an obsessive memory that will not go away, such as seeing an alien face or a strange baby, or an examination table or needles?

28. Have you had dreams of passing through a closed window or a solid wall?

29. Have you had dreams of nonhuman doctors or strange medical procedures?

30. Do you have memories that you suspect may not have happened the way you recall them?

Observations

31. Does your home have unexplainable sounds, apparitions, or unusual events that have been attributed to ghosts?

32. Do you have a strong interest in and a compulsion to read about the subject of UFO sightings or aliens, or a strong aversion toward the subject?

33. Do you sometimes hear a very high-pitched noise in one or both ears?

34. Have you ever seen a UFO in the sky or close to you (within a short walking or driving distance)?

35. If you have seen a UFO, were you strongly compelled to walk, drive, or stand near it, follow it, or call out to it? Have you felt its occupants were particularly aware of you?

36. Have you ever seen someone with you become paralyzed, motionless, or frozen in time, especially someone with whom you sleep?

37. Do you recall having a special, secret playmate or playmates as a child?

38. Have you had electronics around you go haywire or oddly malfunction with no explanation (such as street lights going out as you walk under them, TVs and radios affected as you move closer, etc.)?

39. Do you frequently see multiple digits, such as 111 or 444, or other repeating number patterns, on clocks, digital displays, or in any other setting?

40. Have you seen balls of light or flashes of light in your home or other locations?

41. Has someone in your life witnessed a ship or alien near you, or claimed you were missing for a period of time?

42. Have you seen a strange fog or haze in one area that is not due to weather and that should not be there?

43. Have you heard strange humming or pulsing sounds around you or coming toward you for which you could not identify the source?

44. Have you been suddenly compelled to drive or walk to an out-of-the-way or isolated area, without knowing why you feel compelled to do it?

Physical and Emotional Symptoms

45. Have you ever had nosebleeds or found blood stains on your pillow for unexplainable reasons?

46. Do you frequently have sinus trouble or migraine head-aches?

47. Have you had X-rays or other procedures reveal foreign objects lodged in your body that cannot be explained?

48. Have you been medically diagnosed with any of the following conditions: chronic fatigue syndrome, sleep disorder resulting from a traumatic brain injury (TBI), Gulf War syndrome, fibromyalgia, Myofascial pain syndrome [muscle pain], Epstein-Barr virus, or another immune disorder?

49. Have you woken up with sore muscles, without having exercised or strained before going to sleep?

50. Have you ever felt paralyzed in your bed or at home for no apparent reason?

51. Have you found unusual scars, marks, or bruises on your body with no possible explanation as to how you received them? (E.g., a small scoop-shaped indentation; a straight

line scar; a pattern of pinprick marks; scars on the roof of your mouth, in your nose, or behind one ear; triangular bruises or fingertip-sized bruises on the inside of your thigh)?

52. Have you had paranormal or psychic experiences, including frequent flashes of intuition?

53. Have you ever felt as though you had received telepathic messages from somewhere?

54. Men and women: Have you had frequent urinary tract infections?

55. Has your drug or alcohol use changed significantly one way or the other?

56. Do you have an unusual fear of doctors, hospitals, or needles, or do you tend to avoid medical treatment?

57. Do you have frequent or sporadic headaches, especially in the sinus, behind one eye, or in one ear?

58. For women only: Have you had false pregnancy or a verified pregnancy that disappeared within two or three months?

59. For women only: Have you had frequent female problems and reproductive difficulties?

Appendix C: Close Encounter Classification System

Aclose encounter is defined as a UFO that comes within 500 feet of the witness or observer. The distance from the observer is important for several reasons: The closer you are, the more likely you are to see greater detail of the object or phenomenon; distance from an object helps to ascertain its size and other reference points; and distance from an object can often determine how safe from physical, emotional, or mental harm you may be.

Dr. Joseph Allen Hynek divided these close-range sightings into three categories:

- Close Encounters of the First Kind—Simple observation.

- Close Encounters of the Second Kind—Sightings where the observed anomaly affects the environment or the witness in some physical way that lasts beyond the actual experience.

- Close Encounters of the Third Kind—These encounters, made famous by Steven Spielberg's 1977 film, are categorized as sightings of "animate beings" (Hynek's careful wording) in association with a UFO sighting.

After these categories were accepted—and without the blessing of the man who had put so much work into creating them—UFO researchers added two more classifications. Sometime in the late 1980s, abduction researchers came up with Close Encounters of the Fourth Kind, which involved UFO abductions. And in the 1990s, Steven Greer's CSETI group created the most recent addition to Hynek's original three categories—Close Encounters of the Fifth Kind, in which successful communication takes place with an extraterrestrial being or species.

Researcher Jacques Vallée built from the CE I–V system and incorporated three other useful areas of classification and sub-classification for far-distant observations and witness credibility. These so-called anomalous events (AE 1–5) are far-distant observations that are divided into two groups: Maneuvers (MA) and Fly-bys (FB) (see table 2). Witness credibility is determined with the SVP credibility rating system. The five categories of anomalous events are explained as follows:

- AE 1 events are anomalies like amorphous lights or unexplained explosions in the sky that do not have lasting physical effects.

- AE 2 reports involve lasting physical effects—poltergeist phenomena, anomalous photographs, flattened grass, or "apports."

- AE 3 cases are anomalies with associated entities. This could involve reports of ghosts or yetis, or other instances of cryptozoology—sometimes even elves or spirits.

- AE 4 designates those anomalous reports in which witnesses describe personal interaction with entities in the reality of the entities themselves. This includes near-death experiences, claims of religious visions, and some cases of out-of-body experiences.

- AE 5 describes the cases in which anomalous injuries or deaths are reported, like unexplained wounds or spontaneous combustion. Claims of permanent healings also fit in this category.

Maneuver categories are explained as follows:

- MA 1 gathers those observations that involve an object with a discontinuous trajectory—a drop, a maneuver, a hovering stop, or a loop.

- MA 2 includes those cases that give rise to physical effects in addition to a discontinuity in trajectory. For instance, an official French report described an object that hovered close to a photocell, triggering an extinction of the town's street-lighting system.

- MA 3 contains the cases of objects with discontinuous trajectories when beings are observed on board.

- MA 4 covers instances of maneuvers accompanied by a sense of transformation of reality for the percipient.

- MA 5 involves reports of permanent injury or death related to a maneuvering object in the sky.

The Fly-by categories are explained as follows:

- FB 1 is a simple sighting of an unexplained object "flying by" in the sky without discontinuity. It is the most frequently reported category.

- FB 2 involves cases of fly-by with physical evidence—a recorded sound or radar tracking, for example.

- FB 3 gathers cases of fly-by in which the report of an object is accompanied by the observation of beings on board. Although rare, this type of sighting is occasionally reported.

- FB 4 represents a fly-by in connection with which the witnesses claim they have undergone a transformation of reality.

- FB 5 has to do with cases in which witnesses of a fly-by suffer serious injuries, as in the well-documented Cash-Landrum medical incident near Houston, Texas, in which two women and a boy were hurt as an unexplained, very bright object flew above them without stopping.

These four major categories (AE 1-5, CE 1-5 system, the MA/FB classifications, and the SVP Credibility Rating system discussed below) work together to comprise a very simple system of twenty codes that are easy to remember and easy to handle statistically, since very little overlap can occur among the categories. An additional benefit for the analyst of this behavior-based classification system is the fact that certain hypotheses to explain the observations are specific to each category. For instance, FB events should be examined for explanations involving meteors or airplanes, which are unlikely to apply in CE cases.

The SVP Credibility Rating System

The first letter of this acronym, "S," indicates the reliability of the source. The second letter, "V," indicates whether or not a site visit took place. The third letter, "P," indicates the probability of natural explanations. Each letter is a placeholder for a rating on a five-point scale.

To rate the reliability of the source:

- 0 means an unknown or unreliable source.

- 1 means a report attributed to a source of unknown reliability.

- 2 means a report from a credible source, but secondhand.

- 3 means a report from a credible firsthand source.

- 4 means a report of a firsthand personal interview with the witness, by a source of proven reliability.

To rate the likelihood of a site visit:

- 0 means there was no site visit, or the answer is unknown.

- 1 means a visit by a casual person unfamiliar with such phenomena.

- 2 means a site visit by a personal familiar with the range of phenomena.

- 3 means a site visit by a reliable investigator with some experience.

- 4 means a site visit by a skilled analyst.

To rate the probability of natural explanations:

- 0 means the data is consistent with one or more natural causes.

- 1 means a natural explanation only requires slight alteration of the data.

- 2 means a natural explanation would demand gross alteration of one parameter.

- 3 means a natural explanation demands gross alteration of several parameters.

- 4 means no natural explanation is possible, given the evidence.

Thus a rating of 222 or better (meaning that each of the three digits is 2 or higher) indicates an event reported through a reliable source, in which a site visit has been made, and where a natural explanation would require the gross alteration of at least one parameter. Equipped with this reliability code and the classifications described above, it is possible to start making sense of the patterns extracted from the mass of unusual aerial phenomena reports.

Table 2. Categories of Sightings

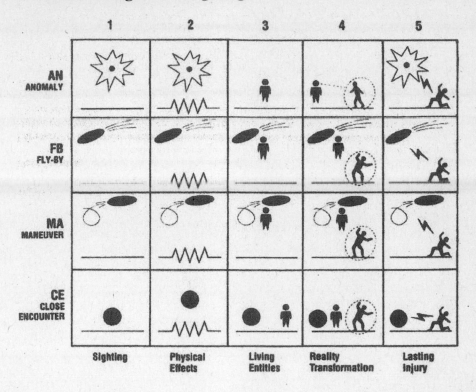

Appendix D:
MUFON Code of Ethics

Since there is no standard code of ethics for the field of ufology, we must look to other professions and their formalized ethical codes. MUFON offers these quick ethical guidelines at *www.mufon.com*:

- Be objective and dispassionate.

- Be honest—make full disclosure to witnesses about the use of any information gathered.

- Always protect your witness. There is a fine line between pushing too hard for information and respecting your source.

- Always solicit investigative help from licensed professionals—a licensed hypnotist, for example.

- Always fully disclose your right to publish any gathered information in the *MUFON Journal*.

Appendix E:
Sources Used in
Writing This Book

Organizations

Center for Physical Trace Research (CPTR) *www.angelfire.com/mo/cptr*

Center for UFO Studies (CUFOS) *www.cufos.org*

Citizens Against UFO Secrecy (CAUS)
www.v-j-enterprises.com/caus.html

Fund for UFO Research (FUFOR) *www.fufor.com*

International UFO Museum and Research Center *www.iufomrc.com*

Mutual UFO Network (MUFON) *www.mufon.com*

National Aviation Reporting Center on Anomalous Phenomena
(NARCAP) *www.narcap.org*

National Investigations Committee on Aerial Phenomena (NICAP) *www.nicap.org*

National UFO Center, NUFOC *www.nufoc.net*

National UFO Reporting Center (NUFORC) *www.nuforc.org*

National UFO Reporting Center *www.ufocenter.com*

Paradigm Research Group (PRG) *www.paradigmresearchgroup.org*

Project 1947 (UFO history) *www.project1947.com*

The Anomalist *www.anomalist.com*

Truckers UFO Reporting Center (TUFORC) *www.tuforc.com*

UFO Investigators Network (UFOIN) Committee for Scientific Investigation of the Paranormal *www.csicop.org*

UFO Links Page *www.ufoinfo.com/ufolink.shtml*

UFO Research Coalition (URC) *www.ufoscience.org*

UFO Research Resources *www.hyper.net/ufo/resources.html*

U.S. Government Sites

Central Intelligence Agency (CIA) *www.cia.gov/*

Defense Intelligence Agency (DIA) *www.dia.mil/*

Department of Defense (DOD) *www.defense.gov/faq/pis/16.html*

FBI FOIA requests *foia.fbi.gov*

Federal Bureau of Investigation (FBI) *www.fbi.gov/*

Kennedy Space Center Visitor Complex *www.kennedyspacecenter.com*

NASA Headquarters *www.hq.nasa.gov*

National Security Agency (NSA) *www.nsa.gov/*

NSA Freedom of Information Act (FOIA) requests
www.nsa.gov/public_info/foia/

Media

Fate Magazine *www.fatemag.com*

Flying Saucer Review (FSR) *www.fsr.org.uk/*

Fortean Times *www.forteantimes.com*

Saucer Smear (UFO Journal) *www.martiansgohome.com/smear*

UFO (United Kingdom edition) *www.ufomagazine.co.uk*

UFO Magazine (Brazil edition) *www.ufo.com.br*

UFO Magazine (United States edition) *www.ufomag.com*

UFO Monthly Magazine *www.ufomonthlymagazine.co.uk*

Internet Resources

www.2012hoax.org/jaysen-q-rand

www.4dreamland.com

www.abduct.com

www.abductedbyaliensthebook.com

www.abductionsite.com

www.abovetopsecret.com

www.acern.com.au

www.accuweather.com

www.adventuresunlimited.com

www.affs.org

www.afu.info

www.alienabductions.com

www.aliendave.com/uufoh_theranch.html

www.alienexperiences.com

www.alienscalpel.com

www.allabouttheoccult.org

www.alliesofhumanity.org

www.altereddimensions.net/places/SkinwalkerRanch.aspx

www.amervets.com

www.amorc.org

www.anndruffel.com

www.anneller.com

www.anomalies-unlimited.com/Bases.html

www.anomalistbooks.com

www.area51.org

www.area51zone.com

www.ashtarcommand.org

www.astronautics.com

www.atlantisrising.com

www.auforn.com

www.backtobentwaters.blogspot.com

www.badastronomy.com/bad/tv/foxapollo.html

www.beatthecourt.com

www.beginnersguide2guns.com

www.bermuda-triangle.org

www.Bielek.com

www.Bielek-debunked.com

www.biomindsuperpowers.com/Pages/2.html

www.bufora.org.uk

www.cafr1.com

www.canadianuforeport.com

www.carlotto.us

www.cefora.com.ar

www.channeling.net

www.cisfo.org/OMIFO.htm

www.cisu.org

www.coasttocoastam.com

www.cobeps.org

www.cohenufo.org

www.conspiracyjournal.com

www.coolmagnetman.com/magmeter.htm

www.coopradio.org

www.creditorsincommerce.com

www.cropcircleresearch.com

www.cropcircles.cc

www.cropcircles.org

www.cryptomundo.com

www.cufos.org

www.danwei.org

www.davidicke.com

www.dccs.org

www.dcsi.net/~bluesky

www.dhs.gov/index.shtm

www.diannerobbins.com

www.drboylan.com

www.dreamlandresort.com

www.earthacupuncture.info/earth_grid.htm

www.earthfiles.com

www.eceti.org

www.edgarcayce.org

www.einhornpress.com/ancientworldhistoryandpictures.aspx

www.enterprisemission.com/

www.esotericguide.com

www.examiner.com/exopolitics-in-seattle

www.exopolitics.com

www.exopolitics.org

www.experiment-resources.com/cognitive-dissonance-experiment.html

www.extra_terrerstrial_association.webs.com

www.farahyurdozu.com

www.floweroflife.org

www.frontsight.com

www.galacticdiplomacy.com

www.galactic-server.com

www.galactic-server.net

www.galdepress.com

www.gaussmeter.info/dc-gauss.html

www.goodtherapy.org/famous-psychologists/daryl-bem.html

www.grahamhancock.com

www.haarp.alaska.edu

www.haarp.net

www.hdrusers.com

www.hermetic.com

www.history.com

www.hyper.net/ufo

www.icrl.org.

inexplicata.blogspot.com

www.integretron.com

www.interdimensionalphotography.com

www.irva.org

www.iwasabducted.com

www.jacquesvallee.net

www.jerrypippin.com

www.joetourist.ca/traveltips/hazards.htm

www.johnemackinstitute.org

www.johnkeel.com

www.johntitor.com

www.jpl.nasa.gov

www.karlaturner.org

www.keyholepublishing.com

www.lasvegasnow.com

www.learnrv.com

www.lighttechnology.com

www.livinginthelightms.com

www.magneticsciences.com

www.majiceyesonly.com

www.merkaba.org

www.metaresearch.org

www.mindreality.com/ufos-and-aliens-are-higher-dimensional-beings

www.monroeinstitute.org

www.moonconnection.com/

www.nancyredstar.com

www.nasa.gov

www.navsea.navy.mil/nuwc/

www.naziufos.com

www.newworldintegrations.com

www.nexusmagazine.com

www.nickpope.net

www.norad.mil/about/cmoc.html

www.nrahq.org/education

www.nrl.navy.mil/clementine

www.nws.noaa.gov

www.occultopedia.com

www.oceanservice.noaa.gov/facts/bermudatri.html

www.onr.navy.mil

www.openminds.tv

opus501.org

www.oto-usa.org/crowley.html

www.ourhollowearth.com

www.ovni.net

www.paranormal.about.com

www.pauldevereux.co.uk

www.phoenixsciencefoundation.org

www.planetxvideo.com

prestondennett.weebly.com

www.probablefuture.com

www.projectcamalot.org/schneider.html

www.psychicinvestigators.net

www.rendalsham-incident.co.uk

www.reptilianagenda.com

www.reptoids.com

www.returnofplanet-x.com

www.roc.noaa.gov/WSR88D

www.roswellbooks.com

www.roswellrods.com

www.saintgermainfoundation.org

www.sanandaseagles.com

www.science.com

science.discovery.com

www.science.howstuffworks.com/ufo-psychology.htm

www.sciencedaily.com

www.selfascension.com

www.self-realization.com

www.sherryshriner.com

www.skybooksusa.com

www.soneya.net

www.spacetimetravel.org

www.spiritual-endeavors.org

www.stantonfriedman.com

www.startinglinks.net/cydoniaufo/11.htm

www.strangemag.com

www.subterraneanbases.com

www.suomenufotutkijat.fi

www.superstringtheory.com

www.survival-goods.com

www.tactrainers.com

www.temple.edu/history/jacobs

www.teslasociety.com

www.theAnunnakiwillreturn.tumblr.com

www.the-bermuda-triangle.com

www.theblackvault.com

www.thelivingmoon.com

www.theoccultnetwork.com

www.thewatcherfiles.com/eisenhower.html

www.theyfly.com

www.think-aboutit.com/Omega/files

time-travelers.org/excerpts.htm

www.timetravelinstitute.com

traveltips.usatoday.com

www.tsl.org

www.ufo.com.br

www.ufo-blogger.com

www.ufocasebook.com

www.ufocongress.com

www.ufocongressstore.com

www.ufodigest.com

www.ufoencounters.co.uk

www.ufoevidence.org

ufohypotheses.com

www.ufoinfo.com

www.ufomag.com

www.ufomaps.com

www.ufomind.com

www.ufomystic.com

www.ufonesia.wordpress.com

www.ufonut.com

www.ufophotoarchives.com

www.ufopop.org

uforeview.tripod.com

www.uforth.com

www.ufos.about.com

www.ufos-aliens.co.uk

www.ufos-co.de

www.ufoseek.com

www.ufoshows.com

www.ufoskeptic.org

www.ufotv.com

www.ufovideo.net/UFODVDS.htm

www.ufoweek.com

www.unexplainedstuff.com

www.usbr.gov/pmts/conveyance/tunnels/tdata.html

www.ushmm.org

www.vortexmaps.com

www.werewolves.com/the-creepy-tale-of-skinwalker-ranch/

www.wilhelmreichmuseum.org

www.williamhenry.com

www.world-famous.com

www.world-mysteries.com/sci_6.htm

www.wovoca.com

www.yogajournal.com

www.yowusa.com

Books

Adamski, George and Desmond Leslie. *Flying Saucers Have Landed* (1953)

Adamski, George. *Inside the Spaceships* (1955)

Allen, D. S. and J. B. Delair *Cataclysm! Compelling Evidence of a Cosmic Catastrophe in 9500 B.C.* (1995)

Allen, James. *As a Man Thinketh* (1902/2011)

Andrews, Colin and Pat Delgado. *Circular Evidence: A Detailed Investigation of the Flattened Swirled Crops Phenomena* (1989)

Angelucci, Orfeo M. *Secrets of the Saucers* (1955)

——————. *Son of the Sun* (1959)

Arguelles, Jose. *The Mayan Factor: Path beyond Technology* (1987)

Arnold, Kenneth and Ray Palmer. *The Coming of the Saucers* (1952)

Atwater, F. Holmes. *Captain of My Ship, Master of My Soul* (2001)

Babcock, Edward J. *UFOs around the World* (1966)

Bach, Egon W. *"UFOs" from the Volcanoes* (1993)

Barker, Gray. *They Knew Too Much about Flying Saucers* (1956)

Barnes, Tom. *The Hurricane Hunters and Lost in the Bermuda Triangle* (2007)

Beckley, Timothy Green and Sean Casteel. *MJ-12 and The Riddle of Hangar 18: The New Evidence* (2003)

Beckley, Timothy Green, ed. *Pioneers of Space—The Long Lost Book of George Adamski: A Trip to the Moon, Mars and Venus* (2010)

——————. *Mystery of the Men in Black: The UFO Silencers* (1990)

—————. *Subterranean Worlds inside Earth* (1992)

—————. *The American Indian UFO–Starseed Connection* (1992)

—————. *Book of Space Brothers* (1969)

—————. *The Conspiracy Summit Dossier: Whistle Blower's Guide to the Strangest and Most Bizarre Cosmic and Global Conspiracies!* (2009)

—————. *The Smoky God and Other Inner Earth Mysteries* (1996)

—————. *Underground Alien Bio Lab at Dulce—Bennewitz UFO Papers* (2009)

Begich, Nick and Jeane Manning. *Angels Don't Play This Haarp: Advances in Tesla Technology* (1995)

Behrendt, Kenneth. *Secrets of UFO Technology* (2007)

Bender, Albert K. *Flying Saucers and the Three Men* (1963)

Berlitz, Charles and William L. Moore. *The Philadelphia Experiment: Project Invisibility* (1979)

Berlitz, Charles. *The Bermuda Triangle* (1974)

—————. *The Dragon's Triangle* (1989)

Bernard, Raymond. *Hollow Earth: The Greatest Geographical Discovery in History* (1969)

Bethurum, Truman. *Aboard a Flying Saucer* (1954)

Birnes, Bill and George Noory. *Worker in the Light: Unlock Your Five Senses and Liberate Your Limitless Potential* (2008)

Birnes, Bill and Harold Burt. *Unsolved UFO Mysteries* (2000)

Birnes, Bill. *Journey to the Light: Find Your Spiritual Self and Enter into a World of Infinite Opportunity* (2009)

—————. *The Day after Roswell: A Former Pentagon Official Reveals the U.S. Government's Shocking UFO Cover-up* (1988)

—————. *The UFO Magazine Encyclopedia: The Most Comprehensive Single-Volume UFO Reference in Print* (2004)

Bishop, Greg. *Project Beta: The Story of Paul Bennewitz, National Security, and the Creation of the Modern UFO Myth* (2005)

Blum, Brian. *Contracts: Examples and Explanations* (2007)

Boirayon, Marius. *Solomon Island Mysteries: Accounts of Giants and UFOs in the Solomon Islands* (2009)

Boylan, Richard. *Close Extraterrestrial Encounters* (1994)

—————. *Labored Journey to the Stars* (1996)

—————. *Project Epiphany* (1997)

—————. *Star Kids: The Emerging Cosmic Generation* (2005)

Bramley, William. *The Gods of Eden: A New Look at Human History* (1989)

BRANTON (Bruce Alan Walton). *Nazi Flying Disks of the German V-7 Development Program.*

—————. *The Omega Files: Secret Nazi UFO Bases Revealed* (2000)

—————. *The Dulce Wars: Underground Alien Bases and the Battle for Planet Earth* (1999)

Brookesmith, Peter. *UFO: The Complete Sightings* (1995)

Bruce, Alexandra. *The Philadelphia Experiment Murder* (2001)

Burt, Harold. *Flying Saucers 101* (2000)

Canada, Steve. *Alien End of Days in 2010* (2009)

—————. *Bible Encoded Crop Circle Gods* (2006)

Cardenal, Ernesto. *Golden UFOs: The Indian Poems* (1992)

Carter, John. *Sex and Rockets: the Occult World of Jack Parsons* (2004)

Casellato, Rodolfo R., Joao Valeria da Silva, and Wendelle C. Stevens. *UFO Abduction at Botucatu* (1985)

Cathie, Bruce. *The Energy Grid* (1990)

———. *The Harmonic Conquest of Space* (1998)

Chamish, Barry. *Return of the Giants* (1999)

Cheney, Margaret. *Tesla: Man Out of Time* (1981)

Childress, David Hatcher. *Anti-Gravity and the World Grid* (1987)

———. *Technology of the Gods: The Incredible Sciences of the Ancients* (2000)

———. *The Time Travel Handbook: A Manual of Practice Teleportation and Time Travel* (1999)

Clark, Jerome. *Encyclopedia of Strange and Unexplained Physical Phenomena* (1993)

———. *Strange Skies: Pilot Encounters with UFOs* (2003)

———. *The UFO Book: Encyclopedia of the Extraterrestrial* (1997)

———. *Unexplained! Strange Sightings, Incredible Occurrences, and Puzzling Physical Phenomena* (2003)

———. *Unnatural Phenomena: A Guide to the Bizarre Wonders of North America* (2005)

Coleman, Loren and Jerome Clark. *Cryptozoology from A to Z* (1999)

Coleman, Loren and Patrick Huyghe. *The Field Guide to Lake Monsters, Sea Serpents, and Other Denizens of the Deep* (2003)

Coleman, Loren. *Bigfoot! The True Story of Apes in America* (2003)

———. *Mysterious America* (2004)

—————. *The Field Guide to Bigfoot and Other Mysterious Primates* (1999)

Collins, Andrew. *Alien Energy: UFOs, Ritual Landscapes and the Human Mind* (1994)

—————. *Government Circles* (2009)

—————. *The New Circlemakers: Insights into the Crop Circle Mystery* (2009)

Commander X and Tim Swartz. *Time Travel: A How-to Insiders Guide* (2001)

Commander X. *Incredible Technologies of the New World Order; UFOs– Tesla–Area 51* (1997)

Constable, Trevor James. *Sky Creatures* (1978)

—————. *The Cosmic Pulse of Life* (1977)

Cooper, William Milton. *Behold a Pale Horse* (1991)

Corrales, Scott. *Chupacabra and Other Mysteries* (1997)

Corso, Philip J. and William J. Birnes. *The Day after Roswell* (1997)

Crowley, Aleister. *Moonchild* (1971)

Dalton, John J. *The Cattle Mutilators* (1980)

Davenport, Marc. *Visitors from Time: The Secret of the UFOs* (1992)

de Lafayette, Maximillien. *460,000 Years of UFO-Extraterrestrials Biggest Events and Secrets from Phoenicia to the White House: From Nibiru, Zetas, Anunnaki, Sumer to Eisenhower, MJ12, CIA, Military Abductees, Mind* (2008)

—————. *Inside the Extraordinary World of the Anunnaki and the Anunnaki-Ulema: What I saw, what I learned, and what I can teach you, Book 1* (2010)

——————. *Anunnaki Chronology and Their Remnants on Earth From 1,250,000 B.C. to the Present Day* (2011)

——————. *Extraterrestrials-U.S. Government Treaty and Agreements: Alien Technology, Abductions and Military Alliance* (2008)

DeMeo, James and Eva Reich. *The Orgone Accumulator Handbook: Construction Plans, Experimental Use, and Protection against Toxic Energy* (2007)

Dennett, Preston. *Extraterrestrial Visitations* (2006)

——————. *One in Forty the UFO Epidemic* (1997)

——————. *UFOs over California: A True History of Extraterrestrial Encounters* (2004)

Devereux, Paul and Peter Brookesmith. *UFOs and Ufology* (1997)

——————. *Earth Lights Revelation* (1989)

Dolan, Richard. *UFOs and the National Security State*, vol. II (2009)

——————. *UFOs and the National Security State: Chronology of a Cover-up, 1941–1973* (2002)

Dong, Paul and Thomas Raffill. *China's Super Psychics* (1997)

Donovan, Roberta. *Mystery Stalks the Prairie* (1976)

Downes, Jon. *Island of Paradise: Chupacabra, UFO Crash Retrievals, and Accelerated Evolution on the Island of Puerto Rico* (2008)

Druffel, Ann. *Firestorm: Dr. James E. McDonald's Fight for UFO Science* (2003)

——————. *How to Defend Yourself against Alien Abduction* (1998)

Elders, Lee and Brit. *UFO . . . Contact from the Pleiades*, vols. I and II (1979, 1983)

Eller, Ann. *Dragon in the Sky: Prophecy from the Stars* (2009)

Emerson, DeAnna. *Mars/Earth Enigma: A Sacred Message to Mankind* (1996)

Emerson, Willis George. *The Smoky God: A Utopian Hollow Earth Classic!* (2009)

Fair, David Robinson. *Uninvited Future Observers* (2010)

Farrell, Joseph. *Secrets of the Unified Field: The Philadelphia Experiment, the Nazi Bell, and theDiscarded Theory* (2008)

Feindt, Carl W. *UFOs and Water: Physical Effects of UFOs on Water through Accounts by Eyewitnesses* (2010)

Ferguson, V. S. *Inanna Returns* (1995)

Flammonde, Paris. *UFO Exist!* (1976)

Flynn, David. *Cydonia: The Secret Chronicle of Man* (2002)

Fowler, Raymond. *Casebook of a UFO Investigator* (1981)

——————. *The Allagash Abductions* (1993)

——————. *The Andreasson Affair* (1979)

——————. *The Watchers* (1990)

——————. *UFOs: Interplanetary Visitors* (1974)

France, Melanie. *Chasing Orbs: An Adventure into the Mysterious World of Orbs* (2010)

Freer, Neil. *Breaking the Godspell* (1987)

——————. *God Games* (1998)

Friedman, Stanton T. and Don Berliner. *Crash at Corona* (1992)

Friedman, Stanton T. and Kathleen Marsden. *Captured! The Betty and Barney Hill UFO Experience* (2007)

——————. *Flying Saucers and Science* (2008)

————. *Science Was Wrong* (2010)

Friedman, Stanton T. *Top Secret/Majic* (1996)

Fuller, John G. *The Interrupted Journey* (1966)

Gilliland, James. *Becoming Gods 2* (1997)

————. *Becoming Gods: A Reunion with Source* (1996)

Glenday, Craig. *The UFO Investigator's Handbook: The Practical Guide to Researching, Identifying, and Documenting Unexplained Sightings* (1999)

Glickman, Michael. *Crop Circles: The Bones of God* (2000)

Good, Timothy, ed. *Alien Update* (1993)

————. *Alien Liaison: The Ultimate Secret* (1991)

————. *Need to Know: UFOs, the Military and Intelligence* (2007)

————. *Above Top Secret: The Worldwide UFO Cover-up* (1987, fully revised and updated as *Beyond Top Secret: The Worldwide UFO Security Threat* [1996])

————. *Alien Base: Earth's Encounters with Extraterrestrials* (1998)

————. *Unearthly Disclosure: Conflicting Interests in the Control of Extraterrestrial Intelligence* (2000)

Gray, John. *Men Are from Mars, Women Are from Venus: A Practical Guide for Improving Communication and Getting What You Want in Your Relationships* (1993)

Greene, Brian. *The Fabric of the Cosmos: Space, Time, and the Texture of Reality* (2005)

Greenfield, Allen. *Secret Cipher of the UFOnauts* (1994)

Greenfield, Jerome. *Wilhelm Reich vs. the U.S.A.* (1974)

Greer, Stephen. *Disclosure: Military and Government Witnesses Reveal the Greatest Secrets in Modern History* (2001)

——. *Extraterrestrial Contact: The Evidence and Implications* (1999)

——. *Hidden Truth: Forbidden Knowledge* (2006)

——. *Cosmic Deception: Let the Citizen Beware* (2002)

Hamilton III, William F. *Time Travel Now* (2005)

Hancock, Graham. *The Mars Mystery: Secret Connection between Earth and the Red Planet* (1998)

Hand Clow, Barbara. *Alchemy of Nine Dimensions: The 2011/2012 Prophecies and Nine Dimensions of Consciousness* (2004)

Harris, Paola. *Exopolitics: All the Above* (2009)

——. *Exopolitics: How Does One Speak to a Ball of Light* (2007)

Harris, Richard. *The UFO Phenomena and the Behavioral Scientist* (1979)

Haselhoff, Eltjo H. *The Deepening Complexity of Crop Circles* (2001)

Hausdorf, Hartwig. *The Chinese Roswell: UFO Encounters in the Far East from Ancient Times to the Present* (1998)

Heinemann, Klaus and Gundi Heinemann. *ORBS: Their Mission and Messages of Hope* (2010)

Hendry, Allan. *The UFO Handbook: A Guide to Investigating, Evaluating, and Reporting UFO Sightings* (1979)

Heselton, Philip. *Ley Lines: A Beginner's Guide* (1999)

Howard, Dana. *Diane: She Came from Venus* (1956)

——. *My Flight to Venus* (1954)

——. *Over the Threshold* (1957)

—————. *Vesta: The Earthborn Venusian* (1959)

Howe, Linda Moulton. *Animal Mutilations: The UFO Factor* (1988)

Hurtak, J. J. with Desiree Hurtak. *The Book of Knowledge: The Keys of Enoch* (1973)

Hynek, Joseph Allen. *The Hynek Report* (1977)

—————. Joseph Allen. *The UFO Experience: A Scientific Inquiry* (1972)

Icke, David. *Alice in Wonderland and the World Trade Center Disaster: Why the Official Story of 9/11 is a Monumental Lie* (2002)

—————. *The Biggest Secret* (1999)

—————. *The David Icke Guide to the Global Conspiracy* (2007)

Imbrogno, Phillip. *Interdimensional Universe: The New Science of UFOs, Paranormal Phenomena and Otherdimensional Beings* (2008)

Jacobs, David. *Secret Life: Firsthand Accounts of UFO Abductions* (1992)

—————. *The Threat: Revealing the Secret Alien Agenda* (1999)

Janssen, Bert. *The Hypnotic Power of Crop Circles* (2004)

Jessup, Morris K. *UFOs and the Bible* (1956)

Joyce, Judith. *The Weiser Field Guide to the Paranormal: Abductions, Apparitions, ESP, Synchronicity, and More Unexplained Phenomena from Other Realms* (2011)

Jung, C. G. *Flying Saucers: A Modern Myth of Things Seen in the Skies* (1978)

Kaku, Michio. *Physics of the Impossible: A Scientific Exploration into the World of Phasers, Force Fields, Teleportation, and Time Travel* (2008)

Kannenberg, Ida and Lee Trippett. *My Brother is a Hairy Man* (2009)

Kanon, Gregory M. *The Great UFO Hoax: The Final Solution to the UFO Mystery* (1997)

Kasten, Len. *The Secret History of Extraterrestrials: Advanced Technology and the Coming New Race* (2010)

Kaysing, Bill. *We Never Went to the Moon: America's Thirty Billion Dollar Swindle* (1974)

Kean, Leslie. *UFOs: Generals, Pilots and Government Officials Go On the Record* (2010)

Keel, John. *Martian Prophecies* (1975)

——————. *Our Haunted Planet* (1968)

Keith, Jim. *Casebook on the Men in Black* (1997)

Kenyon, Tom. *The Great Shift: Co-Creating a New World for 2012 and Beyond* (2009)

Keyhoe, Donald E. *Aliens from Space* (1973)

——————. *Flying Saucer Conspiracy* (1955)

——————. *Flying Saucer: Top Secret* (1960)

——————. *Flying Saucers Are Real* (1950)

——————. *Flying Saucers from Outer Space* (1953)

Klimo, John. *Channeling: Investigations on Receiving Information from Paranormal Sources* (1987)

Knapp, George and Colm Kelleher. *Hunt for the Skinwalker: Science Confronts the Unexplained at a Remote Ranch in Utah* (2005)

Knight, Christopher and Alan Butler. *Who Built the Moon?* (2005)

Knight, Sirona. *Celtic Traditions: Druids, Faeries and Wiccan Rituals* (2000)

Komarek, Ed. *Exopolitics: A Comprehensive Briefing* (2008)

Koppang, Randy. *Camouflage Through Limited Disclosure* (2006)

Kusche, Larry. *The Bermuda Triangle Mystery—Solved* (1995)

Lammer, Helmut. *MILABS: Military Mind Control and Alien Abduction* (1999)

Lapseritis, Kewaunee. *The Psychic Sasquatch and Their UFO Connection* (1997)

——————. *The Sasquatch People and Their Interdimensional Connections* (2010)

Larkin, Lisette. *Talking to Extraterrestrials: Communicating with Enlightened Beings* (2002)

LaViolette, Paul. *Secrets of Anti-Gravity Propulsion: Tesla, UFOs and Classified Aerospace Technology* (2008)

Ledwith, Miceal and Klaus Heinemann. *The Orb Project* (2007)

Leir, Roger. *Casebook: Alien Implants* (2000)

——————. *UFO Crash in Brazil* (2005)

Leviton, Richard. *The Emerald Modem* (2004)

Lloyd, Andy. *Dark Star: The Planet X Evidence* (2005)

Long, Greg. *Examining the Earthlight Theory: The Yakima UFO Microcosm* (1990)

Lyne, William R. *Occult Ether Physics: Tesla's "Ideal Flying Machine" and the Conspiracy to Conceal It* (2010)

——————. *Space Aliens from the Pentagon* (1994)

Maccabee, Bruce and Edward Walters. *UFOs Are Real, Here's the Proof* (1997)

Maccabee, Bruce. *Abduction in My Life* (2000)

——————. *The UFO/FBI Connection* (2000)

MacGregor, Rob and Bruce Gernon. *The Fog: A Never Before Published Theory of the Bermuda Triangle Phenomena* by (2005)

Mack, John. *Abduction: Human Encounters with Aliens* (2004)

—————. *Passport to the Cosmos: Human Transformations and Alien Encounters* (1999)

Marcel, Jesse Jr. *The Roswell Legacy: The Untold Story of the First Military Officer at the 1947 Crash Site* (2008)

Marciniak, Barbara. *Bringers of the Dawn: Teachings from the Pleiadians* (1992)

Massachusetts Institute of Technology. *Alien Discussions: The Proceedings of the Abduction Study Conference* (1994)

Maxwell, Jordan. *The Matrix of Power* (2000)

McKenna, Terence. *The Archaic Revival* (1991)

McMoneagle, Joseph. *Remote Viewing Secrets* (2000)

—————. *The Stargate Chronicles* (2002)

Melchizedek, Drunvalo. *The Flower of Life*, vols. I and II (1999, 2000)

Michel, Aimé. *Flying Saucers and the Straight-Line Mystery* (1958)

Moon, Peter. *The Black Sun: Montauk's Nazi-Tibetan Connection* (1997)

—————. *The Montauk Book of the Dead* (2005)

Moore, Judith and Barbara Lamb. *Crop Circles Revealed: Language of the Light Symbols* (2001)

Moore, Michele Marie. *Oklahoma City: Day One* (1996)

Moosbrugger, Guido. *And Yet . . . They Fly* (2001)

Myers, Craig R. *War of the Words: The True but Strange Story about the Gulf Breeze UFO* (2006)

Nelson, Buck. *My Trip to Mars, the Moon, and Venus* (1959)

Newton, Michael. *Hidden Animals: A Field Guide to Batsquatch, Chupacabra and other Elusive Creatures* (2009)

Nichols, Preston and Peter Moon. *The Montauk Project* (1992)

——————. *Montauk Revisited: Adventures in Synchronicity* (1994)

——————. *Pyramids of Montauk: Explorations in Consciousness* (1995)

——————. *The Music of Time* (2000)

O'Brien, Christopher. *Secrets of the Mysterious Valley* (2007)

Osborn, Maurice. *The Essence of the Notes* (2005)

Overall, Zan. *Gulf Breeze Double-Exposed: The "Ghost Demon" Photo Controversy* (1990)

Pavlevsky, Nicolette. *Who's Who in UFOs and ETs: The Need for Discernment* (2003)

Pringle, Lucy. *Crop Circles: Art in the Landscape* (2007)

Quasar, Gian. *Into the Bermuda Triangle* (2005)

Radke, Larry Brian. *Astronomical Revelations on 666: A Scientific and Historical Study of Asteroids and Comets with Respect to the Apocalypse* (1997)

Rand, Jaysen Q. *The Cosmic Blueprint for After* (1989)

——————. *The Return of Planet-X: Wormwood and Its Effects on Mother Earth, A Natural Disaster Survivor's Manual* (2007)

Randle, Kevin and Don Schmidt. *UFO Crash at Roswell* (1991)

Randle, Kevin D. *Crash: When UFOs Fall from the Sky: A History of Famous Incidents, Conspiracies, and Cover-Ups* (2010)

Randles, Jenny. *Alien Contact: The First Fifty Years* (1997)

————. *Alien Contacts and Abductions* (1994)

————. *Breaking the Time Barrier: The Race to Build the First Time Machine* (2005)

————. *Controversy of the Circles* (1989)

————. *Crop Circles: A Mystery Solved* (1990)

————. *From Out of the Blue* (1993)

————. *Mystery of the Circles* (1983)

————. *The Complete Book of Aliens and Abductions* (2000)

————. *The Little Giant Encyclopedia of UFOs* (2000)

————. *The Rancher's Nightmare: Mysterious Murder of Livestock* (2006)

————. *The Truth behind Men in Black: Government Agents—or Visitors from Beyond* (1997)

————. *The UFO Conspiracy* (1987)

————. *UFO Reality* (1983)

Rawls, John. *A Theory of Justice* (1971)

Red Star, Nancy. *Legends of the Star Ancestors: Stories of Extraterrestrial Contact from Wisdomkeepers around the World* (2002)

————. *Star Ancestors: Indian Wisdomkeepers Share the Teachings of the Extraterrestrials*(2000)

Redfern, Nicholas. *The NASA Conspiracies: The Truth behind the Moon Landings, Censored Photos, and the Face on Mars* (2010)

————. *On the Trail of the Saucer Spies: UFOs and Government Surveillance* (2006)

Reich, William. *Contact with Space: ORANUR, Second Report* (1951–1956)

Ress, Patricia Griffin. *Stranger Than Fiction: The True Time Travel Adventures of Steven L. Gibbs—The Rainman of Time Travel* (2001)

——————. *Why I Believe the HDR Unit Works and Time-Travel Is Possible!* (2010)

Rickard, Robert and Richard Kelly. *Photographs of the Unknown* (1980)

Robbins, Dianne. *Messages from the Hollow Earth* (2003)

——————. *Telos: Original Transmissions from the Subterranean City beneath Mt. Shasta* (1996)

Robbins, Peter and Larry Warren. *Left at East Gate* (1997)

Rowe, Kelvin. *A Call at Dawn: A Message from Our Brothers from the Planets Pluto and Jupiter* (1958)

Ruppelt, Edward J. *Report on Unidentified Flying Objects* (1956)

Sagan, Carl and Thornton Page. *UFOs: A Scientific Debate* (1972)

Sagan, Carl. *Contact* (1997)

——————. *Cosmic Connection: An Extraterrestrial Perspective* (2000)

——————. *Dragons of Eden: Speculations on the Evolution of Extraterrestrial Intelligence* (1977)

——————. *The Demon-Haunted World: Science as a Candle in the Dark* (1997)

Salla, Michael. *Exopolitics: Political implications of the Extraterrestrial Presence* (2004)

——————. *Exposing U.S. Government Policies on Extraterrestrial Life* (2010)

Sanchez-Ocejo, Virgilio and Wendelle C. Stevens. *UFO Contact from Undersea* (1982)

Sauder, Richard. *Hidden in Plain Sight: Beyond the X-Files* (2010)

——————. *Underground Bases and Tunnels: What is the Government Trying to Hide?* (1995)

Sauder, Richard. *Underwater and Underground Bases: Surprising Facts the Government Does Not Want You to Know!* (2001)

Schoch, Robert and Logan Yonavjak. *The Parapsychology Revolution* (2008)

Scully, Frank. *Behind the Flying Saucers* (1950)

Sherwood, John. "Gray Barker: My Friend, the Mythmaker," *Skeptical Inquirer* (May/June 1988)

Shriner, Sherry. *Entrances to Subterranean Tunnels: Underground Alien Bases* (1990)

Silva, Jose and Philip Miele. *Silva Mind Control Method* (1977)

Sitchin, Zecharia. *Divine Encounters* (1995)

——————. *The 12th Planet* (1976)

Smith, Paul H. *Reading the Enemy's Mind: Inside Stargate, America's Psychic Espionage Program* (2005)

Solarion, Robertino. *Planet X Nibiru: Slow-Motion Doomsday* (2004)

Solomon, Steve. *Visitors to the Inner Earth: True Tales of Subterranean Journeys* (2011)

Spence, Richard. *Secret Agent 666: Aleister Crowley, British Intelligence and the Occult* (2008)

Steckling, Fred. *We Discovered Alien Bases on the Moon: Documented with 125 NASA Photographs and Area Blowups* (1981)

Steiger, Brad. *UFO Abductors* (1988)

Steinman, William S. and Wendelle C. Stevens. *UFO Crash at Aztec: A Well-Kept Secret* (1986)

Stevens, Henry. *Hitler's Flying Saucers* (2003)

Stevens, Wendelle C. and Edward James. *UFO Contact from Planet Venus: We Are Not Alone* (2004) (available only as a PDF)

Stevens, Wendelle C. and Omnec Onec. *UFO: From Venus I Came* (1990)

Stevens, Wendelle C. and Paul "Moon Wai" Dong. *UFOs over Modern China* (1983)

Stevens, Wendelle C. *Contact from the Pleiades: A Preliminary Report* (1982)

—————. *Contact from the Pleiades: A Supplementary Report* (1983)

—————. *Message from the Pleiades: The Contact Notes of Eduard Billy Meier Volumes I–IV* (1988–1995)

—————. *UFO Abduction at Botucatu* (1985)

—————. *UFO Contact at Maringa* (1984)

—————. *UFO Contact from Planet Acart* (1987)

—————. *Weapons Development Program* (2007)

Stone, Bradford and Kristen David Adams. *Uniform Commercial Code in a Nutshell* (2008)

Story, Ronald D. and William R. Lyne. *The Mammoth Encyclopedia of Extraterrestrial Encounters* (2001)

Story, Ronald D. *Space Aliens from the Pentagon* (1994)

Stranges, Frank. *Stranger at the Pentagon* (1972)

Strieber, Whitley. *Communion* (1987)

Stringfield, Leonard H. *Retrievals of a Third Kind* (1978)

——————. *Situation Red: The UFO Siege* (1977)

——————. *The Fatal Encounter at Fort Dix–McGuire* (1985)

——————. *The UFO Crash/Retrieval Syndrome* (1982)

——————. *UFO Crash/Retrievals: Amassing the Evidence* (1982)

——————. *UFO Crash/Retrievals: Is the Cover-up Lid Lifting?* (1989)

——————. *UFO Crash/Retrievals: Search for Proof in a Hall of Mirrors* (1994)

——————. *UFO Crash/Retrievals: The Inner Sanctum* (1991)

Summers, Ian. *Cattle Mutilations* (1980)

Summers, Marshall Vian. *The Allies of Humanity* (2001)

Swartz, Tim R., ed. *Reality of the Inner Earth: Return to the Caverns with Richard Shaver* (2005)

Tesla, Nikola. *My Inventions: The Autobiography of Nikola Tesla* (2010)

Thomas, Steven. *The Moon Landing Hoax: The Eagle That Never Landed* (2010)

Tonnies, Mac. *After the Martian Apocalypse: Extraterrestrial Artifacts and the Case for Exploration of Mars* (2004)

Torres, Noe, et al. *The Ultimate Guide to the Roswell UFO Crash: A Tour of Roswell's UFO Landmark's* (2010)

Turner, Karla and Ted Rice. *Masquerade of Angels* (1994)

Turner, Karla. *Into the Fringe* (1992)

—————. *Taken—Inside the Alien-Human Abduction Agenda* (1994)

Uriarte, Ruben and Noe Torres. *Mexico's Roswell: The Chihuahua UFO Crash* (2007, 2008)

Uriarte, Ruben. *The Other Roswell: UFO Crash on the Texas-Mexico Border* (2008)

Vallée, Jacques. *Confrontations: A Scientist's Search for Alien Contact* (2008)

—————. *Dimensions: A Casebook of Alien Contact* (2008)

—————. *Messages of Deception: UFO Contacts and Cults* (2008)

—————. *Passport to Magonia: On UFOs, Folklore and Parallel Worlds* (1968)

—————. *Revelations: Alien Contact and Human Deception* (2008)

—————. *The Invisible College: What a Group of Scientists Have Discovered about UFO Influences on the Human Race* (1975)

van Tassel, George. *I Rode a Flying Saucer* (1952)

—————. *Into This World and Out Again* (1956)

—————. *Science and Religion Merged* (1968)

—————. *The Council of Seven* (1958)

—————. *When Stars Look Down* (1999)

van Vlierden, Carl and Wendelle C. Stevens. *UFO Contact from Koldas* (1986)

van Vlierden, Carl. *The Twelve Planets Speak* (1989)

von Daniken, Erich. *Chariots of the Gods* (1968)

Walter, Pierre F. *The Science of Orgonomy: A Study on Wilhelm Reich* (2010)

Walters, Edward and Frances. *The Gulf Breeze Sightings: The Most Astounding Multiple Sightings of UFOs in U.S. History* (1989)

——————. *UFO Abductions in Gulf Breeze* (1994).

Webre, Alfred Lambremont. *Towards a Decade of Contact* (2000)

——————. *Exopolitics: Politics, Government, and Law in the Universe* (2005, eBook first edition 2000)

Wedd, Tony. *Skyways and Landmarks* (1961)

Weiss, Chuck. *Abducted by Aliens* (2008)

White Song Eagle. *Teluke: A Bigfoot Account* (2008)

Wilson, Colin. *The Mind Parasites* (1967)

Wood, Ryan S. *MAJIC Eyes Only: Earth's Encounters with Extraterrestrial Technology* (2005)

Yurdozu, Farah. *Confessions of a Turkish Ufologist* (2007)

——————. *Life is a Horror Movie/Yaşam Bir Korku Filmidir* (1999)

——————. *Love in an Alien Purgatory* (2009)

——————. *UFO Truths and Lies/UFO Gerçekleri ve Yalanları* (1999)

——————. *UFO Forbidden Zone/UFO Yasak Bölge* (2008)

——————. *UFOs are Coming/UFOlar Geliyor* (1993)

——————. *You Are Your Soulmate* (2007)

About the Author

Bret Lueder is a journalist, author, and filmmaker living in Chico, California. He earned a degree in journalism from Chico State University and has since written over 600 articles on music, spirituality, and UFOs for the *Chico News & Review*, *Magical Blend Magazine*, *UFO Magazine*, and other publications. He is the author of the Esoteric Guide to the Reggae Vibe series, which includes *Song in Your Heart: The Story of the Search for the Lost Note*, and he produced the three-volume DVD series Esoteric Guide to the Bay Area UFO Expo.

Visit him at *www.bretlueder.com* or *www.esotericguide.com*.